Beyond Fundraising

Beyond Fundraising

A Complete Guide to Congregational Stewardship

Wayne B. Clark

Unitarian Universalist Association of Congregations
Boston

Printed in the United States.

Cover design by Robert Delboy.

ISBN 978-1-55896-523-2

4
13 12

Library of Congress Cataloging-in-Publication Data

Clark, Wayne B. (Wayne Berton)
  Beyond fundraising : A complete guide to congregational stewardship
/ Wayne B. Clark.
     p. cm.
  Includes bibliographical references.
  ISBN-13: 978-1-55896-523-2 (pbk. : alk. paper)
  ISBN-10: 1-55896-523-8 (pbk. : alk. paper) 1. Church fund raising.
2. Unitarian Universalist churches—Finance. 3. Stewardship,
Christian. I. Title.
  BV772.5.C53 2007
  254'.8—dc22
                          2006037590

This book is dedicated to the thousands of congregational leaders and professional religious leaders with whom I have worked. Each has taught me something important about stewardship, even though that precise word has seldom been used. This book is also dedicated to Unitarian Universalist fundraising consultants, whose guidance has been instrumental in its development. They include Carole Czujko, Martha Easter-Wells, Tricia Hart, Tamsin Kemos, Jerry King, Jeri Moulder, Laura Nagel, Frankie Price-Stern, David Rickard, Aggie Sweeney, and Larry Wheeler.

CONTENTS

Introduction

Beyond Fundraising is a coming-of-age story. It moves congregations beyond the restrictive myth of scarcity that pervades many American faith communities and leads them toward a reality of abundance. It suggests that we discard some old congregational beliefs like:

- "Our congregation is poor, we have always been poor, and we will always be poor."

- "We simply don't have a good enough (or large enough) facility to invite new people to join us."

- "Except for a very small core group of committed leaders, no one else is willing to step up to the plate."

Those of us who belong to these congregations are convinced that we will never have enough of whatever it is that we desire. At best, the glass is always half empty.

We need to replace our old beliefs with positive, more accurate statements of abundance, such as "Our congregation has a clear mission, we are publicly passionate about that mission, and we *will* secure enough resources (people, time, and money) to successfully implement our mission." A congregation with a culture of abundance believes in the reality that there can always be enough. They believe that diligent stewardship will provide everything needed. The glass is at least half full. Sometimes there are several glasses. Sometimes they even overflow.

Focusing on abundance requires a new vocabulary, one that diminishes our focus on money. This vocabulary puts fundraising under the umbrella of stewardship. Rather than discussing the goal of raising money, congregations should discuss money as no more than a means to an end. Money is most meaningful when we can move from thinking of it as a way to pay the bills and regard it as a way to fulfill the ministry of the congregation.

Beyond Fundraising contends that a new and comprehensive stewardship development program, Forward Through the Ages, puts the annual budget drive in perspective by making it just one of five components, along with stewardship education, joyful giving, ministry and good works, and planned giving. Forward Through the Ages walks congregations through a sequence of activities that dramatically alters congregants' understanding of money. Because money is presented as just one piece of a whole, it becomes a less emotionally charged issue. Money becomes just one stewardship tool to help accomplish the ministry of a faith community, rather than a topic to avoid and a barrier to a fulfilling congregational ministry.

All congregations, regardless of religious beliefs, can create a culture of abundance by taking an approach called Appreciative Inquiry, which starts with clarifying what already is going well. Rather than focusing on problems to solve, congregations are encouraged to build upon their existing strengths. This book does not suggest that congregations put on rose-colored glasses and ignore problems, but it does suggest that problems become much easier to address when the initial focus is on currently successful internal programs and global ministries.

Throughout the book there are references to creating and maintaining spiritual relationship. Congregants are frequently reminded to ask whose voices need to be heard and how to include a diverse group of congregants on any team. Leaders of teams are reminded to create a covenant of spiritual relationship —written promises about their agreed-upon mutual responsibilities to each other—as one of their very first tasks. Congregants are reminded that being in spiritual relationships means welcoming and respecting each other and creating and maintaining an environment that builds connections, renews spirit, and inspires action.

Much of our old money-related language has become a barrier to focusing on abundance, continually dragging us back into the darkness of perceived scarcity. The new vocabulary represents more than semantic gymnastics; it allows us to begin with a blank sheet and to fill that sheet in a way that supports the excitement of new possibilities. Gone are the terms *annual canvass*, *canvasser*, and *pledge*. They are replaced with *annual budget drive*, *visiting steward*, and *financial commitment*. Instead of *canvasser training*, *equal giving*, and *religious education classrooms*, the new vocabulary includes *orientation workshop*, *proportional giving*, and *congregational program spaces*. The new vocabulary limits fundraising to raising money in support of an annual budget or capital campaign, while *stewardship* is used to represent the much broader concept of growing, nurturing, promoting, and building our gifts, call, and spiritual vocation. A complete glossary of terms is found beginning on page 115.

The book also makes a case for widespread congregational buy-in to stewardship develop-

ment. Widespread buy-in provides the necessary ownership of congregational ministry that increases the likelihood of successfully fulfilling stewardship goals.

Even when there is widespread congregational buy-in, most congregations can benefit from the services of a consultant. The concept of spiritual stewardship is so alien to many congregations, and the vocabulary is so unfamiliar, that an external consultant can be a valuable investment, especially in the early stages of the Forward Through the Ages program. A qualified consultant can help to create a strategic plan and implement a comprehensive stewardship development program.

Searching for the Future, explained in Chapter 3, is a series of participative workshops designed to identify a congregation's vision and mission. It is often helpful for a consultant to model the workshop with congregational facilitators before these lay leaders facilitate their own workshops with other congregants. Following the workshops, a consultant can help to create a congregation-wide mission statement as well as help to prioritize goals and activities that support the mission.

A consultant should always guide congregations through a capital campaign. (A capital campaign is a major fundraising effort that has a purpose other than supporting the annual operating budget, such as funding a building project.) The risks are so great, and the opportunities to run amok are so plentiful, that it is a wise investment to hire a consultant in the very early stages of thinking about a capital campaign. If a capital campaign is launched without the assistance of a consultant, a congregation might miss a few integral steps or fail to sequence the steps for maximum results. If a capital campaign fails to reach its financial commitment goal, construction plans would need to be revised and the project could be postponed or possibly cancelled.

Certainly each capital campaign is different, and hiring a consultant cannot guarantee success, but a consultant with extensive experience with faith community capital campaigns can dramatically increase the chances of success.

In some cases, the suggestions in *Beyond Fund-*

raising represent the best congregational practices observed by Unitarian Universalist fundraising consultants over the past twenty years. In other cases, the suggestions come from my conviction that it is time to expand our conversation beyond the narrow confines of fundraising, toward the more encompassing language of stewardship. Our historical focus on fundraising has been largely unsuccessful at facilitating congregational growth. *Beyond Fundraising* has been written specifically for Unitarian Universalist congregations. However, with relatively little "translation," the book can be a helpful guide to faith communities of other denominations. The book is not necessarily intended to be read from cover to cover. It is organized in such a way that readers can easily access specific topics of immediate interest.

Several resources at the back of the book provide examples that can be adapted to particular congregational needs. In addition, a thorough list of books and websites for further reading is provided. While these do not represent a complete list of stewardship resources, they offer the best examples of stewardship-related information available as this book reached publication.

My fondest hope for this book is that it accomplishes more than teaching you about best practices for raising money. Ideally, it should help your congregation to articulate and commit to a dream for the future, one that inspires its members to joyfully contribute their gifts to its fulfillment.

CHAPTER ONE

The Spiritual Roots of Stewardship

We have the opportunity to use resources to help care for others and those less fortunate than ourselves as a sign of our gratitude, and the essential question is not how much we can afford to give, but how much we can afford to keep.

—Stephen Gray

Some of today's healthiest faith communities focus more on stewardship than fundraising. While *fundraising* refers specifically to money-raising efforts, *stewardship* is an attitude that is reflected in all of the congregation's efforts. Fundraising emphasizes the need of the recipient; stewardship addresses people's spiritual need to give. Stewardship must precede fundraising.

Healthy faith communities see stewardship as a vital component of their ministry. They understand that stewardship is an act of worship. Worship includes the joyful sharing of gifts (aptitude, ability, and money), call (willingness to proclaim the congregation's spiritual message), and spiritual vocation (willingness to take up volunteer efforts to support the faith community). Note that *gifts* has a wider meaning than money exchanged for the internal programs and external ministries of a faith community. For example, one's gift to the faith community might be to serve on the finance committee because one has a good understanding of financial matters. Or a member with landscaping ability might agree to become the caretaker of the memorial garden. All kinds of gifts should be valued and considered meaningful.

Stewardship, then, is the growing, nurturing, promoting, and building of the gifts, call, and spiritual vocation of the members of a faith community. Stewardship is not necessarily the things

people do, but the spirit that influences the things they do.

In order to nurture a healthy sense of stewardship, you and your fellow congregational leaders must take a close look at false assumptions about why people give. You must also understand the real reasons for giving so that you can determine the best ways to encourage generosity.

Myths About Giving

Outdated beliefs can prevent a faith community from moving toward a culture of abundance. These prevalent myths can sometimes cause congregations to become paralyzed and resign themselves to living lives of eternal scarcity. Here are a dozen of the most common myths with the corresponding truths.

Myth Those in low-income households don't have money to contribute, so they offer their time instead.

Truth The myth that people contribute money *or* time has been disproved. Recent research conducted by Ian Evison, formerly of the Alban Institute, shows that, in general, financial contributions *follow* an investment of time. Those who give more time also give more money. In addition, anecdotal observations by fundraising consultants indicate that people with limited income often contribute a higher percentage of that income than do those with larger incomes.

Myth Because baby boomers (those born just after World War II) are generally self-centered, materialistic, and achievement-driven, they do not give much money to faith communities or other charities. Furthermore, they do not have the time to offer their call or spiritual vocation to their congregations.

Truth Research conducted in 1994 by the Barna Research Group indicates that baby boomers were the most generous generation of the twentieth century. Barna states, "If we compare their giving to that of prior generations when those people were the same age, boomers emerge as more generous." His research indicates that boomers might be willing to give more to faith communities if furnished with sufficient motivation to do so. It is this "show me what difference my contribution will make" mindset of many boomers that often frustrates older congregational leaders. In contrast, these older congregants come from a generation that sees giving as an obligation and an expectation. When older leaders fail to understand the motivation of boomers, they are unsuccessful at raising money from boomers and often unsuccessful at recruiting them for leadership roles.

Myth During periods of economic downturn, people can't be expected to give as much money to their faith community.

Truth When faced with limited discretionary income, people choose their charitable organizations more carefully. If a compelling case is made in support of the annual budget drive or a capital campaign, they will make significant financial commitments. If a compelling case is not made, potential donors think that the faith community does not deserve to get their money.

Myth Now that so many organizations are asking for contributions, people have decreased giving to their faith community in order to disperse contributions among many organizations.

Truth This is a favorite myth espoused by Unitarian Universalists, but there is no research to support this claim. Those congregants who have become disciplined stewards tend to contribute to many organizations, including their faith community. Ian Evison has concluded that congregations and the programs they administer are receiving a greater share of charitable contributions than in the recent past.

Myth Because many people are suffering from information overload, they do not want to know how the congregation is using their contributions.

Truth Many people, although overwhelmed with information in their daily lives, are also well educated and a bit skeptical. They are less likely than previous generations to have blind faith that the congregation is using their money wisely. They want to know that their contributions are making a difference, and they are interested in the facts and figures as well as the narrative that explains the ways that their financial gifts are being used. (Note that this does *not* necessarily mean they want to see long columns of numbers as found in a detailed line-item budget.)

Myth People want to make their contributions without getting involved in the messy decision-making process of the congregation.

Truth Many want to share their opinions about how the faith community's internal programs and global ministries are conducted. For some, having an opportunity to provide decision-making input is a tangible benefit of giving. It is a way of investing in the programs and ministries of the faith community.

Myth Generous givers feel entitled to complain loudly when things do not go their way. They attempt to "hold the congregation hostage" by threatening to eliminate their financial and volunteer support.

Truth There may be a few generous givers who feel entitled, but not many. Fundraising consultants have an axiom that says, "People who give the most complain the least; those who give the least complain the most." People are more committed to faith communities when they give joyfully of their aptitudes, abilities, and money (their gifts), when they willingly proclaim the faith community's good works (their call), and when they participate in the work (spiritual vocation) of their faith community. With few exceptions, the most committed congregants are those who are helpful and supportive to a fault. The people who are vocal obstructionists often lead with their heels, giving little of their gifts, call, or spiritual vocation to their faith community.

Myth If people only understood the dire financial straits of the church, they would feel guilty and increase their annual financial commitment.

Truth In spite of Garrison Keillor's notion that "guilt is the gift that keeps on giving," nobody wants to throw money at a sinking ship. Emphasizing a financial problem may actually drive people away from the faith community. It is more effective to focus on the positive ways that annual contributions will be used once the money has been received. Have a discussion about the successes of current giving. Talk about how the money is being used and emphasize how much better the programs and ministries will be when the giving is increased. Again, people want to know what difference their financial contribution will make.

Myth The church newsletter is a good place to include current financial commitment fulfillment information because it prods people to keep their payments up-to-date.

Truth People usually know the fulfillment status of their annual commitment. If I am current with my payments, a public newsletter article bemoaning the sad state of payments may only cause me to be upset at others who are not up-to-date. If I have fallen behind, I *know* that I have fallen

behind and don't need a public reminder in the newsletter. It is fine to send monthly personal reminders to all donors, and it is a caring gesture to make pastoral phone calls to those who have fallen behind, but avoid public broadcasting. Besides, financial fulfillment rates are often 95 percent or more of the initially committed amount. A lower fulfillment rate indicates a problem that won't be resolved in the monthly newsletter. It often reflects the impersonal way in which people were asked to contribute.

Myth As long as a fellowship event (to launch an annual budget drive or a capital campaign) provides a free meal, people will attend the event and give generously of their gifts, call, and spiritual vocation. A beautiful brochure with a clever slogan and attractive logo will further increase giving.

Truth A free meal is not enough. When people reserve time in their busy schedules, they expect more than just some mediocre food and an average after-dinner program. They want a well-planned event that includes an opportunity to interact with other congregants. They also want to have fun. Many fundraising consultants have determined that the best entertainment *involves* the attendees. For example, a program of group singing is preferable to having the choir perform for the gathering. (See page 44 for more details on planning a fellowship event.) Nevertheless, keep in mind that the format and promotion of the event matter less than the message. A well-planned fellowship event, a beautiful brochure, and a clever slogan will add absolutely nothing to financial commitments unless a clear and compelling case for stewardship has been made.

Myth Because people don't like to talk about money, annual financial commitments must be sought in an indirect way. It is best to send financial commitment forms through the mail and ask recipients to return them by mail. In this way, they will not be offended, embarrassed, or angry.

Truth The more indirect the approach, the less money will be contributed. Personal stewardship conversations (explained in detail in Chapter 5) are most effective. Getting groups together is a less direct approach, but it can provide an occasional break from the stewardship conversations. Telephone calls and mail solicitations are the most ineffective ways to ask for money. If you are uncomfortable talking about money, the solution is to find ways to become more comfortable talking about it, not to avoid direct, personal conversations.

Myth A financially healthy faith community is one that receives all of its operating budget money from congregants' annual financial commitments.

Truth Not necessarily. Fundraising consultants suggest that annual financial commitments should represent at least 80 percent of the total operating budget, but there is one other important factor: the distribution of those financial commitments. A financially healthy church has an annual *median* commitment that is almost the same amount as its annual *average* commitment.

There are likely more myths about giving than are listed here, so be vigilant. Question the factual basis of pronounced "truths" that might actually be myths. Fundraising consultants, such as those available through the UUA Office of Congregational Fundraising Services, work with this information every day. They work with many congregations and have firsthand stewardship experience. Ask them! (Chapter 2 describes the steps for hiring a fundraising consultant.)

Remember that financial commitment *follows* an investment of time. As lay leaders, you must give congregants an opportunity to serve the faith community. You must ask for call and spiritual vocation in addition to financial gifts. And you must make a compelling case for the annual budget drive or capital campaign, remembering that congregants all want to know what difference their contributions will make. Make it easy to get involved. Emphasize the positive ways in which contributions will be allocated. The more direct the approach, the more successful the fundraising effort will be.

Why We Give

In a 1998 seminar, Stephen Gray, the Indiana-Kentucky Conference Minister for the United Church of Christ, said,

> All we have is just on loan. Whether it be our next breath, the food we eat, what is in our pocketbooks; it is on loan and we cannot take it with us when we go. We have the opportunity to use these resources to help care for others and those less fortunate than ourselves as a sign of our gratitude, and the essential question is not how much we can afford to give, but how much we can afford to keep.

Assuming Gray is right, if we can't afford to keep much, why do we give? There are at least six positive reasons for giving.

Out of a sense of gratitude. Giving can be a way of saying thanks for the gifts that have been bestowed upon us. We give because we acknowledge that we are fortunate to have already received many gifts. Giving can feel like an act of worship, a celebration of abundance.

To add meaning to our lives. There is really nothing bad about feeling good. Giving is truly one of the great joys of life. Giving provides a depth of purpose that peels away several layers of our day-to-day superficiality. Giving takes us away from navel gazing and helps us to focus beyond our personal boundaries.

Because we like to help people. We are, by nature, predisposed to be helpful. If we believe in the case that is being made, we will be motivated by the benefit that others will receive from our gift.

In response to people we trust. The most spiritual stewardship is relational and personal rather than institutional. We give our gifts, call, and spiritual vocation to people we admire, to people who have a high level of integrity. We will give a financial gift, for example, to someone who we believe has already given a meaningful gift of her own. This implies, of course, that people cannot ask us to give something *before* they have given abundantly of *their* gifts, call, and spiritual vocation.

Because we believe in an organization's mission. When we are passionately connected to our faith community, we readily give of ourselves. Even if we are not closely attached to our congregation, we will give if a strong mission-driven case is presented to us.

Because someone asks. It should not be surprising that many of us find it hard to ask others for gifts, call, and spiritual vocation. But we often give willingly to someone who musters the courage to ask. Asking is the single most important factor in securing stewardship support for faith communities.

A Culture of Giving

People are not born with a giving gene. Because joyful giving for the sake of the giver is a worthy goal, faith communities want to help their congregants discover their own personal generosity. To do so requires focusing on the joy of giving, on being self-giving rather than self-serving. Recruiting volunteers and raising money can be almost incidental to creating a healthy culture of giving.

In *Giving and Stewardship in an Effective Church*, church consultant and minister Kennon Callahan writes that the purpose of stewardship is giving, not fundraising, and that stewardship actually provides a service to the giver. The role of those leading a stewardship campaign, he believes, is to help people discover their own generosity.

Callahan proposes a four-year program to increase giving. He suggests that a congregation focus on growing the donor base in the first year and increasing the number of volunteers who work on the annual budget drive in the second year. He recommends that the third year be devoted to increasing the giving level of specific current households. He believes that the cumulative result of the first three years should create a quantum leap of giving during the fourth year.

While Callahan's plan offers a well-conceived sequence, the first step is to find a way to talk about giving. The conversations can't be specifically about money. They must include talk about call and spiritual vocation. A person might share his call (willingness to proclaim the good works of the faith community) by talking about his passion for one of the congregation's programs or ministries at a new-member reception. A congregant might demonstrate her spiritual vocation (willingness to take up the spiritual work of the faith community) by participating in a Habitat for Humanity project or volunteering to teach English to a group of recent immigrants.

If your congregation is entrenched in a culture of scarcity, develop an intentional plan to explore the meaning of giving. By initiating conversations about giving, you can introduce the topic and reinforce the concept until it slowly becomes part of the congregation's way of life.

Conversations about giving can be initiated in many ways. Use the pulpit, guest speakers, the newsletter, the website, the worship service, and committee discussions. Convene small groups before or after the Sunday service for several weeks. Invite the finance committee to participate in a conversation with congregants about the meaning of spiritual stewardship in contrast to the meaning of fundraising. Make "giving" a major theme at annual budget drive orientation workshops. Prepare visiting stewards (the term we prefer instead of *canvassers*) to discuss the concept of giving during their conversations with donors.

You may also want to invite a fundraising consultant to facilitate a Mission and Giving Retreat. Focus on these questions during the retreat:

- What is the difference between stewardship and fundraising?

- What relationship can we construct among giving, compassion, and community?

- In what ways can we grow and invest the gifts we have received?

- How can we turn the gifts we receive into gifts for others?

- What does generosity mean to us? How do we define the term? How will we know if we are being generous? What will it look like?

- What will we do with increased giving? What difference will it make?

- How can we make spiritual stewardship a year-round conversation?

- How can we frame conversations to focus less on the need for money and more on giving as a way to implement our mission?

- How can we help our society move away from an increasing culture of materialism?

Helping congregants discover their own personal generosity will create joyful givers. Joyful givers will help create healthy congregations that view spiritual stewardship as a vital component of their ministry and that believe that sharing one's gifts, call, and spiritual vocation is an act of worship.

Learning to Receive

Religious educators are fond of telling children that it is better to give than to receive. Does that mean it is less blessed to receive? Certainly not. It is important to receive gifts unapologetically and with gratitude, letting others experience the joy of being givers. In fact, receiving gifts is often harder than giving them. In his book *Giving and Stewardship in an Effective Church*, Kennon Callahan expresses his belief that "the key to giving is receiving, for in receiving, we learn how to give." The following suggestions have worked well for those who shared these stories. This sampling of individual stories illustrates how these congregants have learned to value the art of receiving. As such stories are shared in a congregation, the concept that receiving precedes giving will become part of the culture of your faith community.

Allow someone to give you a gift without attempting to repay them. A congregant from the Pacific Northwest tells the story of his two young-adult daughters who wanted to take him to the theater one evening. He was hesitant at first because he knew that the tickets were very expensive. The show was wonderful, and they all thoroughly enjoyed it. And he realized that a big part of his daughters' fulfillment was seeing how much he enjoyed it.

Check your motives for giving. Another congregant shared a story from a recent holiday. A friend surprised her with a gift. They had not exchanged gifts in the past, and she had not bought her friend a gift. She felt embarrassed, then guilty, and was ready to create an excuse for not having a gift to give in return. She thought of saying, "I've ordered a gift for you, but it hasn't yet arrived." Fortunately, before she spoke, she remembered advice from an article written by Bonita Joyner Shield, an assistant editor of the *Adventist Review*. Shield said, "If the only reason you would buy them [a gift] is because they bought you one, forget it! Humble yourself, and allow them the joy of giving." She joyfully thanked her friend for the gift.

Take people at their word. A California congregant shared that a friend was struggling with a terminal illness. The friend was feeling especially weak one day and called to ask for a ride to a medical appointment. The congregant explained how pleased he was that his friend called and that it felt like he was giving his friend a gift. The friend accepted this, and the congregant felt good knowing that he was taken at his word.

Accept compliments. "In the past," another congregant explained, "I would frequently rebuff a compliment with a self-deprecating remark. Someone would compliment me on a meeting I had facilitated and I would respond with, 'Gee, I didn't really do a very good job. I forgot to mention an important point, and I allowed the group too much time to discuss another point.' I never realized it, but my response would deflate the person giving me the compliment. I am better at accepting compliments now and am more likely to respond by saying, 'Thanks. I am pleased that the meeting was helpful.'" The congregant has learned how to accept compliments.

Kennon Callahan says, "Gracious receivers become joyful givers." When we receive a gift graciously, we can see how it gladdens the giver. Perceiving this joy, we are more likely to give to others. And when we appreciate the gifts we receive, we are more likely to invest and grow those gifts so that we have the ability to share our wealth.

Until the congregants of a faith community are willing to initiate conversations and share stories about receiving and accepting, growing and investing, giving back, and joyfully giving their gifts, call, and spiritual vocation, they will be unable to change their culture of scarcity.

Sharing the Responsibility

Appreciating and receiving with joy the gifts that others offer is a way to honor those gifts. But if we don't allow those gifts to inspire our own generosity, it's easy to fall into the trap of taking generous people for granted. This can happen in a congregation when a few members carry too much of the financial responsibility for the community. In a healthy distribution of financial giving, the top 25 percent of financial commitments (the top quartile) is given by 10 percent of donors, with 15 percent of donors giving the next highest quartile, 35 percent giving the third highest, and 40 percent of donors giving the last quartile.

Unfortunately, consultants find that in many Unitarian Universalist congregations, the first quartile of giving comes from 5 percent of the donors. The second quartile often is given by 10 percent, the third quartile is given by 25 percent, and the fourth quartile is given by 60 percent of the donors. With this distribution, the congregation is more vulnerable. If just a few top contributors stop giving, the consequences to the congregation's fundraising efforts are severe.

Here's how to determine the annual financial commitment distribution of your congregation:

1. List all of the current financial commitments from largest to smallest, top to bottom.

2. Add the first commitment to the second commitment, the second to the third, and so on down the list until you reach 25 percent of the total dollars committed. The people who contributed this top 25 percent of the total represent the first quartile of givers.

3. Continue down the list of commitments until you have reached 50 percent of the total dollars committed. The donors who contributed this second 25 percent of the total represent the second quartile of givers.

4. Continue the process by going down the list of commitments until you reach a dollar amount equal to 75 percent of the total dollars committed. The people who contributed this third 25 percent of the total represent the third quartile of givers.

5. The remaining commitments are the final 25 percent of the total dollars. These donors represent the fourth quartile of givers.

Now that you know more about why and how people are motivated to give generously to their congregations, how do you effectively go about the business of asking them? First, evaluate your own congregation's attitude toward giving. Decide whether you have a culture of abundance or a culture of scarcity. What Myths do your members hold on to about giving? How well does your congregation acknowledge gifts? When you understand the meanings that your congregation attaches to money and how you can change the conversation about money to one about stewardship and the congregation's mission, you can inspire both joyful giving and joyful receiving.

CHAPTER TWO

Hiring a Fundraising Consultant

The thing I remember best about successful people I've met all through the years is their obvious delight in what they're doing . . . and it seems to have very little to do with worldly success. They just love what they're doing, and they love it in front of others.

—Fred Rogers

Historically, fundraising consultants help congregations achieve financial goals for an annual budget drive (canvass) or a capital campaign. Consultants typically tell congregations how to organize a fundraising team, create a fundraising calendar, and develop communication materials. Most consultants will conduct a financial feasibility study for a capital campaign. Often they will facilitate orientation workshops for visiting stewards (canvassers).

Unitarian Universalist congregations can take advantage of a model that is considerably more expansive than most other fundraising consultant programs. UUA fundraising consultants offer a holistic approach that puts fundraising within the context of a congregation's mission. Consequently, the consultants frequently help congregations clarify their mission and guide them through the creation of a comprehensive strategic plan.

The UUA fundraising consultants have worked with hundreds of congregations since 1985. They have learned the value of an initial assessment visit to begin their relationship with a congregation. During a long weekend, the consultant meets with several key congregational leaders, asking enough questions and gathering enough information to present verbal recommendations by the end of the weekend. Within two weeks after the visit, the consultant sends a written summary of the recommendations to the congregational leaders. After the assessment visit, consultants often guide a congregation through a mission clarification process and the development of a comprehensive strategic plan. Sometimes they help to revitalize (or create) a planned giving program and develop an endowment fund. Complete information about the UUA fundraising consultant program is found on the UUA website.

UUA fundraising consultants are most effective when they join a project before any significant plans have been made. When helping to plan an annual budget drive, they like to begin consulting at least nine months prior to the launch date. They prefer to begin capital campaign consulting about two years before the anticipated launch date. Throughout the project, they work steadily with congregational leaders, combining on-site visits with telephone conference calls and e-mail exchanges.

The Office of Congregational Fundraising Services has used a guiding and coaching model (as opposed to the on-location management of a fundraising effort) since the program began. The model allows congregations to get assistance with their fundraising effort while maintaining ownership of the effort. The model requires lots of congregational volunteers so that ownership clearly resides with the congregation, not the consultant.

The good news is that a fundraising consultant provides a faith community with the expert guidance and coaching needed to run a successful fundraising effort. The consultant provides counsel and objectivity that congregants cannot offer. The bad news is that a fundraising consultant can never guarantee the amount of money that will be raised.

At this writing there are eight consultants in the program, each of whom is a member of a Unitarian Universalist congregation. Each has taken a leadership role in fundraising efforts in his or her local congregation. Each consultant works collegially with the other consultants, bringing the combined expertise of all eight consultants to a congregation. The Mission Statement and Code of Ethics for Unitarian Universalist Fundraising Consultants on page 118 shows the consultants' mission statement and code of ethics.

The consulting program charges a flat per diem fee. The fees are never based on the amount of money raised. Historically, Unitarian Universalist consulting fees represent between 2 cents and 5 cents of each dollar committed to a fundraising effort. A fundraising consultant could guide and coach a congregation through a strategic planning process, an annual budget drive, a capital campaign (including a financial feasibility study), and some endowment program development, with the total consulting costs unlikely to exceed 5 percent of the money committed to the annual budget drive and the capital campaign. The consulting program pays for all expenses, including airfare, ground transportation, lodging, meals, and materials.

Every consultant must undertake the five primary tasks listed below. The second through fifth are based on tasks identified by Allan Arlett, principal of the Arlett van Rotterdam Partnership. They have been adapted to relate more specifically to congregational fundraising efforts.

- Guide the congregation toward determining their mission so that fundraising can be put within the context of the congregation's preferred future.

- Compile and produce an analysis and realistic assessment of the congregation's fundraising capacity.

- Help the congregation make appropriate choices about fundraising methods without imposing a consultant-created plan.

- Help the congregation to internalize the proposed course of action so that they take ownership and responsibility for the effort.

- Work with congregational leaders to prepare for the fundraising effort.

When to Hire a Consultant

There are some specific situations in which a fundraising consultant is helpful to a congregation. Consider hiring a consultant when:

- The congregation lacks a clear vision and is without a consensus about direction.

- The congregation needs a fresh perspective from an external, impartial expert.

- Help is needed to create a culture shift from a myth of scarcity to the reality of abundance.

- Congregational leaders understand that money spent on a consultant can be a wise investment.

- In the recent past, few congregants have been willing to work on a fundraising effort.

- Even fewer congregants have been willing to assume a leadership role.

- No one in the congregation has experience as a fundraiser for religious institutions.

- The congregation has someone with fundraising experience who is willing to lead a fundraising project, but the person's previous efforts have not been very successful.

- There is conflict about which fundraising method to use.

- The leaders are unsure about what needs to be done.

- A proposed capital campaign project is too big to rely totally on volunteers.

- A capital campaign project has been proposed, and a consultant is needed to determine how much money can be expected from congregants.

- There is no active planned giving program.

- There is no endowment fund, or the existing fund is moribund.

- The congregation has a small endowment fund that represents less than three times the annual operating budget.

Some faith communities may have situations that suggest caution in hiring a consultant. Caution is advisable when:

- Hiring a consultant will cost more money than the congregation can or should spend. The consultant's expertise and the cost of services need to be balanced.

- The congregation is not ready to listen to a fundraising consultant. For example, if the congregation is in serious conflict, it is probably an inappropriate time to bring in a fundraising consultant.

Twelve Steps

Some congregational leaders will not want to take the time that is required to walk through each of the following twelve steps in the process of hiring a consultant. They are cumbersome. Many congregations will be able to streamline the process, especially when hiring a consultant to guide and coach them through an annual budget drive. But all twelve steps are vital when preparing for a building project and a subsequent capital campaign.

Unitarian Universalist congregations that are hiring a Unitarian Universalist Association (UUA) fundraising consultant may not have to complete all twelve steps. Because the program has been around since 1985 and is so well known, completing the first three steps, plus Step Ten (checking references), will likely provide all the information needed.

Step One: Create a Consultant Review Task Force

To begin the search for a fundraising consultant, ask the governing body to appoint five congregants who have had experience with consultants and who have some knowledge about the world of fundraising for religious institutions. When considering team members, remember to keep two questions in mind: Whose voices need to be heard? How can we include people of varying backgrounds, cultures, races, ages, abilities, genders, and sexual orientations, as well as people from historically marginalized groups?

Next, determine the parameters of the assignment. Do the task force members have the responsibility to interview fundraising consultant candidates, while the governing body retains the authority to make a final hiring decision? Or do the members have the responsibility to interview candidates and the authority to hire a consultant? Be sure to clarify ownership, whatever the decision-making process.

Step Two: Create a Covenant of Spiritual Relationship

As the consultant selection process begins, create a written set of promises about how you want to work with one another and with consultant candidates. (For more about covenants of spiritual relationship, see page 22). Start by discussing and agreeing upon how to work together. For example, task force members might agree to start and end all meetings on time and to always have a written agenda distributed prior to the day of the meeting. Extend the covenant to include treating consultant candidates in a responsible way. In *Selecting and Working with Consultants*, Thomas J. Ucko reminds us, "Acting responsibly with candidates means treating them with decency and respect—as if consultants were human beings with feelings, just like you!" Part of the covenant might include agreeing to return candidates' phone calls or e-mail messages within a specified length of time and agreeing to notify candidates of a hiring decision within a specific time frame.

Step Three: Define the Ideal Fundraising Consultant

Match the required skills of a consultant with the expectations of the congregation and the specific project being planned. Ask each member of the task force to answer the following questions. Later, when members compare their answers, the definition of an ideal consultant will become clear.

Relevant experience. Should the consultant have extensive experience with projects similar to the currently proposed project? Is it okay if the consultant has only some relevant experience, or even little experience?

Consultations with other congregations. Does the consultant need to have had experience with other congregations? How important is it that the other congregations were of the same denomination or were located in a specific geographical region?

Affiliation with colleagues. Does the consultant work independently? Is the consultant affiliated with colleagues and part of a larger network?

Image and style. What personal characteristics are necessary for a consultant to be welcomed by the congregation? Should the consultant be reserved or outgoing? Easygoing or tough? Will the consultant need to look, act, or dress in a certain way?

Location. Must a local consultant be hired, or is the best consultant needed, regardless of location?

Reputation. How important is the consultant's reputation? Is the reassurance that comes with a well-known and respected consultant needed? Or is it preferable to hire a dedicated consultant who is still building a reputation?

Project goals. Is it best to hire a consultant who will come in and raise money for the congregation, or is it preferable to seek a consultant who will teach fundraising techniques for future use?

Availability. Is it all right if the consultant has several other clients and may not be available on short notice?

Response time. What response time (to e-mail and phone messages) will you expect from the consultant?

Contract and payment. Will you require that a consultant work from a written contract? What schedule of payments will work best for the congregation?

When each member of the task force has answered these questions, compare notes and create a priority list of important consultant characteristics. It is unlikely that the perfect consultant will be found. By defining the characteristics of a perfect consultant, however, the task force is more likely to find the *right* consultant.

If the congregation is seeking a UUA fundraising consultant, the next step is to appoint a congregational contact person to have a telephone conversation with the UUA director of congregational fundraising services. After the conversation, the director matches the congregation's expectations with the skills and characteristics of a consultant in the program. Then the consultant contacts the congregation. During a telephone conversation, a congregational representative should ask the consultant enough questions to be comfortable. If the conversation goes well, they then plan an assessment visit, and a contract is developed between the UUA and the congregation. The contract covers only the assessment visit. It puts the congregation under no obligation for future consulting services with the consultant or any other consultant in the program. The remaining steps, except for Step Ten, may not be necessary in this situation.

Step Four: Create a Pool of Candidates

If you choose not to have a Unitarian Universalist fundraising consultant, start by asking your denominational headquarters for recommendations. In some cases, they will recommend a consultant or a consulting program. Also check with the leaders of other faith communities in the local area. Explore whether each consultant has:

- Demonstrated knowledge, expertise, and capability related to specific fundraising needs.

- Experience with similar fundraising projects.

- A respected track record and a high level of credibility.

- A work style, process, and approach that includes an ability and willingness to customize to meet specific needs. Avoid consultants who want to sell a generic, off-the-shelf approach to fundraising.

- A demonstrated capacity to assess a congregation's readiness to begin a fundraising effort.

Don't eliminate candidates from consideration because of their distance from your community. To provide an effective consulting experience, consultants are willing to supplement on-site visits with e-mail correspondence and telephone conference calls.

Step Five: Preliminary Evaluation

Next, narrow down the choices to a list of three to five candidates. Create a set of core questions, and then telephone each candidate.

Many fundraising consultants are individual entrepreneurs or part of very small firms, so you may need to leave a message. If so, make the message concise. Include the nature of the project, the size of the campaign, and the date on which the consultant's services are needed. Pay attention to how long it takes for a consultant to return the phone call. A slow turnaround time (more than twenty-four hours) may indicate that the consultant will not be responsive to future consulting needs.

In the telephone conversation, ask about experience with similar fundraising efforts and the results. Also ask about the fee structure. Take notes during the telephone conversations so that it will be easier to remember candidates' answers. In addition to the answers, note the willingness to answer questions. If a candidate seems vague or hesitant, it may indicate a lack of interest or a lack of experience needed for the project. Of course, it might just indicate a degree of caution. At the end of each call, ask the candidate to send an in-troductory sample of materials, a résumé, a list of references, and a client list.

Most fundraising consultants have a website. Review the site to get a sense of the services offered and of the quality of those services. We still recommend that the first contact be made by telephone because it is hard to get a feel for a consultant's personal style by exchanging e-mail messages.

Step Six: Evaluate Materials

Wait no longer than five working days to receive materials from candidates. As with slow telephone message returns, late-arriving materials may predict a lack of timely responsiveness in the future.

Once the materials have arrived, review and evaluate them. Did the candidate send the materials requested? What is the quality of the materials? Would you feel comfortable sharing these materials with the congregation? Would you feel comfortable sharing these materials with potential large donors? Did the candidate include a personal note with the materials? Did she or he encourage more questions if the materials were unclear?

After evaluating the materials, meet with other task force members and compare notes. Narrow the field of candidates to a couple of the most promising. However, if there has been discomfort with any of the preliminary phone conversations and none of the materials meet expectations, consider eliminating all of the candidates from consideration. It is much better to delay a project than to hire the wrong fundraising consultant.

Step Seven: Prepare for Interviews

Before interviews are conducted, make each task force member aware of the following guidelines.

- Create a relaxed and informal climate. The goal is to gather relevant information rather than create undue stress in the candidates.

- At the start of each interview, indicate the format to be used. Do not allow candidates to turn the interview into a sales pitch.

- Be sure to ask all the relevant questions, even if the candidate has to be politely interrupted.

- During each interview, plan on listening at least 75 percent of the time. It is hard to learn while talking.

Before conducting interviews, decide which core questions to ask. Select open-ended questions that cannot be answered in one word—questions that start with "tell me about," "how," "what," "when," or "why." Plan to ask the same core questions at each interview. Also decide who will ask each question, dividing them up among team members. In that way, the responsibility is shared, and the other members can take notes while the person asking the question maintains eye contact with the candidate.

The following core questions are helpful (although we certainly don't recommend asking all of them):

- Why are you interested in consulting with our congregation?

- What consulting strengths do you possess, especially those that will be helpful to our project?

- How will you apply those skills?

- What similar consulting have you done?

- What success stories can you share? Why were they successful?

- Have you had any unsuccessful experiences? Why were they unsuccessful? What did you learn from them? What would you do differently if you could repeat the experience?

- What other congregations are you currently working with? How much time is needed with each?

- What specific parts of our fundraising effort will you be responsible for?

- What "deliverables" (for example, an assessment visit written report, leadership role descriptions, guidelines for creating a case statement, financial feasibility report) will you provide?

- What will our responsibilities include?

- How much will your services cost? How will you determine the costs? How will you expect to be paid?

- Who will be responsible for your expenses, including airfare, ground transportation, lodging, meals, and preparation of materials?

- Based on your current information about our project, what challenges do you anticipate?

- What is your availability to complete this project within our time frame? Are there other consultants who will be working with you? Who are they? When can we interview them? How will the consulting tasks be divided?

- Why should we hire you rather than any other consultant?

- What other questions should we be asking you? What great answer had you planned to share if we had only asked the right question? What else would you like to tell us?

Step Eight: Interview Candidates

The task force is now ready to schedule interviews with the most promising candidates. If seeking a consultant for an annual budget drive, plan one hour for each interview. Reserve a longer amount of time to interview capital campaign consultants.

If a candidate is local, schedule a personal interview. If a candidate resides beyond your geographic region, conduct a telephone interview. When interviewing by telephone, limit the local participants to three members of the task force. If you have access to a high-quality speakerphone, all task force members can be in the same room. The results of each phone conversation can then be easily processed immediately after the call. On the other hand, speakerphones often provide a low level of quality that can be frustrating to everyone.

Step Nine: Evaluate the Candidates

After each interview, use the following evaluation factors:

Personal chemistry and trust. Do the task force members feel comfortable with the candidate? Trust your instincts here.

Interest in the project. Does the candidate seem to view this as just another job or demonstrate genuine interest in the project?

Concern for the congregation. Is the candidate sensitive to the congregation's needs and concerns.

Integrity. Is the candidate direct and straightforward? How does he or she speak about former clients? Is confidentiality maintained?

Step Ten: Check All References

Contact the references that the candidate provided. In addition, contact other clients on the candidate's client list, even if they are not included on the reference list. Here are some suggested questions to ask:

- How did you like working with the consultant?

- How would you describe your project?

- What methods, techniques, and solutions did the consultant provide?

- Did you successfully achieve your goal? How are you defining success?

- Did the consultant stay within your budget? If not, what caused the overrun?

- Did the consultant complete the project on time?

- How well did the consultant understand the unique culture of your congregation?

- How well did the consultant communicate in person, in writing, during telephone conversations, and in e-mail exchanges?

- Were the consultant's responses always timely? Sometimes? Seldom? Never?

- What do you perceive as the consultant's strengths and weaknesses?

- How does this consultant compare with previous consultants you have used?

- Was confidentiality maintained regarding the level of financial commitments from specific donors?

- In what ways was widespread participation encouraged?

- Would you hire the consultant for future fundraising efforts?

Step Eleven: Select a Fundraising Consultant

Once the interviews have been completed and references have been checked, select a consultant to work with the congregation. If one of the candidates meets all of the criteria and his or her references indicate a high level of satisfaction, the decision (or recommendation to the governing body) may be easy to make.

On the other hand, in spite of his or her strengths, the top candidate might not be the best fit for the congregation. The website of the Department of Human Resources at Yale University offers this suggestion: "The very best determination of whether a consultant will be successful is how comfortable you feel with that person and the degree to which you think there will be a personal fit with your organization. Since a good client-consultant relationship is ultimately based on trust, you need to have a good personal fit." This subjective intangible may trump all of the quantifiable data that you have gathered.

Of course, it is also possible that the task force will not be comfortable with any of the candidates. If this happens, you may be tempted to settle for a consultant who is almost just right, since there has already been a lot of time and energy invested in this chore. In this situation, you have a few options:

- You could decide to settle for the consultant who comes the closest to being the right one for the project. This option is not recommended. In the long run, the success of the fundraising effort may be compromised.

- You could give a candidate a trial run by offering a smaller fundraising project. The consultant will expect to be paid for these services, but this option might prove to be a valuable investment.

- As a last resort, you may have to start the process over again.

Step Twelve: Develop a Contract

Regardless of the congregation's size and regardless of the scope of the fundraising effort, use a written contract that is signed by the consultant and a congregational representative. Do not begin any consulting arrangement until both parties have signed the contract. Include the following components in the contract:

Identification. The official name of the congregation and the official name of the consultant's firm.

Date. The date when the contract is signed by the congregational leaders and the consultant.

Term. The starting date of the consultation and the ending date.

Services. A description of the services to be provided by the consultant.

Ownership. The person who owns the deliverables after the contract has ended.

Confidentiality. The consultant's agreement to keep sensitive information, such as the list of donors, confidential.

Primary contact person. A congregant, not a professional religious leader. This policy will prevent a professional religious leader from getting too many steps ahead of the congregation.

Location. Where the consultation will occur.

Compensation. The fee arrangement with the consultant. Do not agree to a fee structure in which the consultant receives a percentage of the money raised. It is unethical and may result in the consultant placing undue pressure on donors.

Cancellation policy. The agreement of terms if the fundraising effort is cancelled before the consultation begins.

Termination. How the contract can be terminated if necessary.

Signatures. The signatures of the consultant and an officially designated person in the congregation.

A sample contract for consulting services is provided on page 119.

The Assessment Visit

An assessment visit by a UUA fundraising consultant offers an opportunity for a Unitarian Universalist congregation to invite an objective consultant to gather information about the congregation. The consultant gathers enough information to gain a clear understanding of existing congregational strengths and opportunities, as well as identifying areas of weakness and potential threats. The consultant may want to meet with the following constituents:

- Minister(s)
- Professional religious educator
- Other staff members (secretary, sexton, coordinator of volunteers, new member coordinator)
- Finance committee chair
- Chair of planned giving
- Annual budget drive chair
- Building and grounds committee chair
- Members of the governing body

By the end of the visit, the consultant develops a sequence of actions to help the congregation reach its desired future. The sequence of actions includes specific recommendations to get "from here to there." Based on all the information gathered, the consultant lists the steps necessary for the congregation to attain its long-term goals. The recommendations are given verbally at the end of the assessment visit and are followed by a written summary within two weeks of the visit. The recommendations may address the following issues:

- Clarifying the congregation's vision
- Congregational growth issues

- Annual budget drive

- Capital campaign

- Financing options (for a capital project)

- Five-year strategic plan

- Facilities planning

- Planned giving program

- Endowment program development

- UUA loans, loan guarantees, and grants

An assessment visit also clarifies how the UUA fundraising consultant program may be helpful to the congregation after the assessment visit is completed.

With the assistance of an experienced consultant, you are now ready to embark on strategic planning. The next chapter will explore a new approach to this process that encourages congregants to focus on the positive aspects of their faith community and collaborate on fulfilling its promise.

CHAPTER THREE

Searching for the Future:
The First Step of Strategic Planning

Vision without action is a daydream. Action without vision is a nightmare.
—Anonymous

Searching for the Future is a weekend strategic planning process that has been used successfully in dozens of organizations, including faith communities and nonprofit organizations, for twenty years.

A Searching for the Future weekend consists of three segments:

Modeling workshop. On Friday evening, a consultant models the program with a carefully chosen group of lay leaders.

Congregational workshops. On Saturday, members of the congregation are grouped into workshops of no more than fifteen participants each. The lay leaders who were workshop participants on Friday evening become workshop facilitators on Saturday. Following the same agenda used on Friday evening, each workshop group, guided by a facilitator, drafts a mission statement and a set of brainstormed goals.

Wrap-up. On Sunday afternoon, the facilitators and the consultant meet to combine the results of the Saturday workshops. The final product is a single mission statement and a collated list of brainstormed goals.

These three components will be explained more fully a bit later. First, however, it is helpful to understand the ideas on which Searching for the Future is based.

Appreciative Inquiry

Searching for the Future is based on a concept called Appreciative Inquiry, created by David L. Cooperrider (with Jane Magruder Watkins and others). In Cooperrider's words, "a faith community is not a problem to be fixed but a mystery to be embraced." While traditional problem-solving processes separate, dissect, and pull apart, Appreciative Inquiry generates affirming images that pull people together.

Participants in the Searching for the Future workshop affirm what the faith community already does well. They are encouraged to tell a short story about their faith community, starting with "I remember the time when. . . ." Participants then focus on moving forward by building on those positive images. Following this process of discovery, participants work with what has been learned, nurture growing enthusiasm, and open the way to co-create the future of their congregation. The process is always collaborative and is generated out of strong personal relationships.

Problems are not ignored in this appreciative environment. However, rather than starting with defining the problems, the workshop leader helps participants reframe core issues. The reframing turns away from understanding what's wrong and shifts to moving toward the best future opportunities possible. Reframing instantly changes the tone and atmosphere of each workshop. The conversations focus on the most promising, appreciated, valuable images of the faith community.

Appreciative Inquiry, as applied to Searching for the Future workshops, provides an opportunity for congregational transformation by allowing participants to live in the present what they most desire in the future. Positive change occurs as images and visions of a desired future are enacted in the present.

Four core appreciative questions are asked during the workshop. They have been adapted from Diana Whitney, co-author (with Amanda Trosten-Bloom) of *The Power of Appreciative Inquiry: A Practical Guide to Positive Change*.

- Who are we at our best, when the congregation is most alive, engaged, and committed?

- What is our positive core, our life-giving center from which our best thinking and contributions emerge?

- What are our most courageous dreams for the future of this faith community?

- What are our greatest possibilities for making a spiritual difference in our world?

These questions are designed to elicit answers that reveal appreciation, achievement, and success. The questions seek the commendable and steer away from judgment. They shift conversations from evaluation to valuation, bringing a shift in spirit with significant increases in trust.

Several Appreciative Inquiry resources are included in the list of resources for further reading that begins on page 159. More information can be found at **www.centerforappreciativeinquiry.net**.

Guiding Principles

In addition to Appreciative Inquiry, Searching for the Future is based on several of the following strategies:

Quick and dirty. Searching for the Future begins with an assumption that we are all busy people. We are volunteers, squeezing church activities into a limited amount of discretionary time. The program is offered without apology for the compact, intense approach that allows congregations to complete the workshop in one weekend.

Teach people to fish. A consultant models the program with a group of carefully chosen congregational leaders. After completing the modeling workshop, the congregational leaders are responsible for facilitating workshops with other congregants. In this way, lay leaders feel personally invested in the program and are able to replicate it in future years, often without the guidance of a consultant.

The more the merrier. The program is grounded in a commitment to a high level of congregational participation. The more congregants who become involved, the more ownership and buy-in the strategic plan will have. The only limitation to the level of congregational participation is the number of available facilitators (two facilitators are required for every fifteen participants).

Guided participation. The program is a carefully guided process that allows for contributions from all participants while maintaining a clear focus on the outcome. The program is not a series of unstructured conversations.

Personal vision first. Each workshop begins with participants exploring their personal vision of the future. After personal visions have been clarified, a group vision is determined. A draft mission statement evolves from the shared vision, and a prioritized set of goals is established for later use by a strategic planning team.

Resources last. When the congregational vision has been clarified, a mission statement has been developed, and goals have been determined, the strategic planning team turns its attention to the resources (people, time, money) needed to implement the strategic plan. There is a rationale for placing resources last. When congregations gather the energy to explore their vision, the enthusiasm starts to build and increases through the mission statement, goals, and activities stages of the process. Because of this energy, it is more likely that the necessary resources will be found.

Identify leaders. Often, new lay leaders are discovered during Searching for the Future workshops. People are identified who might become valuable members of a strategic planning team.

Process as well as product. The workshop should be replicated at least once every three years. Because the workshop is fairly short and because lay leaders will have learned how to facilitate the program, it is relatively easy to keep the process alive.

Terminology

Before a Searching for the Future weekend, all congregants must have a common understanding of appreciative strategic planning terminology:

Strategic planning. Taking a clean-slate approach to the future—perhaps resulting in a new direction —after clarifying congregational vision and mission. Strategic planning differs from long-range planning, which is the process of simply adding incremental steps to the current direction without considering any significant changes in vision or mission.

Vision. The imagination that gives inspiration and direction to a congregation. A congregational vision is a picture of a preferred reality that captures the overriding essence of the faith community. It identifies how the church will be different and better in the future.

Mission statement. A statement that becomes the foundation of a strategic plan. It is crafted using the congregational vision as a starting point. It is the written expression of the congregation's ideal for itself, offering just enough detail to provide direction and guidance.

Goals. What must be done to fulfill the unique mission that has been crafted. Goals describe the specific themes to be addressed, state who (or what) will be the recipient of the ministry, and provide an elaboration of the themes generated during the visioning process.

- **Activities.** Descriptions of specific and measurable actions identified as the best path toward implementing the chosen goals.

- **Resources.** People, time, money, and facilities needed to implement the activities.

Preparation

Having facilitated many Searching for the Future workshops, Unitarian Universalist fundraising consultants have developed suggestions to help ensure a successful program:

- Arrange for a fully accessible workshop space.

- Provide child care and transportation when needed.

- To recruit people to participate in the workshops, publicize well in advance. Use a telephone tree to ensure that everyone receives an invitation to participate. The website (with a sign-up link), the newsletter, the Sunday order of worship, and short announcements during the Sunday service can all be used. Set up a registration table during coffee hour.

- If your congregation has 500 or more members, use a representative democracy approach. Recruit members who represent specific constituencies (for instance, the worship and music committee, lifespan religious education committee, finance committee, and building and grounds committee).

- Ask members of the governing body (as well as other lay leaders) to be Saturday workshop facilitators, providing a way for them to visibly and actively support the program.

- Be clear about the time commitment required. The Saturday workshops take three and a half hours. Facilitators must commit to an additional three and a half hours on Friday evening, plus two hours in the afternoon on Saturday or Sunday.

- Assign two facilitators to each Saturday workshop. While one facilitator is leading the workshop, the other can take notes on an easel pad and handle any miscellaneous issues that surface. Two facilitators can also be helpful to guide participants when they meet in small groups.

- To determine the number of Saturday workshops, figure on five to fifteen participants per workshop. With more than fifteen participants, it becomes difficult to manage discussion and finish the workshop in the allotted time. With fewer than five participants, it is hard to create and maintain a meaningful level of interaction. If there will be 105 congregational participants on Saturday, for example, you will need at least seven workshop groups and fourteen facilitators.

- A couple of days before the workshops, place a reminder phone call to each participant and facilitator.

- If all the Saturday workshops are conducted at the same location, schedule breaks at the same time, creating an opportunity for informal discussions among all of the participants. Serving a light lunch at the end of the workshops creates another opportunity for informal discussion.

Sample Workshop Agenda

The core elements of the Friday and Saturday workshops are described below. This sample agenda is offered as a brief overview only. Consultants adjust the program to meet the unique needs of each congregation.

Social time. The first half hour is reserved for socializing and refreshments. The social time helps participants transition from their workday into the workshop and also leaves a margin of error for latecomers.

Overview and introductions. Each participant is given a written copy of the agenda and a handout of definitions. The facilitator (the consultant on Friday, a lay leader on Saturday) summarizes the plan for the workshop. It is never safe to assume that participants know each other, so distribute name tags and make introductions.

Set the tone. Participants, as they are willing, are encouraged to share a short personal story about their relationship to the faith community. Ask them to start their story with "I remember the time when . . . ."

Create personal visions. The facilitator reads several sentence fragments and asks participants to complete them using a maximum of three words. Sentence fragments might include:

- My most spiritual experience as part of this congregation was when . . .

- The most fun I've ever had with this congregation was when . . .

- Right now I am most proud of . . .

As participants complete the sentence fragments, the facilitator uses an Appreciative Inquiry approach that helps participants build upon what is already working well in their faith community. By focusing on memories of the congregation at its best, the participants begin to shape the church's future.

Create a group vision. For the second exercise, participants are divided into groups of three to seven each. Each small group is responsible for reaching consensus in answering several questions provided by the facilitator. For example, the participants might be asked: What would we miss if this faith community disappeared? What makes us different from other local religious institutions? Sometimes, participants are asked the questions mentioned on page 18.

Collate personal vision information. While the small groups are at work, the facilitator arranges the personal vision information into identifiable themes. Although the themes differ from one workshop to another, five themes are often uncovered during a visioning exercise:

- *Worship and music:* a worship service that incorporates music to offer a cohesive whole, a vision that one is supportive of the other.

- *Lifespan religious education:* a cradle-to-grave religious education program that logically and systematically flows from one segment to the next, meeting the needs of each age group.

- *Congregants worshipping, playing, and working together:* For many congregations, this is the easiest picture to capture and consistently generates lots of energy and enthusiasm.

- *Outreach/Ministry:* congregational focus on local, national, and global issues.

- *Denominational connection:* an awareness that the congregation is part of a larger whole (except in nonaffiliated, independent churches). Participants acknowledge that they are not isolated and find comfort in their relationship with a larger entity.

Share. When the small groups have reached consensus in the group vision exercise, they share the results. The facilitator adds that information to the existing themes from the personal vision exercise.

Draft mission statements. With guidance from the facilitator, the same small groups create first-draft mission statements. If your congregation has an existing mission statement, it is best not to use it. The program is designed as an interactive workshop that begins with a clean slate. The process is at least as important as the end result.

A mission statement is specific enough that congregants recognize their faith community and simple enough that nonmembers want additional information. A mission statement is similar to a résumé. It is a tease. It leaves the reader wanting to know more and generates inquiries. Consider these guidelines:

- Use an absolute maximum of fifty words.

- Write for accuracy, not cosmetics.

- Write about where the congregation wants to go (as opposed to where it might go).

- Avoid tentative words like *try*, *seek*, *influence*, and *encourage*.

- Answer the question: Why do we exist?

- Identify what difference the congregation makes in the wider world.

- Differentiate the church from other faith communities; express uniqueness.

- Do not use jargon, acronyms, or insider terminology.

- Solicit ends, not means; results, not effort or righteous exertion.

- Identify opportunities.

- Generate enthusiasm.

- Describe what the congregation will be remembered for.

Healthy congregations create mission statements that clearly define the boundaries of their mission. They make no apologies for sticking to those boundaries. They recognize that there are some ministries they can't address. Healthy congregations know when to say no.

Create a new mission statement. The small groups share their mission statement drafts. Similarities begin to surface. Guided by the facilitator, the participants create a single second-draft mission statement, using the first-draft statements from the small groups as a foundation.

Brainstorm. Using the themes and the second-draft mission statement as guides, participants brainstorm a list of activities that could help to fulfill the vision described in their mission statement draft.

Review the workshop. At the end of the Friday evening workshop, the consultant answers any questions and distributes the materials the participants will need to facilitate their own groups on Saturday.

Workshop Follow-Up

Suppose there are seven workshop groups on Saturday. By the end of Saturday, there are eight second-draft mission statements (one from Friday evening and seven from Saturday) and eight sets of brainstormed activities.

After the Sunday morning worship service, the Saturday workshop facilitators share lunch with the consultant and tackle the final piece of the program. Their task is to create one third-draft mission statement and one copy of the collated brainstormed activities. The process is usually completed in a couple of hours. (If all the Saturday workshops are completed in the morning, it might be possible to conduct this final piece of the program on Saturday afternoon.)

As soon as possible, preferably on that Sunday evening, the third-draft mission statement, along with the collated list of activities, is presented to the governing body for its review. A couple of weeks later, the congregation is asked to adopt the mission statement. Assuming that the mission statement accurately reflects the input from the workshops, the congregation will readily adopt it. Do not let the congregation "wordsmith" the mission statement by proposing changes. The congregation either votes to adopt the mission statement or votes not to adopt it. In the unlikely event that the mission statement is not adopted, send it back to the governing body for revision.

The Strategic Planning Team

Once the mission statement has been adopted, the governing body forms the strategic planning team. When considering team members, keep two questions in mind:

- Whose voices need to be heard?

- How can we include people of varying backgrounds, cultures, races, ages, abilities, genders, and sexual orientation, including people from historically marginalized groups?

Under the umbrella of these two questions, recruit members for the strategic planning team who are actively involved in the faith community and are fully committed to the value of appreciative strategic planning. Start by conferring with the consultant. Ask who stood out among the Searching for the Future participants. Quite often the consultant observes program participants who would be wonderful members of the strategic planning team.

Effective team members are those congregants willing to make a time commitment of about six months. They have credibility with the congregation and are good communicators, willing to keep in touch with the congregation. They are comfortable with a big-picture approach to the future. Since most of their work concerns shades of gray rather than black-and-white issues, they are comfortable with the ambivalence that comes with that territory. And perhaps most importantly, they are willing to have some fun as they develop a strategic plan for their congregation.

Once the strategic planning team is formed, its members should consider the following tasks and guidelines as they begin their work:

Create a covenant of spiritual relationship. A *covenant* is a written set of promises that people make in mutual responsibility and agreement. To be in spiritual relationship means to welcome and respect each person and to create and maintain an environment that builds connections, renews spirit, and inspires action.

Before writing the covenant, each team member can ponder six questions (adapted from *Practicing Right Relationship: Skills for Deepening Purpose, Finding Fulfillment, and Increasing Effectiveness in Your Congregation* by Mary Sellon and Dan Smith):

- What do I want my relationship with each team member to be?

- What attitudes and values do I want to honor while I am with this team?

- What must I let go of to appreciate each team member?

- What is the goodness in each team member that I will see and trust?

- How will I acknowledge to each team member the goodness that I see in her or him?

- What will I dare to ask of each team member?

The answers to these questions are likely different for each member, but sharing the answers with teammates helps to shape the covenant. Once the covenant is written, there will probably be moments when team members fail to live up to the promises. But the nature of covenant means that team members grant one another the right and responsibility to call teammates back to the promises they have made. Given that mutual relationship, the promises made and the promises that people want others to make are inseparably bound together, one and the same.

Here is an example of a covenant of spiritual relationship. It was developed by Second Unitarian Church of Chicago and reported by Sue Stukey, a member of the governing body, at the 1999 Unitarian Universalist General Assembly:

> We covenant to build a community that challenges us to grow and empowers us to hold faithful to the truth within ourselves. We will be generous with our gifts and honest in our communication, holding faithful to a love that embraces both diversity and conflict. Called by our living tradition, we will nurture spirituality within a vision of the eternal, living out our inner convictions through struggles for justice and acts of compassion.

Additional sources of information about covenants of spiritual relationship are included in the list of resources for further reading that begins on page 159.

Clearly define the task. Strategic planning team members are charged with taking the recently created mission statement and the starter list of activities and creating an outline of a five-year strategic plan. Their task is to accurately reflect back to the congregation what the congregants have already provided during the Searching for the Future workshop. Strategic plan outlines can take many different forms. A popular form takes the shape of a chart that lists the goals (as determined from the Searching for the Future process) for each of the next five years. Within each goal, possible activities are listed (see page 139).

Once the chart has been built, and after it has been adopted by the congregation, the governing body adds specificity to the outline by creating an action plan that determines responsibility for each activity, the date upon which the activity will be completed, help that is needed, and what the measurable outcomes will be.

After the first year of the plan, the task is more manageable. In each subsequent year, the team members fine-tune the second, third, fourth, and fifth years of the plan, and they are responsible for adding only one new year to the plan.

Project income and expenses, both operating and capital. These projections should be part of the strategic plan for the next five years. When income is projected, use conservatively low numbers. When expenses are estimated, use high numbers. Show both income and expenses in round numbers, with lots of zeroes. There will be time later in the process to get specific about income and expense projections. If a capital campaign is being considered during the next five years, project capital campaign income and expenses separately from operating budget projections. (For more information about projecting income and expenses, see page 92.)

Create conservative projections for membership growth. "Pastoral-size" congregations are those that see as many as 150 congregants on a typical Sunday. "Program-size" congregations average between 150 and 350 congregants on a typical Sunday, and "corporate-size" congregations have an average Sunday attendance of 350 or more. Pastoral-size congregations sometimes show annual growth of 10 percent or more, since this can be accomplished with just a few new congregants. Program-size and corporate-size congregations seldom experience more than 10 percent sustained annual growth. The few congregations that sustain that degree of growth have specific growth plans and actively implement those plans.

Consider future staff, program, and facility needs. These three major components of a strategic plan are determined by the congregational vision and mission. It is usually easy to see the need for new facilities or renovation of current facilities. Strategic planning team members find it more difficult to consider future program and staff needs. This difficulty is an example of the shades of gray mentioned earlier. Team members must be comfortable wrestling with the more uncertain future staff and program needs.

Create a balanced five-year plan. When strategic planning teams create a five-year plan for the first time, they tend to front-load the plan by projecting too many accomplishments in the first two years. It is more realistic to distribute the goals and activities evenly among the five years. The more even distribution will make it easier to provide the necessary resources and will diminish burnout in the first few years of the program.

Communicate. Seek feedback from the congregation. The strategic planning team should ask on a regular basis, "Are we accurately reflecting your wishes as expressed during Searching for the Future?"

Design activities for measurable results. A congregational vision informs the mission statement. The mission statement helps determine the goals, and the action plan describes the activities chosen to support the goals. The action plan also answers the following questions:

- What are our goals?

- Who will be primarily responsible for completion?

- When will activities be completed?

- What resources will be needed to complete each activity?

- How will outcomes be measured?

- How are we defining success?

- What barriers are we likely to encounter?

- What sources of help exist?

Note that the person who is primarily responsible for an activity is not necessarily the person who will actually complete it. The person who is primarily responsible may delegate the activity to someone else, but is still responsible for completion. If an activity is identified and no one can be found to take responsibility for its completion, a congregation would be wise to delete the activity from consideration. If the activity is really important, someone will tackle it.

At the end of this process, congregants should feel empowered to articulate and contribute to a common dream for the faith community. This unified vision will provide the basis for conversations about giving when the time comes for the annual budget drive or capital campaign.

CHAPTER FOUR

Annual Budget Drive

Money has everything to do with religion, with the choices that we make about how to be in relationship with ourselves, our neighbors, and with the divine. Religion is about life, and life, it seems, has a whole lot to do with money.

—Lynn Ungar

The annual budget drive is more than just an opportunity to raise money for the congregation's programs and ministries. It is also a chance to nurture stewardship among the church's members, to help them feel ownership of the congregation's mission. The way that you approach conversations about money carry a message about your faith community's theology of abundance and generosity. Several models for the budget drive are outlined in this chapter, and some accomplish this purpose better than others. Remember that money conversations need to occur within the context of a congregation's mission. This is a fundamental change from "If you don't give us enough money, the sky will surely fall" to "When we reach our financial goal, we will be able to (*fill in the blank*) so that we can better fulfill our congregational mission."

No matter which model you decide to use for the annual budget drive, often the first and most important step is to make a separate appeal to leadership donors. *Leadership donors* are often defined as those who are expected to contribute the top 10 to 15 percent of total financial commitments. Some congregations expand the definition to congregants who indicate they are giving a certain percentage of their income. And some expand the definition further to include members of the governing body, regardless of the size of their financial commitment. Create a definition

that works for your congregation. Professional religious leaders, regardless of their financial commitment, should always be considered leadership donors.

However leadership donors are defined, they are asked for a financial commitment in an early phase of the annual budget drive, before the rest of the congregation is asked. This early phase is referred to as the leadership gifts phase (or sometimes, the "silent phase"). Typically, the leadership donors are invited to a reception to celebrate the beginning of this phase and to hear about the plans for the funds that will be raised. (Guidelines for planning the leadership reception are given in Chapter 5.) During the next couple of weeks, the leadership donors are individually asked to make a financial commitment. No matter which method is used for the rest of the budget drive, the personal stewardship conversation method (described below) is always used with leadership donors. Asking leadership donors to make an early financial commitment helps ensure that the budget drive gets off to a good start.

Here is an overview of eight methods to consider for an annual budget drive. They offer a range of possibilities from personal to impersonal, efficient to time-consuming, and high probability of success to low probability of success. Each method is first described and then followed by a list of strengths and challenges. Some methods are recommended over others. Even those methods that are not recommended at all are described here in an effort to present a thorough picture of annual budget drive techniques—including some that congregations may have tried in the past, but hopefully will not use in the future.

The symbols after each method indicate the probability of success. Five stars (*****) indicate a high probability of success; one star (*) indicates a low probability of success.

Stewardship Conversations *****

This model of fundraising relies on individuals who are recruited to have personal conversations with prospective donors. These volunteers, called visiting stewards, focus their conversations on the mission of the congregation rather than on a request for money.

The commitment to talk with every donor requires lots of planning and careful scheduling. A leadership team must be formed; all visiting stewards must attend an orientation workshop; progress toward the financial goal must be monitored; and a follow-up program must be implemented to collect the unreturned financial commitment forms (previously called pledge cards).

In spite of the hard work, stewardship conversations provide the best way to give personal attention to the spiritual growth of the congregation. These conversations build and enhance the community through personal contacts. They provide feedback on how well the congregation is meeting the spiritual expectations of its congregants, and they gather the financial commitments essential to strengthening the congregation and the larger community.

We recommend using personal stewardship conversations as the foundation of a stewardship development program. Conducting an annual budget drive using personal stewardship conversations is discussed in depth in Chapter 5. Perhaps it goes without saying, but stewardship conversations are the only method to use in a capital campaign (as discussed in Chapter 11).

Strengths

- Deepens personal relationships within the congregation.

- Provides a vehicle for in-depth dialogue with congregants, including opportunities for questions, answers, and feedback.

- Offers a forum to provide stewardship education and interpretation.

- Creates a confidential, informal setting for frank dialogue.

- Produces a high level of financial response.

- Engages every donor in taking responsibility for giving financial support to the church.

- Gives all donors the opportunity to engage in a personal conversation.

- Can be completed in a fairly short time.

- Relatively cost effective, even with the guidance of a fundraising consultant.

- Helps to clean up the membership database.

- Over time, facilitates personal growth and acceptance of talking about money, giving, scarcity, and abundance.

Challenges

- Requires a corps of volunteers committed to having stewardship conversations.

- Requires visiting stewards who are mature and sensitive.

- Requires the guidance of an external fundraising consultant, especially in the first year.

- Requires a significant amount of time and energy from the annual budget leaders.

- Follow-up not as easy as with other methods.

- Requires coordination in getting all visiting stewards to attend an orientation workshop.

- Can be hindered by apprehension about discussing money, especially when used for the first time.

Commitment Sunday ✳✳✳✳

This method is sometimes called Dedication Sunday, Miracle Sunday, or Consecration Sunday. The method can be used successfully as an alternative approach to personal conversations once every few years. It can also be used as a "close the gap" Sunday if the annual budget drive falls short of the financial goal.

This method assumes that Sunday worship is the one event each week that draws the largest number of congregants. Commitment Sunday activities can take place before, during, or after the service. A religious professional, lay leader, or even guest preacher offers a motivational "Sermon on the Amount" that is relevant to your specific congregation. Testimonials are shared. Someone (usually the budget drive chair) announces the financial commitment to date (the amount already committed by leadership donors, as explained below). Congregants are asked to complete a financial commitment form during the service.

Don't be misled into thinking that Commitment Sunday is an easy, quick way to raise money for the next operating budget. The actual day of Commitment Sunday is preceded by lots of planning, publicity, and opportunities for the congregation to ask questions and raise concerns about the upcoming fiscal year. Three key components must be completed before the day of Commitment Sunday.

- Schedule several mailings, small-group meetings, and pulpit announcements. Make a compelling case that can be shared with the congregation.

- Talk with leadership donors and get their financial commitment *before* Commitment Sunday. Then announce the leadership donors' total financial commitment during the service to provide incentive to the rest of the congregation. It is unreasonable to rely on Commitment Sunday alone to secure all of the needed financial commitments.

- Before choosing a motivational speaker for Commitment Sunday, talk to representatives of congregations on the speaker's list of references. Explain that you are looking for someone to excite the congregation about fulfilling its vision through financial support of the operating budget. Look for a speaker who inherently brings a positive, upbeat, can-do attitude; who takes an Appreciative Inquiry approach by helping the congregation build on its strengths; and who promotes an attitude of abundance and generosity.

Be aware of the amount of follow-up required after Commitment Sunday. For the next couple of Sundays, before or after the service, offer congregants additional opportunities to financially support the church. Insert financial commitment forms into the order of service. Designate one person to collect the forms, and make sure that everyone knows where to find that person. After a couple of weeks, contact those who were not at Commitment Sunday and have not yet made their financial commitment.

Strengths

- Brings a skilled motivational speaker to the faith community.

- Promotes the concept of stewardship in a visible way.

- Convenient—financial commitment forms can be turned in directly during a Sunday service.

- Fairly easy to promote.

- Economical (although a guest speaker will want to receive an honorarium plus money for expenses).

Challenges

- Requires several information-sharing meetings and different types of publicity before Commitment Sunday.

- Relies heavily on many donors attending the service on one particular Sunday.

- May result in a Sunday service that some consider to be lacking in spirituality.

- Is unlikely to pique the interest of marginal congregants.

- Can lead to a higher "slippage rate" (the gap between commitments and money received), as people commit in a moment of exuberance rather than from careful consideration.

Cottage Meetings ✳✳✳✳

Cottage meetings are informal small-group meetings at the homes of congregants. The goal is to get each congregant to attend one cottage meeting. Sometimes the host provides snacks or dessert. Occasionally the meetings are scheduled as a potluck meal.

Two people from the annual budget drive team attend each meeting and make a presentation about the upcoming church fiscal year. The presentation uses a brochure that includes a case statement, a suggested fair-share giving guide, and an essential gifts chart. (These materials are explained in Chapter 6.) Other interpretive materials, such as informative handouts and posters, may also be used. Consider developing a presentation using software such as PowerPoint or Keynote to ensure consistency among all the cottage meetings.

At the end of the presentation, the budget drive team members entertain questions and address any concerns. They then distribute financial commitment forms, with an envelope for confidentiality. They collect the completed forms and deliver them to the budget drive treasurer.

Strengths

- Strengthens community and fellowship.

- Creates a low-key, informal approach to the annual budget drive.

- Stimulates small-group conversations.

- Is a good stewardship education tool.

- Can be a comfortable setting for newer congregants.

- Can be organized by geography, affinity group (such as choir, religious education teachers, women's alliance, etc.), or time availability.

- Requires a limited number of leaders, which increases consistency of the message.

- Is very cost-effective.

Challenges

- Engages only a few leaders to promote financial stewardship, thus limiting "ownership" in the process.

- Requires extensive telephone conversations to arrange attendance and to remind people (reservations are an absolute must).

- May not reach less-committed congregants.

- Can allow negative voices to hijack meetings unless the presentations are well managed.

- Requires a number of cottage meetings within a short time.

- Becomes more logistically difficult as congregations grow in membership.

Annual Congregational Dinner ✳✳✳

An annual dinner, in addition to providing congregants with a special night out to socialize with one another, can serve as the venue for asking for a financial commitment in an annual budget drive. The dinner may be held in the fellowship hall of the church or elsewhere, and may be catered or a potluck. At the end of the evening, entertainment is provided. In the interval between the dinner and the entertainment, the budget drive program is presented. Team members distribute and explain the annual drive brochure, the case statement, the suggested fair-share giving guide, and the essential gifts chart (if one is being used). Two or three congregants may be asked to deliver short testimonials. If the leadership donors have already made their financial commitment, the total amount to date is announced.

If the congregational dinner is to be the main method of conducting the annual budget drive, the financial commitment forms and envelopes are distributed. Congregants complete the forms and then turn them in.

A similar congregational dinner (usually called a fellowship event) can serve as the kickoff for a budget drive that uses personal stewardship conversations. In that case, the financial commitment forms are not distributed that evening. Instead, during the next few weeks the forms are brought to each donor by visiting stewards. Chapter 5 provides more information about this approach, including guidelines for planning the event.

Strengths

- Sends a clear message that this event is special.

- Works well as an occasional alternative to personal stewardship conversations or to launch a personal stewardship conversation drive.

- Requires only one evening to collect many financial commitment forms (if the dinner is the primary method used for the budget drive).

- Provides the congregation with an enjoyable night out together, with the food, setup, breakdown, and cleanup all done by others.

- Builds a stronger sense of community.

- Requires a relatively small number of people to plan the event.

- Ensures a consistent message because only a few people make presentations.

- Can include the housebound and parents with young children if transportation and child care are provided.

- Is easy to promote.

Challenges

- Can be expensive if not held at the church or at another local faith community.

- Is not personal because there are no face-to-face conversations between one donor and one visiting steward.

- Depends on all congregants being available on one evening. (*Hint:* Reserve the date and location a year in advance to ensure a good venue and so that people can put the date on their calendars.)

- May require two dinners to accommodate everyone in a large congregation.

- Is unlikely to entice marginal congregants, although personal invitations are helpful.

- May overemphasize social atmosphere and entertainment, obscuring the stewardship education purpose of the evening.

- May not be conducive to asking questions or raising concerns.

- Requires follow-up to contact all who did not attend.

Faith Promise ❋❋

This method emphasizes personal faith rather than the operating budget. Individual capacity for giving is the criterion for financial commitment. The faith promise approach is unique in that the donor makes a personal covenant with God. The donor is accountable to God rather than to the congregation. The approach stresses the need of the donor to give, as opposed to the need of the faith community to receive. E. Barent Grevatt, a United Church of Christ minister, describes this method: "Faith promise provides participants with an instrument with which to express their identity as persons in a partnership that is both human and divine."

In this approach, donors are asked to make a faith promise during a motivational and emotionally charged worship service. As with Commitment Sunday, a motivational speaker is asked to lead the service. Unlike Commitment Sunday, the dollar amount of the faith promise is not a financial commitment, but represents the amount of money each congregant will strive to be able to give as the Lord blesses his or her life.

Congregants are asked to place the amount of their faith promise on a card. They are asked to indicate the frequency with which the faith promise will be given and the percentage of their income that it represents. The congregant's name is not put on the card. In a separate act of commitment, congregants are asked to submit a card with their name, indicating that they have made a faith promise, but not indicating the amount. With that information the annual budget drive team contacts those who have not made a faith promise.

We do not recommend this method for Unitarian Universalist congregations. The faith promise is better suited for evangelical congregations.

Strengths

- Can be a financially rewarding and spiritual experience for congregations that have had previous experience with this method.

- Can promote a healthy awareness that financial stewardship is congruent with a faith life.

- Can be quickly implemented with minimal cost.

- Appeals to the spiritual strength of people.

- Can have a significant Biblical motivation.

Challenges

- Can result in a significant gap between the amount of the faith promise and the actual contribution, leading to serious budget problems. Congregational leaders must know how much to "discount" faith promises.

- Is highly impersonal.

- Impossible to follow up with reminder letters or monthly/quarterly statements.

- Does not reach housebound people or others not attending the Faith Promise Sunday.

Pony Express *

This method is known by several different names, including personal delivery, Paul Revere's ride, whistle stop, run for the roses, up and running, and circuit rider. The method is simple and methodical, but generally ineffective. It requires dividing the congregation into teams (sometimes called families, trails, chains, or tracks) of ten households each. The process begins with each team leader delivering a packet of interpretive information, including a financial commitment form, to the second donor on the list. The team leader talks a bit about the church's needs during a short visit when the packet is delivered.

The second person reviews the material, completes a financial commitment form, and either mails the form to the annual budget drive treasurer or returns the form (sealed in an envelope) to the packet. In some drives the donor is asked to hold the completed form until a Sunday worship service at which all the forms are accepted. In any case, the second person delivers the packet to the third person on the list. The process continues until the tenth donor has received the packet and completed the financial commitment form. Assuming all the teams start at the same time and make two visits per week, the pony express could be completed within five weeks.

Strengths

- Encourages every family to take responsibility for the financial health of the church.

- Treats every donor equally, unless some are not visited.

- Allows household visits to be completed in a relatively short period of time.

- Requires little training.

- Helps to clean up the membership list.

- Can be fun, stimulating, and foster a playful spirit.

Challenges

- Assumes that every donor agrees to be visited and agrees to visit another donor.

- Can be difficult to manage, with delays or significant breakdowns in the delivery of packets.

- Almost always results in inconsistency when some teams are unable or unwilling to complete their visits.

- Creates difficulty in getting the completed financial commitment forms returned.

- Does not provide an opportunity for questions to be asked or concerns to be addressed.

- Can be impersonal.

- Limits dialogue about the mission of the congregation.

- Offers little or no opportunity for stewardship education.

- Creates uncomfortable situations in which the team leaders can be viewed as using guilt to coerce donors into making larger financial commitments.

- Does not offer homebound people the opportunity to fully participate.

- Prevents the congregation from having open discussions about money and moving toward a culture of abundance.

Telephone Appeal *

Although this method is still used by public broadcasting networks, it is rapidly losing support and becoming obsolete in faith communities' annual budget drives. The concept is that a team of callers, preferably all located in one call center, seeks financial commitments over the phone. With answering machines, voice mail, caller identification, and call screening, it has become increasingly difficult to speak to people over the phone, and only a small percentage of people ever return calls. While a telephone approach is not recommended as a primary method, it has some merit as a follow-up technique, as described in Chapter 5.

Strengths

- Can be effective as a follow-up to other, more direct methods.

- Provides a way to reach congregational alumni (those congregants who have moved away but want to stay in contact).

Challenges

- Is highly impersonal.

- Depends on persons answering the phone rather than screening their calls.

- Requires many repeat phone calls, taking an inordinate amount of time.

- Makes the potential donor responsible for returning the call.

- Presents a risk of calling at an inopportune time.

- Requires careful training of the telephone callers.

- Does not produce a written financial commitment, opening the door for misunderstanding and increasing the chances of an unfulfilled commitment.

Direct Mail Appeal *

Do not be misled by the term *direct*. Direct mail is the most indirect, and consequently the least effective, way to approach an annual budget drive. Some congregations have tried to make direct mail more personal by including a handwritten note with the letter. The personal note does help, but some congregants are disappointed to receive a written request for money from their own faith community.

One exception to this approach: Send a letter to members who have moved away but want to maintain some connection to the church. These alumni occasionally surprise congregations when they return a significant financial commitment.

Strengths

- Doesn't require many people to develop and administer.

- Is inexpensive and doesn't require much time or energy.

- Can be quickly implemented.

- Guarantees consistency and accuracy in presenting the message.

- Provides a way to reach congregational alumni.

Challenges

- Is highly impersonal.

- Does not provide for discussion, questions, or sharing of concerns.

- Does not guarantee that budget drive materials will be viewed or read. Some people simply do not open direct mailings, even from their own faith community.

- Tends to have response rates of less than 20 percent.

- Requires a major follow-up plan.

The personal stewardship conversations method has the most advantages of all the strategies that could be used in an annual budget drive. Personal stewardship conversations are important, and not only for the purpose of asking for money. They provide an opportunity to build on current congregational strengths, to share success stories, to build community, and to begin a move toward a culture of abundance.

Having said that, we do not recommend using personal stewardship conversations in every annual budget drive. The level of success often drops dramatically as the congregation becomes matter-of-fact about the process. After three consecutive years of personal stewardship conversations, use a Commitment Sunday model for the fourth year. In the fifth year, conduct cottage meetings. Repeat the five-year sequence in the sixth through tenth years. (Of course, personal stewardship conversations are the *only* method that should be used for capital campaigns, as discussed in Chapter 11.)

With so many advantages, personal stewardship conversations must become a vital part of each congregation's ministry. The next chapter will take a closer look at the process of using personal stewardship conversations in an annual budget drive.

CHAPTER FIVE

Personal Stewardship Conversations

It is a rare and high privilege to be in a position to help people understand the difference that they can make not only in their own lives but in the lives of others by simply giving of themselves.

—Helen Boosalis

Experience has shown that the stewardship conversations model is generally the most successful approach to fundraising for an annual budget drive, This chapter will provide a detailed explanation of how to implement this strategy and avoid some common pitfalls. (Guidelines for using personal stewardship conversations for a capital campaign are detailed in Chapter 11.) Every annual budget drive is unique, and the specific process varies from one congregation to the next. However, in the interest of simplicity, this discussion operates on several assumptions:

- The congregation is committed to using the personal stewardship conversations method.

- The congregation has decided to use a fundraising consultant to guide them through the budget drive. (This decision is especially wise if the congregation has no recent history with stewardship conversations or if the congregation has not reached its annual budget goal in recent years.)

- The consultant is scheduled to make between three and six on-site visits to the church.

- The key decision makers are the people on the annual budget drive leadership team.

The Leadership Team

Recruiting the best annual budget drive leaders greatly increases the likelihood of success. Recruiting is helped by the fact that there are specific role responsibilities for each leadership position. Be sure that the governing body provides the list of co-chair responsibilities when they are recruiting those two people. Once recruited, the co-chairs can then use the remaining role descriptions to recruit the rest of the leadership team. (Preparing written fundraising materials, which are included in several of these descriptions, is described in more detail in Chapter 6.)

The annual budget drive co-chairs manage the drive, from recruiting teammates to planning the final celebration. It is best to have two co-chairs, each agreeing to a two-year term, with the terms staggered so that continuity can be maintained from one year to the next. Ask a professional religious leader or the governing body president to recruit the annual drive co-chairs, looking for these characteristics:

- Thorough understanding that financial giving is an example of stewardship

- Previous financial commitment to the faith community

- Significant time and energy to complete the tasks

- Strong leadership and organizational skills

- Understanding of the relationship between financial giving and stewardship

- Ability to inspire others

- History of completing tasks on time

- Solid relationship with the professional religious leaders

- Willingness to work collaboratively with the rest of the leadership team

- Ability and willingness to delegate

- Commitment to work closely with the fundraising consultant

Specific responsibilities of the co-chairs are to:

- Recruit the rest of the annual budget drive leadership team

- Develop the essential gifts chart (with help from the congregational treasurer and one or two long-time congregants)

- Help develop the annual program budget (with the finance committee chair and the governing body president)

- Oversee development of the case statement (or they may ask a task force to create the statement)

- Supervise creation of the written summary of programs and ministries (or they may ask a couple of governing body members to create the summary)

- Develop the fact sheet

- Approve details of the suggested fair-share giving guide (see the UUA guide on page 130)

- Direct creation of the brochure (constructed by the publications team)

- Write a brief final report

The leadership gifts co-chairs focus on activities related to soliciting gifts from leadership donors (those who will be asked to make a substantial financial commitment). They also lead by example, contributing two of the largest annual budget drive gifts. The leadership gifts co-chairs:

- Plan a leadership reception and sometimes host it

- Write a letter to the congregation

- Recruit team leaders for the leadership gifts part of the drive

- Help team leaders match visiting stewards with specific donors

- Help team leaders monitor the stewardship conversations

- Write a brief final report

The general gifts co-chairs oversee the process by which congregants other than the leadership donors are visited. Strong organizational skills are needed, plus an ability to recruit and inspire. But the most important qualities of general gifts co-chairs are to be supportive of the project and to have a willingness to share their passion. The general gifts co-chairs:

- Recruit group leaders if the drive is big enough. Group leaders recruit team leaders, who in turn recruit the general gifts visiting stewards

- Supervise the group leaders during the weeks of the general gifts stewardship conversations, offering encouragement and guidance and reminding the group leaders to maintain contact with their team leaders

- Write a brief final report

The fellowship event chair is responsible for the congregation-wide event that launches the annual budget drive. (The event is described on page 44.) The chair needs several team members, so he or she must have good organizational skills and the ability to delegate responsibility. The fellowship chair writes a brief final report after the event has concluded.

The publicity chair is responsible for presenting the annual budget drive information to the congregation. The chair announces the orientation workshops for visiting stewards. The publicity chair also develops a comprehensive publicity strategy and implements the strategy as the fundraising effort gains momentum.

To raise awareness, use several of the following publicity options.

- Inserts in the Sunday order of worship
- Church newsletter articles
- Weekly website updates
- Banners and posters
- Bulletin board displays
- Three-dimensional displays (scale model for a building project)
- Local radio and television
- Creative songs and jingles
- Skits
- Balloons, badges, bookmarks, travel mugs, pens, souvenir hard hats
- DVDs and videotapes
- PowerPoint presentations
- Local newspapers

The publications chair manages all of the annual budget drive publications, ensuring continuity and consistency of all materials. A team is recruited and is responsible for publishing (but not creating) seven pieces of budget drive information (discussed in detail in Chapter 6):

- Case statement
- Summary of programs and ministries
- Program budget charts
- Essential gifts chart
- Suggested fair-share giving guide
- Brochure

- Financial commitment form

The follow-up chair is needed because even in the most successful fundraising efforts, there are unreturned financial commitment forms at the end of the general gifts phase. The follow-up chair is responsible for getting the rest of the commitment forms returned. He or she recruits a team of three to seven people to help complete the task. Team members need creativity, sensitivity, and good judgment in determining the best way to approach each situation. Suggestions for ways to follow up begin on page 46.

The budget drive treasurer is responsible for creating and maintaining the data input and retrieval systems that provide all the necessary financial information. The budget drive treasurer needs to be good with details and able to create computer spreadsheets. Because the budget drive treasurer handles confidential financial information, the person must have the trust of the congregation.

Once the budget drive is launched, the budget drive treasurer should be ready to receive the donor-signed financial commitment forms from the annual budget drive co-chairs, the leadership gifts co-chairs, the leadership gifts team leaders, the general gifts co-chairs, the general gifts team leaders, and the visiting stewards. To accomplish this task, the budget drive treasurer obtains from the administrative support chair a master list of all congregants who are being asked for financial commitments. The list is essential to keep track of all the commitment forms.

The budget drive treasurer also:

- Provides regular cash flow reports to the budget drive co-chairs and answers questions
- Coordinates sending confirmation letters to all donors
- Creates a final financial report and submits it to the budget drive co-chairs. The report should include an accurate accounting of the total amount committed to the fundraising effort
- Transfers all financial data to the church trea-

surer after the final financial report has been submitted

The administrative support chair manages all administrative tasks related to the annual budget drive. There are so many administrative tasks to complete that it is unrealistic to think that a church administrator can absorb them all. The administrative support chair and team are responsible for three main tasks:

- Create and maintain the donor databank (see page 38)

- Prepare mailings

- Put together information packets (see page 41) for the visiting stewards

Calendar

First Month

1. Professional religious leader and governing-body president recruit annual budget drive co-chairs.

2. Co-chairs recruit other leadership team members.

3. Consultant makes first on-site visit; meets with leadership team; introduces stewardship conversations method.

4. Co-chairs, the Finance Committee chair, and governing-body president start to develop program budget for next fiscal year.

5. Co-chairs and the consultant develop a six-month calendar with specific launch date and closing date.

6. Publicity team creates comprehensive public strategy; takes pictures for brochure and fellowship event.

7. Fellowship Event Team reserves location for fellowship event (if not already done).

Second Month

1. Publicity Team completes comprehensive publicity strategy.

2. Budget drive treasurer and Finance Committee complete program budget.

3. Task force (selected by budget drive co-chairs) develops first-draft case statement and shares with Leadership Team.

4. Fellowship Event Team plans fellowship event meal.

5. Administrative support chair compiles donor contact list (from the donor data bank).

6. Leadership Team meets to review progress.

Third Month

1. Leadership Team gathers information for the brochure and Publications Team starts to construct the brochure.

2. Consultant makes second on-site visit and meets with Leadership Team.

3. Leadership Team approves final case statement.

4. Leadership gifts co-chairs plan leadership reception and recruit leadership gifts visiting stewards.

5. Budget drive treasurer develops financial commitment form and submits to Publications Team.

6. Publications Team begins development of other publications.

7. Fellowship Event Team plans program and entertainment.

8. Governing body approves program budget.

9. Co-chairs send first letter to all congregants.

Fourth Month

1. Consultant makes third on-site visit and meets with Leadership Team.

2. Two governing-body members (selected by budget drive co-chairs) develop summary of programs and ministries.

3. Publications Team continues to develop brochure.

4. Co-chairs develop fact sheet and give to Publications Team.

5. Leadership gifts co-chairs write fellowship event invitations.

6. General gifts co-chairs write fellowship event invitations.

7. Administrative Support Team mails invitations.

8. Fellowship Event Team recruits table hosts and hostesses.

9. Leadership gifts co-chairs complete plans for leadership reception.

10. Leadership gifts co-chairs recruit their visiting stewards.

11. General gifts co-chairs recruit their visiting stewards.

12. Minister writes second letter (to alumni, with financial commitment form enclosed).

13. Administrative Support Team mails leadership reception, fellowship event invitations, and second letter.

14. Minister preaches sermon on stewardship.

15. Leadership Team meets to review progress.

Fifth Month

1. Publications Team shares draft brochure with consultant.

2. Publicity Team publicizes orientation workshops.

3. Governing-body president writes third letter (to all congregants except alumni).

4. Publications Team mails third letter.

5. Minister preaches second sermon on stewardship.

6. Leadership Team meets to review progress.

Sixth Month

1. Leadership gifts co-chairs write fourth letter (to all congregants except alumni).

2. Consultant reviews *all* materials *before* printing.

3. Budget drive co-chairs, leadership gifts co-chairs, general gifts co-chairs, and congregational treasurer match each visiting steward with four donors.

4. During a worship service, a verbal commitment is made between the congregation and the visiting stewards. (See page 123 for a sample covenant).

5. Administrative Support Team prepares orientation workshop materials.

6. Consultant conducts orientation workshop for all visiting stewards.

7. Leadership reception is held.

8. Leadership gifts visiting stewards have stewardship conversations with leadership donors.

9. Fellowship event is held, signifying launch of the annual budget drive.

10. General gifts visiting stewards have stewardship conversations with remaining donors.

11. Minister preaches third stewardship sermon.

12. Budget drive treasurer collects financial commitment forms and enters information into donor database.

Seventh Month

1. Follow-Up Team pursues unreturned financial commitment forms.

2. Budget drive treasurer computes financial commitments and writes final report.

3. Each leadership team writes final report.

4. Close-out meeting: Leadership teams meet with consultant for evaluation and to lay foundation for next year's budget drive.

5. Volunteers celebrate end of the budget drive.

6. Book is closed on annual budget drive.

Donor Databank

The administrative support chair gathers full information (name), mailing address, phone number, and e-mail address) for each donor who is asked to participate in a stewardship conversation with a visiting steward. The list should indicate if each household has had one, two, or more donors making separate contributions in the previous year. The list *should not* include the amount of any previous financial commitments to the operating budget. As explained later in this chapter, it is helpful if visiting stewards are unaware of a donor's financial commitments to previous annual budget drives.

Letters to the Congregation

Four letters to the congregation are an integral part of an annual budget drive:

First letter. The fundraising co-chairs write the first letter, which is sent to all congregants.

- Make the case for financial support of next year's annual programs and ministries.

- Indicate the financial commitment goal for the annual budget drive.

- Explain the personal stewardship conversations process.

- Summarize the current financial condition of the faith community.

- Request the most generous financial gifts ever given.

Second letter. A professional religious leader writes to congregational alumni (those congregants who have moved away but want to stay in contact).

- Include information similar to that in the first letter.

- Request a financial commitment. Enclose a financial commitment form and a stamped envelope, and ask for the financial commitment form to be returned to the church.

Third letter. The governing body president writes to all congregants (excluding alumni).

- Share a summary of the current programs and ministries and the desired new programs and ministries.

- Reiterate the plan for stewardship conversations between visiting stewards and donors.

Fourth letter. The leadership gifts co-chairs write to all congregants (excluding alumni).

- Provide a personal testimony.

- Reinforce the plan for stewardship conversations.

- Ask congregants to be receptive to the visiting stewards and to welcome the conversations.

Remember to focus on the positive in each letter. Use the letters as an opportunity to apply the concept of Appreciative Inquiry (see page 17). Share confidence that the congregation will achieve the financial goal. Personalize each letter by using creative and colorful imagery while sharing personal thoughts and convictions. Keep the letters to an absolute maximum of one full page, remembering the words of Blaise Pascal: "I have made this letter rather long only because I have not had time to make it shorter."

Leadership Reception

Whether planning an annual budget drive or a capital campaign, hold a reception for all of the potential leadership donors—those expected to make a substantial financial commitment. (For more details about how leadership donors are defined, see Chapter 4.) The leadership reception is designed to accomplish five goals:

- To gather together all of the potential leadership donors.

- To celebrate the launch of the silent phase (the first phase during which leadership financial commitments are made) of the fundraising effort.

- To share the brochure and hear about plans to be undertaken when the financial commitments have been received.

- To ask each donor to consider making a large financial contribution.

- To announce that each donor will be asked for a financial commitment in a personal stewardship conversation during the next couple of weeks.

Send personal invitations to the potential leadership donors. A sample invitation is provided on page 124.

The reception is often scheduled for a Sunday afternoon or an early evening in the home of one of the leadership donors. Provide light refreshments. If alcohol is served, also offer nonalcoholic beverages. Begin with an opening prayer, reading, or centering exercise. Distribute the campaign brochure, provide a brief summary of the project, and have two or three short testimonials (no more than three minutes each). Explain the importance of financial commitments from this group, and prepare them for upcoming conversations with the visiting stewards.

Do not solicit financial commitments during the reception. Secure all commitments during stewardship conversations between the visiting stewards and the leadership donors during the few weeks after the reception.

How Many Visiting Stewards?

Whether the congregation is planning a relatively small fundraising effort or a larger effort, the coordination philosophy is the same: Conduct as many stewardship conversations as possible, assigning each visiting steward a maximum of four donors. The more visiting stewards that can be recruited, the more stewardship conversations can occur.

It is sometimes difficult to recruit enough visiting stewards to conduct conversations with every donor. If this is the case, it is best to maintain the four-to-one ratio even if means that some donors

will not have the benefit of a stewardship conversation. Some of these donors may be invited to a cottage meeting or contacted by phone to make their financial commitments.

We don't recommend asking visiting stewards to conduct more than four stewardship conversations. The visiting stewards' job becomes more time-consuming and the number of completed conversations diminishes. Requiring too much of the visiting stewards also makes it more difficult to recruit visiting stewards the following year.

The process of coordinating stewardship conversations is the same, regardless of the size of the fundraising effort and regardless of whether the effort is to raise money for an annual budget drive or a capital campaign. Larger efforts just require a few more steps.

Let's take the example of coordinating stewardship conversations in a congregation of 397 donors. During the leadership gifts phase:

- The fundraising consultant has a stewardship conversation with the fundraising chair (1 conversation).

- The fundraising chair has a stewardship conversation with the minister (1 conversation).

- The fundraising chair has a conversation with the leadership gifts chair (1 conversation).

- The leadership gifts chair has an individual conversation with the 2 team leaders (2 conversations).

- Each of the 2 team leaders talks with 4 visiting stewards (8 conversations).

- Each of the 8 visiting stewards talks with 4 donors (32 conversations).

During the general gifts phase in the same example,

- The fundraising chair has an individual stewardship conversation with each of the 2 general gifts co-chairs (2 conversations).

- Each of the 2 general gifts co-chairs has an individual conversation with 2 group leaders (4 conversations).

- Each of the 4 group leaders has an individual conversation with 4 team leaders (16 conversations).

- Each of the 16 team leaders talks with 4 visiting stewards (64 conversations).

- Each of the 64 visiting stewards talks with 4 donors (256 conversations).

The example can be contracted or expanded by decreasing or increasing the number of group leaders, team leaders, and visiting stewards as needed. But remember to assign visiting stewards to a maximum of four stewardship conversations.

Recruiting Visiting Stewards

In spite of their best efforts, some congregational leaders have difficulty finding enough visiting stewards. They may be tempted to lower their recruiting standards to fill their roster, or to ask visiting stewards to talk with five or more donors instead of four. It is better to maintain the four-to-one ratio and, if necessary, to move forward with an incomplete roster, even if it means that some donors will not have conversations with a visiting steward. Similarly, even though asking for a financial commitment by phone is a poor substitute for asking in person, it is better to seek commitments by phone than to select visiting stewards who are not fully committed.

Many people are hesitant to become visiting stewards. They may fear the scope of the task, thinking that the role requires them to extricate more money than the donor is comfortable giving. Or they may think that they must know every detail about the fundraising effort if they are going to ask others to contribute to it.

Fortunately, these assumptions are incorrect. In fact, annual budget drive visiting stewards will be unable to talk about budget specifics, because a line-item budget doesn't get developed until *after* the budget drive has been completed. They can refer to a program budget chart (see page 50), but nothing more specific. (Similarly, visiting stewards for a capital campaign will certainly need to understand the proposed project, but the scope of the project, the attending details, and the cost of the project will not be determined until *after* the capital campaign financial commitments have been totaled.)

Still, it can be difficult to recruit volunteers, especially the first year that a congregation uses personal stewardship conversations. The in-person approach is the best way to recruit. A telephone conversation is a distant second option. A written request (letter or e-mail) is clearly the least effective approach and will generate the smallest number of volunteers.

When asking people to volunteer, emphasize these points:

- It is an honor to be asked to be a group leader, team leader, or visiting steward. Only congregants who are deeply committed to the faith community and the proposed project can fill these integral positions.

- Stewardship conversations are experiences of fellowship and sharing. Visiting stewards do not use any type of pressuring activity. A one-hour conversation should include only a few minutes of talking about money.

- Visiting stewards are not expected to do any negotiating with potential donors. In fact, most donors will have already decided upon their financial commitment before the visiting steward talks with them.

- The time commitment is relatively short. Group leaders and team leaders can expect about a four- to six-week commitment. Visiting stewards can expect about a three- to four-week commitment, depending on the total number of conversations with donors.

- The experience of being a group leader, team leader, or visiting steward can enhance the faith development of those who volunteer for those roles.

To make the recruiting of visiting stewards easier, ask recruits for only one commitment: to attend an orientation workshop. At the end of the workshop, if they feel comfortable about the visiting steward role, they will be asked to have stewardship conversations with a maximum of four donors. If they are uncomfortable with the role, they are under no further obligation.

Matching Visiting Stewards with Donors

Prior to the orientation workshop, the budget drive co-chairs, leadership gifts co-chairs, and general gifts co-chairs match each visiting steward with four donors. Contrary to conventional wisdom that visiting stewards and donors are most comfortable if they know each other well, visiting stewards often prefer to avoid talking to their friends about money. In fact, it is helpful to match visiting stewards with unfamiliar donors. Unfamiliarity promotes genuine conversation with the donor. Through these interactions, new friendships are created. Talking with unfamiliar people provides an opportunity to expand the faith community.

We are not suggesting the random matching of visiting stewards with specific donors. The annual drive co-chairs, the leadership gifts co-chairs, the general gifts co-chairs, and the congregational treasurer have enough knowledge about most of the donors to make good matches. Three criteria, in descending order of importance, for determining a good match are:

* Comparable giving levels.

* Similar degree of current participation in the congregation.

* Geographic proximity of the visiting steward and the donor.

The first two criteria help create a peer relationship during conversation between the donor and the steward. The third criterion, location, would be a bigger issue if all conversations had to occur in donors' homes, but conversations can occur wherever it is fairly quiet and the two are unlikely to be interrupted. Favorite locations include breakfast cafés, lunchtime restaurants, parks, the beach, or a quiet spot at church during off-peak hours.

When matching a visiting steward with four donors, the first of the four donors should be someone who is easy to talk with and who is likely to provide a successful first conversation for the visiting steward.

Orientation Workshops

Orientation workshops are a way for the visiting stewards to learn from the fundraising consultant. The four goals for attendees are:

* To understand the role of the visiting steward.

* To maintain the dignity of each visiting steward.

* To practice stewardship conversations in a safe atmosphere.

* To have some fun.

The orientation workshop is one of the most important elements of a stewardship conversation approach to a fundraising effort. Each workshop helps participants overcome their anxieties about asking for money. It provides a nonthreatening venue in which participants can maintain their dignity as they practice their approach to donors. And it ensures that all visiting stewards get the same information so that there is some uniformity about the way they approach their stewardship conversations.

Because of the participative nature of orientation workshops, schedule a minimum of ten and a maximum of twenty participants for each workshop. If there are fewer than ten, it's hard to maintain lively interaction. If there are more than twenty, it's hard for the consultant to manage the workshop and answer all the questions.

Careful attention to the following elements will help ensure successful workshops and significantly increase the number of workshop participants who agree to become visiting stewards.

Information Packets

Before the workshops occur, ask the Administrative Support Team to prepare an information packet for each visiting steward. The fundraising consultant will distribute the packets during the workshop. Include the following items in each packet. (Guidelines for preparing most of these items are found in Chapter 6.)

- A contact list with the name, address, phone number, and e-mail address of each of the four donors to which the steward has been assigned. The list should indicate whether the household had one, two, or more donors making separate contributions in the previous year. The list *should not* include the amount of any previous financial commitments to the operating budget.

- Essential gifts charts (for the packets of leadership gifts visiting stewards only)

- The suggested fair share giving guide. (For a capital campaign, substitute the financial commitment request level for each donor.)

- Four copies of the fundraising brochure. Although donors may have already seen the brochure, they may have lost it or forgotten what they read. The visiting steward can give the donor a new brochure if needed

- Four copies of the case statement, if not included in the brochure

- Four summaries of current congregational programs and ministries

- Four financial commitment forms

- Four envelopes (to ensure privacy of the completed financial commitment forms)

- Four lined index cards for recording any donor commendations or concerns

- Four thank-you note cards with envelopes

Publicity

The publicity team is responsible for announcing the orientation workshops well in advance. The better the publicity, the easier it is to recruit workshop participants. A representative from the publicity team can collaborate with the fundraising consultant to plan various publicity pieces. These might include a congregation-wide mailing and short articles for the order of service, the newsletter, and the website. Focus publicity on the purpose and importance of the workshops, and include a description of the visiting stewards' role.

Planning and Logistics

The annual budget drive co-chairs are responsible for recruiting a small team of volunteers to manage the logistics of the orientation workshops. If public transportation is available, schedule the workshop time around that schedule, or arrange carpooling for people who cannot drive to the workshop.

Consult the church calendar to ensure the availability of a meeting room. Be sure the room is barrier-free, with enough space for wheelchairs and scooters to maneuver. It should also have good lighting, adjustable heating and cooling systems, and easy access to bathrooms. The room needs to be large enough for twenty people to sit comfortably at tables arranged in a horseshoe shape. Tables are helpful because many participants take notes during a workshop.

Some fundraising consultants use presentation software, such as PowerPoint or Keynote. They will bring their own LCD projector but will need a projection screen. The fundraising consultant also needs an easel pad and a set of colored markers. If items will be written on an easel pad, consider using a "scribe" system so that one person writes on the easel pad, while a second person, facing the workshop participants, speaks the words that are being written. The scribe system is helpful for people who can't see or hear well.

Provide food and beverages for each workshop. At a morning session, offer bagels or muffins, coffee, and tea. For an early afternoon or evening workshop, offer soup and sandwiches or pizza, soft drinks, coffee, and tea. Provide fruit, crackers, cheese, cookies, and bottled water in every workshop. Attention to these details will send a message that this work is important and that you are committed to taking good care of all the congregants who volunteer to help with the fundraising effort.

Workshop Content

The orientation workshops offer participants suggestions for scheduling and conducting a stewardship conversation. Each workshop employs the best practices of adult learning. The consultant explains and demonstrates the skills of a visiting steward using an Appreciative Inquiry approach (see page 17). For example, although workshop participants are not asked to put on a pair of rose-colored glasses, they learn how to acknowledge the positive aspects of their faith community and how to invite donors to share their positive experiences. Two-way communication is encouraged throughout the workshop. The consultant shares case studies from previous fundraising efforts, and the participants are given practical experience when they participate in simulations.

As the workshop unfolds, participants start to shape their own style, picking and choosing from a variety of options. There is no script to memorize, no one-and-only way to complete the task. A visiting steward who is "reading off some other person's page" will sound uncomfortable, and that awkwardness will be apparent to the donor. In contrast, visiting stewards who feel comfortable about their role and speak from their heart will be effective. The next section of this chapter gives guidelines for stewardship conversations.

The most helpful part of the workshop—and the part that sometimes causes participants the most angst—is the time devoted to simulations. Toward the end of the workshop, participants pair up, retire to a quiet corner or to another room, and simulate scheduling and conducting a stewardship conversation. Each participant gets to simulate the visiting steward and the donor.

When the simulations have been completed, the participants have fun discussing their experience with each other. The consultant asks, "What went well? What didn't go so well? Were there any surprises? Did you learn something you didn't know before? Did the simulations generate new questions? What will you do differently the next time?" A consultant who is passionate about the role, who feels that the workshop makes a real difference, and who considers this work to be a personal ministry will be able to impart some genuine joy into the workshop.

At the end of the orientation workshop, the consultant reviews the information packets with the participants. The consultant allows time to ask final questions and ensures that the participants are clear about the commitment they are making.

Occasionally, but not often, a workshop participant decides that he or she is not comfortable with the role of visiting steward. The person simply speaks to the consultant during a break before or after the simulations, and the consultant accepts that information gracefully and without question. As disappointing as it may be to lose a potential visiting steward, the leaders are better off knowing now rather than later, when the person may struggle with the task or just never conduct the conversations.

The most important outcome of an orientation workshop is that the congregation takes a step toward becoming more direct about money talk. In so doing, the congregation moves a bit farther away from the myth of scarcity and a bit closer to the reality of abundance.

Guidelines for Stewardship Conversations

With the orientation workshops complete, the visiting stewards are ready to schedule their four conversations. It is preferable to contact the donors by phone rather than by e-mail. Although the scheduling can be done right away, the stewards should not begin visiting donors until after the leadership reception (in the case of leadership gifts visiting stewards) or the fellowship event (in the case of general gifts visiting stewards).

Visiting stewards are encouraged to begin each visit without an expectation of the outcome. Although they certainly ask each donor for a financial commitment, they are discouraged from expecting a certain level of commitment. To have any expectation is really quite presumptuous. Having an expectation means that the visiting steward knows how much a donor *should* give. But based on what? A presumption of the donor's income?

A presumption of their net worth or the amount of their secured assets? An assumption based on the type of car driven by the donor? A visiting steward need not know the income level or the financial responsibilities of the donor. Furthermore, visiting stewards need not know the amount of the donor's financial commitment to previous annual budget drives. Visiting stewards are well served to discard expectations and "shoulds" from their stewardship conversation vocabulary.

Asking for money is simple, but not easy. It should always be done within the context of fulfilling the mission of the faith community. Money is important, but it is nothing more than a means to an end. Money simply helps congregations fund their ministries. We recommend spending 90 percent of the time in a personal stewardship conversation exchanging stories about the church, not talking about money. In orientation workshops, visiting stewards are told that they have missed the point of the conversation if they spend any more than ten minutes (of a one-hour conversation) talking about money.

Visiting stewards use the essential gifts chart as a guide to asking leadership gifts donors for a financial commitment at one of the listed giving levels. They use the fair-share giving guide with all other donors.

Visiting stewards are instructed to finish each conversation with a completed financial commitment form. If a donor can't decide on the amount, the visiting steward schedules another time to get the form completed rather than leaving the form with the donor. There is a dreadfully low return rate when commitment forms are left with donors. Envelopes are included in the visiting steward's packet because donors may prefer the privacy of putting their financial commitment form in an envelope, especially when a stewardship conversation approach is first being introduced.

With the donor's permission, visiting stewards may record any donor commendations or concerns, using the cards provided in the information packet, and forward the cards to the president of the governing body. The president collates the information and identifies themes. The governing body and the professional religious leader(s) then decide how to process the themes. For example, let's assume that there are concerns about the beauty and meaningfulness of a recently constructed memorial garden. The governing body and the minister may choose to publicize the names of those responsible for creating the garden. They may ask for a task force of volunteers to develop a plan for ongoing maintenance. They may ask for input about ways in which to memorialize people. Whatever responses are chosen, they must become public knowledge so that donors will know that their comments were heard. If they feel as though they were not heard, donors will be unlikely to discuss concerns during the next round of visiting steward conversations.

Visiting stewards write a brief note to the donors after the visit—nothing fancy, just a personal note thanking the donors for their time and their financial commitment. The amount of the donors' commitment is not included in the visiting steward's note. The donors will receive confirmation of their commitment amount from the treasurer.

The Fellowship Event

As mentioned earlier, the general gifts visiting stewards wait to begin their visits until after an important event—the congregation-wide fellowship event that launches the fundraising effort. Here's a closer look at that event and how it is planned.

The fellowship event is often held on a Friday or Saturday evening. A few congregations have scheduled their event after the Sunday service or as a Sunday afternoon reception. Find a date and time that are the most convenient for most of the people.

Whenever the event is held, make it a special treat. Congregants should not have to pay for the meal. Nor should they be responsible for setting up the tables and chairs or cleaning up afterwards. Plan the dinner so that, for a change, the congregants won't have to do any of the heavy lifting or reach into their pockets to pay for the evening out.

The fellowship event chair is responsible for planning. Good organizational skills are needed, as well as the ability to delegate responsibility. The event chair must be someone who loves to plan fun-filled parties and can put together the groups needed for the following major tasks.

Reserve a site. The dinner may be held in the fellowship hall of the church. However, reserving an off-site location is one way to send the message that this event is not "business as usual." Because suitable locations for this kind of event are usually in great demand, start pursuing options a year before the event date. Consider reserving the function hall of a local nonprofit organization, a hotel banquet hall, a private room in a restaurant, or the fellowship hall of another local congregation. The latter option has several advantages: it promotes local interfaith relationships, is likely to be cost-effective for your congregation, and allows the other congregation to earn some money from rental fees. The key is to find a location where there is comfortable space for the congregation. Choose a site that is universally accessible and provides a private and comfortable atmosphere.

Arrange for the food. The breaking of bread is an important aspect of a fellowship event. Some congregations plan a catered sit-down meal. Others plan a catered buffet, which is less expensive and less time-consuming. A few offer a potluck meal or a reception with finger sandwiches and snacks. While the food should be nourishing and tasty, it need not be terribly expensive or fancy. What is most important is to get everyone together.

A catered meal is often the most expensive option. Instead of a professional catering company, consider asking another local congregation to cater the meal. They might provide the food for a fairly modest amount.

Address the issue of alcohol at the event. Some congregations specifically avoid it, some offer wine at each table, and a few provide a cash bar. If alcohol is available, provide viable nonalcoholic options as well.

Recruit hosts and invite congregants. The axiom "the more personal, the better" is as relevant for inviting people to the fellowship event as it is for asking them to make a financial commitment.

Rather than simply putting an announcement in the church newsletter, mail an invitation to each individual or family. (A sample invitation is provided on page 125.) In addition, recruit hosts to follow up by telephone. Assign each host, along with an appropriate number of guests, to a specific table. After the invitations have been mailed, the hosts call their assigned guests to confirm that they will be attending the dinner. The phone conversation is also an opportunity to offer transportation and child care if needed.

Although it may be unrealistic to think that everyone will attend, this is an opportunity to challenge yourselves. Set a goal of 100-percent attendance and challenge the congregation to reach it.

Develop the program. Carefully plan the program for the evening. Include the following elements:

- Opening words, spiritual reading, or brief centering activity and a period of meditation, prayer, or centering.

- Distribution and explanation of the annual drive brochure, the case statement, the suggested fair-share giving guide, and the essential gifts chart. Use a presentation that is long on information about programs and ministries and short on detailed information about finances.

- Personal, heartfelt testimonials (three to five minutes each) delivered by two or three especially passionate and well-respected members.

- Recognition of the fundraising team members.

- Announcement of the total amount of financial commitments made in the leadership gifts portion of the budget drive.

- Top-notch participative entertainment. For example, a group sing, using a projector and screen for the words, is preferable to having the choir sing to the attendees. Contra dancing, square dancing, or line dancing is preferable to watching a group dance.

- A "we can do it" finale led by the budget drive co-chairs or some other inspirational speaker.

Do not ask for any financial commitments during the fellowship event, even if someone is prepared to make a contribution that evening. Asking for a commitment during the fellowship event preempts the upcoming stewardship conversations between the visiting stewards and the donors.

Make the fellowship event a defining moment in the life of the congregation. Let the event be a celebration of the first exciting move into the future. Make it a symbol of things to come, a message that things are going to be different. Be bold.

The Follow-Up Phase

The team in charge of following up on unreturned financial commitment forms must have a high level of sensitivity and good judgment. Recruit three to seven people to determine the best way to approach each situation. It is helpful if team members are long-term members of the congregation. They might know of circumstances that could have contributed to an unreturned financial commitment form.

As soon as the follow-up team has been recruited and after the general gifts phase is finished, conduct a meeting of the follow-up team. Sort the names of congregants who have not returned commitment forms into three categories: people who were not contacted, people who declined a stewardship conversation, and people who were contacted but not visited by a steward for some other reason. If careful bookkeeping has been maintained, congregants who haven't returned forms can be easily identified.

Congregants not contacted. Some people may have been away or may not have responded to previous telephone messages. Unless there is additional information, contact them by phone. To increase the likelihood of contact, vary the time of day of making phone calls. Some budget drive committees have established "no-call time zones" during each day. They avoid calling before 8 a.m., when many people are getting ready for work or getting their children ready for school. They also avoid calling between 5 p.m. and 7

p.m. to decrease the chance of interrupting dinner. They often make no calls after 9 p.m. to be sensitive to people who retire early.

In the event that phone messages are left but not returned, continue to leave messages until the follow-up period has ended. This is not to suggest calling and leaving messages every fifteen minutes, but to be persistent until one of three things occurs: the congregant responds to the call and a time is arranged for a conversation, the congregant responds to the call and flatly declines to discuss a financial commitment, or the follow-up time frame ends.

Another effective follow-up technique is to place a financial commitment form on the church website *after* personal conversations have been completed but before making follow-up phone calls. When callers reach a person, they accept the financial commitment over the phone. When they reach an answering machine or voice mail, they leave the web address where the financial commitment form may be found. They may also follow up the phone message with an e-mail that gives the web address. Donors who receive the phone message or the e-mail can complete the online form and e-mail it to the church. This method won't work miracles, but it is worth the time and energy. Be sure not to post the financial commitment form on the website until the follow-up phase of the drive, and remember to delete it six months prior to the next annual budget drive. You don't want next year's donors opting for the online financial commitment instead of a more personal and interactive appeal.

Congregants contacted but unable to schedule a stewardship conversation. Take the same approach as above, but prepare to be flexible and imaginative to work around donors' schedules.

Congregants who declined a stewardship conversation. Some of these people probably asked to have their financial commitment form mailed to them. Since visiting stewards have strict orders not to mail any commitment forms, the potential donor would have already been given that message. It is worth another try to arrange a stewardship conversation. Ultimately, if the potential donor says something along the lines of "Either mail me my commitment form or I am not going to contribute," go ahead and mail the form. But remember: Every time you give up on a stewardship conversation, you miss an opportunity to engage a fellow congregant in a pastoral, pleasant, painless, and pressure-free conversation that builds community and enhances congregational relationships.

The Close of the Drive

Set a specific closing date for the annual budget drive. A specific date brings formal closure and firm financial commitments allow the congregation to focus on implementation of its programs and ministries. Remind all budget drive leaders to write a brief final report to submit to the budget drive chair.

Schedule a close-out meeting for the budget drive leaders and the fundraising consultant. At the meeting, share the final reports, talk about what went well and what problems surfaced, identify potential leaders for next year's drive, and then celebrate the closing of a successful annual budget drive.

If the financial goal has not been met, schedule a congregational meeting and ask the congregants to consider their options. Instead of settling short of the goal, the congregation could decide to conduct a close-the-gap supplementary drive to make up the difference between financial commitments and the financial goal. Let the congregation, rather than the governing body, decide. Plan a close-the-gap drive only if at least two-thirds of the members approve. In nearly all cases, a Commitment Sunday (see page 27) is the most effective approach to use in this situation.

After the drive has formally ended, hold an annual budget drive leaders' dinner and close-out meeting. Make it a special event, with food and drink provided. After the dinner, begin the closeout meeting by starting with a summary of each leader's final report. Discuss what went well for each of the leaders and try to capture the essence of the recently completed drive. The closeout meeting also provides an easy way to begin planning for next year. Have someone take notes to pass along to next year's annual budget drive leaders.

Hold a celebration for completing the annual budget drive. Do it up big! Acknowledge all of the workers who played a vital part in the drive.

CHAPTER SIX

Written Materials

There are three irrefutable rules that will assure your success in fundraising. Unfortunately, no one has ever discovered what they are.

—John Russell

Although each annual budget drive and each capital campaign is unique, all successful fundraising efforts depend on the preparation of written materials. These materials help communicate information to potential donors and generate enthusiasm. For an annual budget drive, these written materials include a case statement, a summary of programs and ministries, a program budget chart, an essential gifts chart, and/or a suggested fair-share giving guide, a brochure (which includes many of the preceding elements, as well as additional information), and a financial commitment form. Many of these written materials are needed in a capital campaign as well.

Case Statement

Making the case is the single most important element in a fundraising effort. A case statement that justifies the reason for the effort will attract significant financial commitments. Most people receive requests for money from many nonprofit organizations. Because they have finite financial resources, people must make careful decisions about which organizations to support. Therefore, they need to be convinced that the faith community is deserving of their financial support.

A case statement provides the written justification for a fundraising effort. The statement defines the mission of the faith community and describes the relationship between the fundraising effort and the mission. It summarizes the components of the effort and explains the goals that will be accomplished when the money is received. An effective case statement motivates people to contribute and provides answers to the following questions:

- In what ways is the fundraising effort compatible with the mission?

- What will be different when the financial goal is attained?

- What internal programs or global ministries will be enhanced?

- What new initiatives will be started?

- What are the sources of projected income?

- How will this effort increase the faith community's role in society?

- What congregational spiritual expectations will be met?

- What spiritual expectations of the wider community will be addressed?

- Who is supportive of this effort (professional staff, the governing body, specific sponsoring groups, special interest groups)?

- Why me? What difference will my contribution make?

Include at least four components in the case statement: shared commitment, shared pride, shared goals, and plans to use the money. The four components do not necessarily need to be listed in the statement, but a reader should be able to spot them easily in the text.

A case statement for an annual budget drive is usually fairly short, often about 200 words, and is placed in the brochure. A case statement for a capital campaign is sometimes several pages longer and may be placed in a separate booklet of its own.

Examples of case statements are intentionally not provided, since each congregation must create a case statement unique to its specific situation. However, fundraising consultant Jerald King, in his *Asking Makes a Difference* workbook, gives suggested guidelines for creating a case statement. The following list of steps has been adapted from his work.

1. Conduct a brainstorming session to create a list of possible case statement ideas. For an annual budget drive, the brainstorming group is the budget drive leadership team, who should gather soon after they have been appointed. For a capital campaign, the group consists of the governing body president, the capital campaign chair, and the publications team chair. (See Chapter 11 for descriptions of specific roles in a capital campaign.) Use the four components listed above as a guide for brainstorming.

2. When the brainstorming session has been completed, combine the individual ideas into five to ten categories.

3. Appoint one editor to create a first-draft case statement from the categories.

4. Send the first draft to the other team members. Ask them to review the first draft for content only: Did the editor accurately capture the essence of the brainstorming session?

5. Have the editor create a second draft from the team members' feedback.

6. Distribute the second draft to the professional religious leaders and the governing body. Ask them: Does this draft statement match your understanding of the purpose for the fundraising effort? If not, what has been missed? Is there anything that should be deleted from the draft statement?

7. After receiving the second-draft feedback, have the editor write a third-draft case statement. Send the third draft to the group members, the professional religious leaders, and the governing body. Ask them to do a final review of the content only.

8. Ask the editor to revise the third draft as needed and to share it, in person, with the group members, who then make suggestions for fine-tuning the wording.

9. Have the editor create the final draft.

10. Team members adopt the case statement. Because of the participatory process, it should be easy to reach consensus on the final wording of the statement.

Summary of Programs and Ministries

Develop a summary of all internal programs and global ministries currently offered by the congregation. The purpose of the summary is to spread the word about the faith community. For some active congregants, the summary serves as a reminder of the breadth and depth of the vision and mission. For less active congregants and the general public, it functions much like a résumé, teasing them with a bit of information that may entice them to find out more about the faith community.

The summary might be titled "Fulfilling Our Mission," "The Ministry of Our Church," "Our Faith Community at Work," or some similar title. When writing the summary, accentuate the positive. (Appreciative Inquiry skills, discussed on page 17, are useful.) Some congregations use categories like

Worship and Music, Lifespan Religious Education, Community Within, Outreach (global ministries), and Denominational Connection. The information may be presented as a single sheet of paper, a pamphlet, or a folder. Put the summary on the website as well. Update the summary periodically, and use it as a communication piece long after the fundraising effort has been completed.

Program Budget Charts

When people are asked to give, they want to know where their money is going and how it will make a difference. At the same time, they don't want to be overwhelmed with too much financial detail. The best solution is to develop a program budget and to communicate it using pie charts.

Program budgeting is a method designed to clarify and simplify the operating budget. A typical church program budget divides annual income into four or five sources and annual expenses into four or five broad categories. Pie charts show the proportion of income from each source and the proportion of expenses in each category.

A program budget does not replace a line-item budget. It serves as an introduction to the proposed budget during an annual budget drive. The program budget proposal is shared with congregants when they are asked to make their financial commitment. The pie charts make it easy to see where financial resources come from and how the congregation chooses to allocate them, including the relative significance of various programs and ministries. These priorities may be altered if the congregation chooses. After the annual budget drive, the pie chart program budget is converted into a line-item budget and presented to the congregation for adoption.

In a program budget, sources of income typically include annual financial commitments, rental income, program fees, and donations. A healthy annual income distribution requires that at least 80 percent of income comes from annual financial commitments. (In many nondenominational evangelical congregations, whose culture

of financial responsibility leads to higher expectations, annual financial commitments make up 90 percent of the operating budget.) A healthy income distribution might look like this:

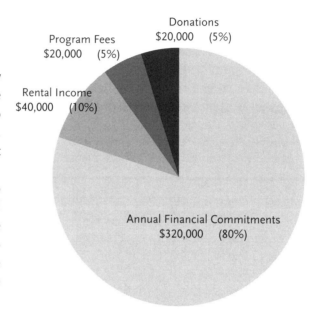

Program Budget Income
$400,000

A healthy congregation does not use money from the endowment fund to balance an annual operating budget. As explained in Chapter 8, endowment fund income is typically designated for capital projects and "rainy day" surprises. Nor should the congregation rely on income from service auctions, church fairs, yard sales, and similar events. Such events offer wonderful opportunities to build community, but they are not cost-effective ways to balance the operating budget. Instead, contribute the proceeds to a local or global community ministry—a worthwhile project or cause focused beyond the walls of the faith community.

For expenses, consider the following categories: worship and music, lifespan religious education, community within, outreach (or global ministries), and denominational connection. In some Unitarian Universalist program budgets, the distribution of expenses might look like this:

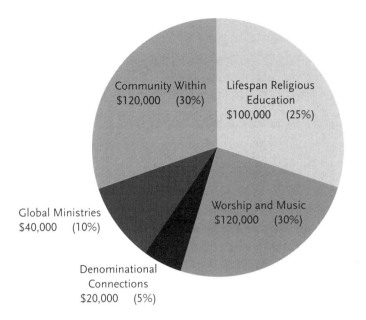

Program Budget Expenses
$400,000

Community Within
$120,000   (30%)

Lifespan Religious
Education
$100,000   (25%)

Global Ministries
$40,000   (10%)

Worship and Music
$120,000   (30%)

Denominational
Connections
$20,000   (5%)

While many Unitarian Universalist congregations allocate up to 10 percent of their operating budget to outreach, many nondenominational evangelical congregations devote 20 percent of their income—as well as many hours of sweat equity—to global ministry programs.

Some congregational finance leaders resist program budgeting, saying that congregants want the level of detail provided by a line-item budget. These leaders often believe that the more information people are given, the more money they will commit. On the contrary, line-item budgets confuse many people. At best, most congregants find them too tedious to explore in detail. Many fundraising consultants believe that there is no direct correlation between the amount of detailed financial information provided and the motivation to make a larger financial commitment. Remember: People give to other people, to programs, to ministries, and to worthy causes. People *do not* give to line-item budgets.

Even if financial leaders are knowledgeable about program budgeting, it is wise to purchase copies of Jerald King's workbook, *Mission-Based Budgeting: A Guide to Program Budgets,* which offers a step-by-step tour of program budgeting. In

addition to purchasing the workbook, invite an external expert to guide and coach the congregation through the first year of the program budget process. Expect to pay for the professional services of a consultant, understanding that the money spent will represent a good investment for the future financial health of the congregation.

Essential Gifts Chart

Sometimes referred to as the gift table or table of gifts, the essential gifts chart is created to show the gift distribution needed to achieve the financial goal of a fundraising effort. In a capital campaign, the essential gifts chart is included in the brochure (see page 53). In an annual budget drive, we recommend that an essential gifts chart be presented to the leadership donors.

An example of an essential gifts chart for an annual budget drive is shown on page 128. The chart is developed by the annual budget chair, with assistance from the congregational treasurer and one or two long-time congregants. To create the first five lines of the chart, the members of this small team make their best guess about the ability and willingness of each leadership donor to make a significant financial commitment. (Later, a visiting steward can use this best guess when asking a donor to consider a commitment in the range of, for example, $8,000 to $10,000.) The rest of the chart is completed by the treasurer, using previous giving history, when available, as a guide.

For a capital campaign, the essential gifts chart is created by the capital campaign co-chairs, the leadership gifts co-chairs, the congregational treasurer, and one or two long-time congregants. As in the previous example, they make their best guess about the amount that each congregant will be able and willing to donate, but they do this for the entire list of potential donors rather than only the top few. This is called a full-list evaluation (see page 127 for an example). The essential gifts chart evolves from that information. An example of an essential gifts chart for a capital campaign is shown on page 128.

People like to feel that they are an integral part of their congregation's financial giving program. The essential gifts chart can be a successful motivator. When approaching leadership donors, use the chart to emphasize the importance of large financial gifts from those who are able and willing to make them. In the case of an annual budget drive, leadership donors can see how their financial commitment can really make a difference in funding next year's programs and ministries. For a capital campaign, donors can see how their gift will help ensure the future viability of the faith community by providing the necessary staffing, programs, ministries, and facilities for the next generation of congregants.

Suggested Fair-Share Giving Guide

We strongly recommend using a suggested fair-share giving guide for each annual budget drive. Unitarian Universalist fundraising consultants have recently created a revised giving guide that is an adaptation and expansion of a model used at the Henry David Thoreau Unitarian Universalist Congregation in Stafford, Texas. The new guide replaces the 1997 version found in *Fundraising with a Vision* by Ed Landreth. The financial commitment levels are still suggestions, but the new guide is different in several respects.

The terms *equal sacrifice* and *proportional giving* are used, replacing the term *equal giving*. The two new terms represent an acknowledgment that asking for a percentage of net worth or salary is more equitable than asking all congregants to increase their annual financial contribution by the same percentage. Asking everyone to increase their annual giving by five percent, for example, sets an unnecessarily low bar for many congregants who have the ability to contribute a higher percentage of their income, while setting an unrealistically high bar for other congregants who are unable to increase their giving by that percentage. The new suggested fair-share giving guide suggests a minimum financial commitment of 2 percent of adjusted gross income for congregants earning up to $10,000. At the other end of the

spectrum—the highest level of giving—the guide suggests a full tithe of 10 percent of income, regardless of a congregant's income level.

Each income line has four suggested fair-share giving levels. For example, if your adjusted gross annual income is $50,000, you can choose one of four fair-share commitment options.

Supporter: The congregation is a significant part of your life, and it promotes your spiritual growth. Your fair-share financial commitment is 3 percent of your $50,000 income—$125 per month or $1,500 per year.

Sustainer: The congregation is central to your identity, and you are committed to sustaining the programs and ministries of the church. Your fair-share financial commitment is 4 percent of your $50,000 income—$167 per month or $2,000 per year.

Visionary: You are committed to both the present and future growth of the congregation. Your fair-share financial commitment is 5 percent of your $50,000 income—$208 per month or $2,500 per year.

Full Tither: You designate 10 percent of your $50,000 income as a way of living out your spiritual principles. Your fair-share financial commitment is $417 per month or $5,000 per year.

This is not to suggest that all congregants should locate their income on the guide and dramatically increase their annual financial commitment during the next annual budget drive. Instead, congregants should be encouraged to make a commitment to *move toward* their suggested financial fair share. It might be a three-year process or even a five-year process for some, but we advocate moving toward a fair-share financial commitment in a steady, intentional way.

The guide can be found on page 130. A worksheet for calculating what income to use in determining a level of fair-share giving can be found on page 131. Give new congregants an opportunity to financially support the faith community as soon as possible. If they have arrived from another faith tradition, they may be accustomed to a different fundraising style and a different set of financial expectations. If the new congregants were unchurched (not previously affiliated with any religious organization), they probably have no idea about the giving expectations of their new faith community. The suggested fair-share giving guide is a helpful tool for all newcomers.

For those newcomers who choose to become members, provide the current annual budget drive brochure and the suggested fair-share giving guide as part of their new member information packet. Within the first month of membership, visit new members and ask for a financial commitment. Do not wait until the beginning of the next fiscal year to get new members involved in making a financial commitment to the church.

Share the guide with long-time members as well. Many of them have historically made small financial commitments. Let the guide remind them that a significant financial commitment is one of the responsibilities of membership. Expect some resistance from this group. Many will remember the good old days when dropping a dollar in the offertory plate was their norm. Regardless of which method is used in an annual budget drive, use the suggested fair-share giving guide to help congregants determine their level of financial commitment to the faith community.

Brochure

The fundraising brochure can be one of the most important fundraising communication tools. It is the piece of information most likely to be seen by all congregants. At its best, the brochure provides a concise summary of information to help the congregation become familiar with the fundraising effort. It includes many of the elements already described, as well as additional content.

Although there are many variations on a theme, the common components found in most effective brochures are:

- A theme and a visual representation of the fundraising goal.

- A brief history of the congregation that gives

just enough information to put the fundraising effort in context.

- The congregational mission statement.

- A compelling case statement.

- The program budget chart (for an annual budget drive brochure) or a similar chart that depicts how the money that is raised will be spent (for a capital campaign).

- The suggested fair-share giving guide (for an annual budget drive brochure), so congregants can determine their own financial commitment based on a percentage of their income.

- The essential gifts chart (sometimes for an annual budget drive brochure and always for a capital campaign brochure), so that congregants can locate the different levels of financial commitment needed to reach the fundraising goal.

- One or two short (fifty-word maximum) testimonials from congregants.

- One or two short (fifty-word maximum) messages from the fundraising chair and the professional religious leader(s) to show their support.

- The names of the fundraising leaders and fundraising consultant.

- The name, address, phone number, e-mail address, and website URL of the congregation.

- Information about how to make a financial commitment.

- The tax advantages of making a financial commitment.

The brochure is used in a variety of ways during a fundraising effort. Give a brochure to each visiting steward during the orientation workshop (see page 41), to each attendee at the leadership reception, and to everyone who attends the fellowship event that launches the public phase of the fundraising drive. Mail the brochure to former members and friends who have moved away but who maintain a connection to the faith community. Place several copies of the brochure in the literature rack, and include one in each new member packet. Don't forget to place the brochure on the website.

For an annual budget drive, some congregations use simple desktop publishing techniques to create an attractive, inexpensive brochure. For a capital campaign, most congregations send their brochure to a printer or hire a professional graphic designer. Some congregations include photos in their brochures. Action photos of congregants at work or play are especially effective. Unitarian Universalists can contact the Office of Congregational Fundraising Services (617-948-4251) for sample brochures.

Remember, however, that the most attractive brochure cannot make up for the lack of a compelling case. Neither can an attractive brochure compensate for a disorganized fundraising effort. An attractive brochure without a vital case statement and without a well-organized plan will not convince people to give their financial support to the faith community.

Financial Commitment Form

The financial commitment form (pledge card) is the formal written and signed document that records each donor's contribution. It is best to have three copies of each financial commitment form: one for the congregational collector or treasurer (for official church records), one for the campaign treasurer or financial management chair (to keep track of which forms have been returned), and one for the donor. Use NCR (no carbon required) paper to allow for the three copies.

For an annual budget drive, include these items on the financial commitment form:

- Name and full address, including e-mail address, of the faith community.

- The name (theme/title/slogan/logo) of the fundraising effort.

- A code number to identify each donor in the church records. Complete contact information (name, mailing address, telephone, e-mail) of the donor).

- Place for the signature(s) of the donor(s).

- Amount of the financial commitment.

- The commitment payment schedule (monthly, quarterly, annually).

- The starting date for payment of the commitment. Information about the option of automatic deduction from the donor's checking account.

- Place to indicate whether the commitment represents a suggested fair-share commitment.

- An exit statement: "It is understood that financial situations sometimes change. If you need to revise your financial commitment, please contact [*name of contact person*]."

Only a few changes are needed for a capital campaign financial commitment form. Two sample forms, one for an annual budget drive and one for a capital campaign, can be found on pages 132-133.

Preparing written materials can be tedious and time consuming, but their importance cannot be overemphasized. Written materials help inform the congregation, generate excitement about the programs and ministries that will be offered, and answer many questions. Quality written materials alone do not guarantee a successful drive, but they are a very important tool.

CHAPTER SEVEN

Forward Through the Ages: A New Stewardship Development Program

I was taught that the world had a lot of problems; that I could struggle and change them; that intellectual and material gifts brought the privilege and the responsibility of sharing with others less fortunate; and that service is the rent each of us pays for living—the very purpose of life and not something you do in your spare time or after you have reached your personal goals.

—Marian Wright Edelman

Chapter 1 discusses the difference between fundraising and spiritual stewardship. To review: Fundraising efforts are those designed to raise money for an annual operating budget or a capital project, while stewardship is the growing, nurturing, promoting, and building of the gifts, call, and spiritual vocation that have been given to us. Stewardship is the spirit that influences the things we do. Good stewardship certainly involves raising money, but raising money must be nestled under the large umbrella of a congregation's vision.

Forward Through the Ages (FORTH) is a multi-year program designed to support a congregation's mission while deepening the commitment to its vision of the future. The program raises awareness of the importance of spiritual stewardship and provides resources for internal programs and global ministries.

FORTH also enables the congregation to identify the relationship between stewardship and ministry. The program helps congregants to place money within the larger context of supporting the mission of the church. FORTH becomes the foundation of the congregation's strategic plan, which outlines its programs and ministries.

The ultimate goal of FORTH is to facilitate growth—not just numerical growth, but maturational, organic, and incarnational growth, as explained in Chapter 9 (page 82).

FORTH has five phases, each with a specific theme. The phases build on one another as a pattern of spiritual stewardship growth is established.

- Phase 1 is devoted to teaching congregants how to accept gifts.

- In Phase 2, the congregation learns how to grow and invest gifts.

- Phase 3 focuses on ways to give back to the faith community.

- Phase 4 is dedicated to activities related to generous giving.

- Phase 5 builds on the previous four phases by encouraging the congregation to apply recent learnings.

Each phase has the same five components:

- Stewardship education

- Joyful giving

- Ministry and good works

- The annual budget drive

- Planned giving

Suggested activities for each component are offered during each phase. For example, during Phase 1, congregational leaders might offer a money management workshop and plan a worship service around the theme of gracious receiving.

To emphasize the concept of joyful giving, a plan to help congregants grow the giving of their gifts, call, and spiritual vocation could be developed. Congregants might be helped to understand appreciative inquiry (see page 17) as a technique to celebrate the ministry and good works of the congregation.

The annual budget drive could be conducted using personal stewardship conversations (see Chapter 5) and a bequest recognition society could be created to begin a planned giving program (see page 77). See pages 134-138 for charts of all five phases.

Although it is presented in a five-year format, the program accommodates congregations by allowing them to move forward at their own comfortable pace. For many faith communities, full implementation will require a significant culture shift, and a change of this magnitude must be made slowly and carefully. Only one component—the annual budget drive—needs to be addressed every fiscal year. FORTH suggests specific budget drive methods for each fiscal year: stewardship conversations in the first three years, Commitment Sunday in year four, and cottage meetings in the fifth year. (See Chapter 4 for an explanation of each method.)

Learning and practicing spiritual stewardship is an undertaking for both religious professionals and lay leaders. FORTH is a congregation-wide program, but creating it, implementing it, and fine-tuning it as the congregation moves through the five phases requires special attention from a team of stewardship development leaders.

Begin by appointing a standing stewardship committee. Making this a standing committee sends a message that stewardship is a spiritual, ongoing way of congregational life. It also allows time for the committee members to focus on all aspects of the program, not just the annual budget drive. Five to seven core members are sufficient. Create staggered two-year terms so that there are veterans and rookies on the team each year. Ask the professional religious leader(s) to participate *ex officio*, without vote, and ask one member of the governing body to serve as an ex officio, nonvoting liaison. Be mindful to ask whose voices need to be heard and to include a diverse group of congregants on the committee.

Once the stewardship committee has been recruited, remind the members to create a covenant of spiritual relationship. Ask them to write a list of promises about their agreed-upon mutual responsibilities to each other. Remind them that being in spiritual relationship means to welcome and respect each team member and to create and maintain an environment that builds connections, renews spirit, and inspires action. To facilitate communication and to ensure common understanding, provide a copy of this book for each stewardship committee member, each governing body member, and each professional religious leader.

Larger congregations are strongly encouraged to hire a part-time director of stewardship development to be responsible for recruiting committee members to help develop Forward Through the Ages. This paid staff position can be a relatively inexpensive investment that will help ensure healthy long-term stewardship development. At the very least, FORTH offers a great opportunity for widespread participation and the development of new lay leaders.

As you read through the following outline of the five phases of FORTH, you will find many ideas for activities. They are suggestions, not mandates. They are designed to stimulate ideas for other, perhaps more exciting, possibilities. Choose activities that will be a good fit for your congregants while also challenging them to stretch.

Phase 1: Accepting

Love cannot remain by itself—it has no meaning. Love has to be put in action and that action is service.

—Mother Teresa

Phase 1 guides congregants through activities that help them learn how to receive before learning how to give. This phase is devoted to the belief that people can best learn how to be generous givers by first learning how to graciously receive gifts. A congregation might focus on Phase 1 for a full church year, perhaps longer.

Stewardship Education

Stewardship education is the first component of each phase of Forward Through the Ages. The goal is to provide programs and informal opportunities to expand the congregation's understanding of stewardship. For Phase 1, when stewardship education is a new concept, consider some of these entry-level activities.

- Offer a class titled "The Art of Gracious Receiving" or "Is It Really Better to Give Than to Receive?" Focus on storytelling and shared learning. Talk about ways to gracefully accept the many gifts that have been given to us. Approach the class with questions and let the group search for answers.

- Plan and present a worship service about giving. The service might be conducted by the minister or a lay leader (perhaps a member of the stewardship committee). Focus on the three aspects of stewardship: gifts, call, and spiritual vocation. Acknowledge and welcome the many different kinds of gifts congregants may have received throughout their life, such as love, family, friendships, health, education, meaningful employment, serenity, and eternal hope. Talk about the stewardship of giving gifts, including aptitude, ability, and money. Explain the stewardship of call (the willingness to proclaim the good works of the faith community) and spiritual vocation (the willingness to take up the religious work of the faith community).

- Offer at least one money management workshop for the congregation during the year. (If the congregational leaders are comfortable doing so, invite members of other local faith communities as well. To ensure a welcoming atmosphere, create a plan to greet them and make them comfortable.) Use the workshop as a tool to foster a spirit of sharing. Present

one new skill at each workshop, matching the topics to the needs of the congregation. A few possibilities include mastering a budget, controlling credit card debt, being sensitive to fraud, preparing for retirement, saving money to purchase a car or a home, and investing money. Invite local experts to speak, but be sure that they avoid promotion of any product. Don't become discouraged if only a few people attend. It takes time for money management workshops to catch on, and even when they do, they will never have standing-room-only crowds. Consider the workshops as one part of a successful stewardship education program, even if they help only a few people.

- At the end of each workshop and class, ask participants to complete a feedback form. Use the feedback to develop future workshops and courses.

Joyful Giving

When we acknowledge our gifts and become graceful recipients of them, we are prepared to become joyous givers. This component of Phase 1 asks: What are the current gifts, calls, and spiritual vocations that the congregants share with each other? Which ones are shared with the local community? Are there some that are shared nationally and internationally? What new gifts, calls, and spiritual vocations might be added?

- Ask the stewardship committee to create a plan to increase the giving of gifts, call, and spiritual vocation. Develop a curriculum to help participants be stewards of self, family, community, and congregation. Focus on stewardship that protects existing resources and nurtures growth to ensure the future. Invite each person to advance his or her spiritual development with good works in the wider world. Challenge congregants to put their faith into action.

- Review *Stewardship: The Joy of Giving*, a curriculum developed by Fia B. Scheyer and Ruth Lewellen-Dix. It includes separate units designed for primary children, intermediate children, youth, and adults, as well as a final unit for a multigenerational group of participants. It is available on the UUA website. Adapt it to fit your own congregation's needs.

Ministry and Good Works

This component promotes the internal programs and global ministries of the faith community, providing a picture of how the congregation's mission is being fulfilled. The focus on ministry and good works makes the case for generous giving by clarifying the relationship between giving and successful programs and ministries.

We often take for granted some of our truly spiritual undertakings. Many of these activities have become so woven into the fabric of the congregation that they go practically unnoticed. In losing sight of our successes, we tend to emphasize our problems. We can become so close to the programs and ministries that we are unable to see the forest of abundant giving through the trees of scarcity.

- To begin the ministry and good works component of Phase 1, conduct a workshop to help lay leaders familiarize themselves with the philosophy of Appreciative Inquiry (see page 17). Rather than looking for and analyzing problems, Appreciative Inquiry asks, "What is already working well in this faith community?" (Appreciative Inquiry resources can be found in the list of resources for further readings that begins on page 159.) Invite a consultant to conduct the workshop, or ask a congregant who understands the philosophy to lead it.

- During the Appreciative Inquiry workshop, share memories of especially meaningful and spiritual moments that have energized the congregation. Explore how the congregation can build on those examples. The goal is to leave the workshop with a renewed sense of commitment, confidence, and affirmation that the congregation is already doing many things well, thus making it easier to move forward.

- Develop a series of one-page inserts to place in Sunday orders of service. Devote each insert to a summary of one church program or ministry. Ask each author to share a personal story using an Appreciative Inquiry approach. For example, one insert might begin, "Because of your gifts, our partner church has been able to buy fifty Bibles, and I was proud to present them when I visited there last year." Be sure to post the inserts on the church website as well.

- On the church website, add a special section specifically reserved for stewardship-related information. Appoint one member of the stewardship committee to be responsible for managing this part of the site.

- Recognize congregants who have shared their gifts, call, and spiritual vocation during the year. Honor the members of the governing body, the lifespan religious education staff and volunteers, leaders of programs and ministries, and any others who have made a special contribution to the faith community. Specifically include the annual budget drive leaders and visiting stewards. Acknowledge all workers who made the drive possible. There are many ways to pay tribute to these important people. Choose a celebration that "stretches the envelope" of the congregational culture and sends a message that we are not doing business as usual. Make the celebration a special event.

Annual Budget Drive

The techniques, approaches, and programs that could be used during the annual budget drive are many and varied, as explained in Chapter 4. In the first fiscal year of FORTH, use personal stewardship conversations as the core approach to the budget drive. Make this budget drive the foundation upon which future drives are built. Expect to put a lot of time and energy into planning the drive this first fiscal year. Have faith that a well-planned drive will result in immediate success, as well as make future drives easier and more successful.

To conduct the budget drive, follow the suggestions given in Chapter 5. In Phase 1, focus on these activities:

- In large congregations, have stewardship conversations with all of the leadership donors.

- In all congregations, have stewardship conversations with as many other donors as possible.

- Call donors who are not having a stewardship conversation with a visiting steward. Expect that it will take time and energy to track down financial commitment forms.

- Follow up using telephone calls and the church website, as explained in Chapter 5 (page 46).

Planned Giving

A well-conceived planned giving program encourages congregants to give their financial support to the long-term fiscal stability of the faith community. Create a planned giving program if none exists. Revitalize an existing program if it has become inactive. During Phase 1, consider the following planned giving activities. Chapter 8 provides more information about each idea.

- Develop a planned giving mission statement.

- Market the planned giving program.

- Prepare and share lists of local professional financial planning options and services.

- Create a bequest recognition society, publish a list of charter members, and create activities to recognize them. Ask them to share their passion with others.

Annual Progress Summary

At the end of the fiscal year, ask the FORTH chair to send a progress summary form, by e-mail, to each stewardship committee member, each member of the governing body, each committee chair, and each professional religious leader. The progress summary form is located on pages 139-140. Ask the recipients to return the completed form, by e-mail if possible, to the chair. Collate the information and use it at the yearly stewardship committee meeting as the foundation for planning Phase 2.

Phase 2: Growing and Investing

Successful stewards not only protect but help something to improve and grow. Their actions are empowering.

—Anonymous

Having taken whatever time was needed to focus on accepting gifts, in Phase 2 the congregation begins activities related to growing and investing the gifts that have been received.

Stewardship Education

Consider these activities in Phase 2:

- Plan another worship service about money, selecting a topic that seems particularly relevant to the congregation.

- Offer at least one money management workshop. Consider repeating the workshop for those not able to attend the first session.

- Plan a Sunday service with a theme of growing and investing gifts. After the service, offer a lay-led workshop to help people learn ways to increase gifts rather than hoarding them. As a starting point, introduce the parable of the talents (Matthew 25: 14-30): A wealthy man was going on a journey and entrusted three of his servants with some of his talents. (A talent was a monetary unit equivalent to 6,000 days' wages for a laborer.) One servant was entrusted with five talents, another with two talents, and a third with one talent. The servant who had been given one talent buried it to keep it from being stolen. He did not do anything to increase the talent. The other two servants doubled the amount they had been given by wisely investing their talents. These two servants each returned not only their master's initial talents but also all the additional talents they had grown. In this parable, each of the three servants had the financial *ability* to manage his master's wealth, but only two of the servants invested the talents wisely. In the workshop, ask: Does the parable of the talents have any relevance in today's world?

- Send a consistent message to the congregation, through worship services and workshops: "The mission of our faith community is even more important during difficult times. Let's find ways to grow our gifts so that we can make an even bigger difference in the world. How can we grow our gifts of life, love, family, friendships, health, education, meaningful employment, serenity, and eternal hope? How can we multiply the giving of gifts, call, and spiritual vocation? How can we express our gratitude?"

- As part of new member orientation, include a workshop that helps new members understand the concept of receiving and giving gifts. Ask congregants who were particularly receptive to the previous receiving and giving program to lead this workshop.

- At the end of each workshop and course, ask participants to complete a feedback form before they leave. Use the feedback to develop future workshops and courses.

Joyful Giving

Finding out about the specific skills of congregants is of vital importance. Small congregations can appoint a coordinator to gather such information and to recruit and manage volunteers. Midsize and large congregations are strongly encouraged to hire a part-time coordinator of volunteers. Whether appointed or hired, having a coordinator of volunteers can be a significant asset. Involving many congregants in the church's ministries will create a sense of ownership among them. The giving of gifts, call, and spiritual vocation will follow.

There are many ways to gather information about congregants' skills. For example, you can create a simple skills identification sign-up sheet by listing all of the ongoing activities that need to be performed. Insert the sign-up sheet into a Sunday worship order of service, ask each congregant to place a check mark next to the activities of interest, and then collect the sheets along with the morning offering. Post the checklist on

the website as well, and encourage congregants to complete and return it by email. As the information is gathered, create a donor databank. Update the data on a regular basis. However, do not gather information about potential volunteers during the annual budget drive. Any questionnaire or survey used during this important time dilutes and draws attention away from the drive.

After information about congregants has been gathered, ask the coordinator of volunteers to match volunteer opportunities to congregants' skills. When the matches have been made, the volunteer coordinator is ready to put the volunteers to work. If a congregant shows a desire to volunteer and indicates specific skills and interests, it is imperative that the congregant's skills be used. Congregations waste valuable resources when willing and capable volunteers are never asked to share their skills and interests.

Ministry and Good Works

Ask a task force of the stewardship committee to organize and host a Mission Fair to promote and celebrate the current programs and ministries of the church. Hold the fair on a Saturday morning or Sunday afternoon. Open the event to the public, and send personal invitations to other local faith communities. Invite the local press as well. Use the fair as a visible way to spread the good works of the congregation into the larger community.

Representatives from each internal program or global ministry can create a table display to show information about their particular activity. Handouts are helpful. Include a sign-up sheet for congregants interested in joining the activity.

Offer refreshments or a light lunch. Ask the youth of the congregation to be responsible for the food, and charge a modest amount for food so that the event becomes a fundraiser for the youth. Don't forget to provide age-appropriate activities for youngsters so that their parents can wander through the displays unencumbered by children tugging at their pants legs.

Invite guests from the denomination's district or national staff and ask them to share information about their programs and ministries. If your congregation is not currently involved with these programs, the fair may spark interest in becoming involved. For example, Unitarian Universalists can invite a representative from the Washington-based Advocacy and Witness staff group, the Holdeen India Program, the Social Justice Internship Program, the Congregational Justice Making Program, the Identity-Based Ministries staff group, or the Lifespan Faith Development staff group.

Videotape the event. Take photographs to insert into the literature rack, new member packets, and the annual budget drive brochure. You can also transform the photos into a slide show to be shown at the next annual fellowship event. Use the Mission Fair as an opportunity to show off a bit. Spread the good news!

Annual Budget Drive

As in Phase 1, conduct the budget drive using personal stewardship conversations. Follow the guidelines in Chapter 5. Refine the process, building upon the experiences of the previous fiscal year to create a more successful annual budget drive. Clean up the donor databank, adding the names of new people and deleting the names of people who have asked to be dropped from the list or who have been inactive for an extended period of time. Update the alumni databank to include people who want to stay in touch even though they have moved away.

Planned Giving

Here are some activities to consider during Phase 2. Additional information is found in Chapter 8.

- Form a planned giving committee. (In small congregations, one committee can perform the duties of both a planned giving committee and an endowment fund committee. Larger congregations can create two separate committees.)

- Clarify checks and balances for the planned giving committee.

- Define planned giving policies and create enabling resolutions.

- Ask the Bequest Recognition Society members to identify and generate a list of potential donors. Remind the society to meet personally with each potential donor at least once a year.

Annual Progress Summary

At the end of the second fiscal year, again distribute the progress summary form (page 139) to all congregational leaders and ask them to return the information to the chair. Collate the information and use it at the yearly stewardship committee meeting as the foundation for planning Phase 3.

Phase 3: Giving

Those who give have all things. Those who withhold have nothing.

—Hindu Proverb

When the congregation is comfortable with the concept of accepting gifts and the concept of growing and investing, it is time to move to Phase 3. Of course, *comfortable* is a relative term. Congregational leaders will need to make a subjective decision about when it is time to move on. Determining the speed at which to proceed is much more of an art than a science. Activities for this phase are related to the idea that we are only stewards of the gifts that we receive, not owners, and that an important reason to grow our gifts is so that we will be able to turn the gifts we receive into gifts to others.

Stewardship Education

In this phase, consider the following activities an extension of the first two stewardship education components:

- Offer at least one money management workshop in Phase 3. Use feedback from Phases 1 and 2 as a guide to developing the workshop.

- Offer a course on the idea that we do not truly own the gifts that we receive. Return to the parable of the talents from Phase 2 and point out that the servants who invested their master's wealth understood that they were stewards of the talents but never owned them. You could also mention that investing the talents meant giving them to someone else, and that it was by keeping the talents moving rather than simply keeping them that the wealth was increased.

- Ask lay leaders to plan and conduct a worship service using the parable of the talents as the theme.

- For new members who join the church during Phase 3, conduct a workshop as part of their new member orientation that helps them understand the concept of accepting gifts, as well as the concept of growing and investing gifts. Ask a couple of previous stewardship education participants to lead this workshop.

- At the end of each workshop and course, ask participants to complete a feedback form before they leave. Use the feedback to develop future workshops and courses.

Joyful Giving

Consider the following ways to encourage congregants to give generously of their time, skills, and resources to your community:

- Update the volunteer skills identification sign-up sheet, placing special emphasis on identifying the skills of new congregants. Find appropriate tasks for the volunteers.

- Sponsor a services auction at which volunteers offer some of their skills to the highest bidder. Contribute the proceeds to a global ministry—a cause or project that supports people other than the congregants.

- Identify new donors. Be intentional, rather than reactionary, about the process. In addition to information about the faith community, include the following items in each new member packet: a volunteer skills identification signup, the most recent annual budget drive brochure, the current essential gifts chart (see page 51), the suggested fair share

giving guide (see page 52), and a note indicating that a visiting steward will soon be in touch.

- Be sure that a specific visiting steward is responsible for asking each new donor for a financial commitment. The same visiting steward can collect the completed skills identification sheet during the stewardship conversation.

- In midsize and large congregations, try to expand the part-time coordinator of volunteers staff position to a full-time position that includes responsibility for membership coordination. The two responsibilities are a good combination for one person. Some congregations have already blazed this trail, so it's possible to adapt existing programs rather than start from scratch. There are many examples, but the following three programs are especially worth noting.

Jefferson Unitarian Church in Golden, Colorado, is a good example of a congregation that has integrated the coordination of volunteers and new members into one staff position. Between 2001 and 2005, the congregation experienced membership growth of about 25 percent, and as of 2007 had more than 700 members. The congregants have moved beyond the concept of one ordained minister who is wholly responsible for their spiritual well-being. They use the concept of shared ministry, in which the congregation creates and owns the ministry of the church. The Jefferson Unitarian Church congregation has fostered a new church culture of welcoming and inclusiveness. They have created a guest registry with written greeter instructions, a formal welcoming statement, and a new member packet of information. The congregation sponsors membership classes during which expectations of financial support are discussed. Complete information can be found at **www.jeffersonunitarian.org/programs**.

The East Shore Unitarian Church in Bellevue, Washington, also had membership growth of about 25 percent between 2001 and

2007. The East Shore program began with a half-time coordinator of volunteers, which has grown to a three-quarter-time position. The coordinator interviews new members to determine their most passionate interests and then passes the names along to the appropriate church leader. As the database increased from 60 to 300 volunteers, the level of inclusiveness increased. About one-third of the 660 members are now involved in a community service project. To learn more, check their website at **www.membership@eastshoreunitarian.org**.

The Unitarian Universalist Congregation at Shelter Rock in Manhasset, New York, currently has 675 members. They have created a membership/volunteer coordinator position designed to support and contribute to the mission of the church by assisting in the inclusion, development, and retention of members into congregational programs and activities. A complete list of role responsibilities can be found at **www.uucsr.org**.

Ministry and Good Works

As before, this component focuses on the internal programs and global ministries of the faith community and how they are helping to fulfill the congregation's mission. In this phase, introduce the finance leaders of the congregation to program budgeting, a method designed to clarify and simplify the operating budget. It is explained in Chapter 6 (see page 50).

Annual Budget Drive

In Phase 3, continue to use personal stewardship conversations as the primary method for the annual budget drive, following the recommendations given in Chapter 5. Ask veteran visiting stewards to help recruit new visiting stewards. By this third fiscal year, it becomes easier to recruit visiting stewards, and the stewardship conversations unfold in an organized, calm, and confident way. More visiting stewards means more stewardship conversations and fewer telephone calls. A greater sense of ownership in the process creates an increased number of donors, as well as a higher financial commitment total. The task is to keep fine-tuning the process.

Planned Giving

The following Phase 3 planned giving activities are described in Chapter 8.

- Clearly define the purpose of the endowment fund.

- Gather and publicize information about financial planning options.

- Create an evaluation tool to identify planned giving successes and shortcomings. Continue personal relationships with potential donors, and identify new potential donors.

Annual Progress Summary

As the third fiscal year ends, distribute progress summary forms (page 139) to all congregational leaders and ask them to return the information to the chair. Collate the information and use it at the yearly stewardship committee meeting as the foundation for planning Phase 4.

Phase 4: Giving Generously

Giving is a simple act
that becomes a great occasion
for the benefits are incalculable.
                              —Fia Scheyer

By the beginning of Phase 4, Forward Through the Ages has taken on a life of its own. Stewardship education has become a vital part of the religious life of the congregation. Giving is becoming a joyful experience. Lay leaders have found ways to promote their internal programs and global ministries. Program budgeting has been introduced but may still be met with some confusion and skepticism. The congregation has completed three fiscal years of successful stewardship conversations to raise money for the annual budget drive. A planned giving program has begun and is starting to generate steady momentum.

The congregation has learned how to accept gifts (Phase 1), how to grow and invest gifts

(Phase 2), and how to return and restore gifts (Phase 3). Worship services have been planned around these themes, and at least one money management workshop has been offered during each of these three phases. Phase 4 focuses on giving generously.

Stewardship Education

In this phase, further refine the stewardship education component by considering these activities:

- Offer at least one more money management workshop. Choose a topic based on experiences of the first three phases. Experience also determines the scheduling of the workshop and the presentation format. To continue local ministry efforts, remember to invite guests from the surrounding community.

- Plan a lay-led Sunday worship service around the theme of generosity. Consider these sermon themes:

  "Prosperity Is Located Within"
  "Give Thanks for Everything: Discard Your Scarcity Mentality"
  "Moving Toward the Reality of Abundance"
  "Building the Gifts of Life"
  "Give Without Remembering; Receive Without Forgetting"
  "Giving Is a Privilege, Not a Duty"

- Plan another stewardship education course, focusing on learning ways to give generously. Consider two core texts: *Growing Givers' Hearts* by Thomas H. Jeavons and Reekah Burch Basinger and *Give to Live* by Douglas Lawson. (See the list of resources for further reading beginning on page 159.) Jeavons and Basinger present a spiritual way of looking at giving, suggesting that fundraising (we would use the term *spiritual stewardship*) can be an opportunity to nurture current and prospective donors, as well as facilitating their growth in faith. They believe that within the context of generosity, congregants from across the theological spectrum can be guided toward making faith-building their first priority. Law-

son advocates a three-part approach to the question "How are we to live and enjoy our lives fully?" He suggests that first we need a purpose to live for. Second, we need to be comfortable with and accept who we are, to be selves fit to live with. And third, we need a faith fit to live by. Either of these two texts can be used as the foundation of a stewardship education course.

- For people who join the church during Phase 4 and those who missed the first time, conduct a workshop about the stewardship education concepts taught during the previous three phases. Be bold. As in the previous phases, make the workshop a requirement for membership. Resist the temptation to take shortcuts during this phase. New members need this background to become conversant about generosity and to feel included in the life of the congregation.

- Remember to ask workshop and course participants to complete a feedback form before they leave. Use the feedback to shape Phase 5 workshops and courses.

Joyful Giving

By now, the concept of joyfully giving gifts, call, and spiritual vocation has been created and implemented, and specific talents of volunteers have been identified. In small congregations, an unpaid coordinator of volunteers and new members has been appointed, and volunteers are consistently used. Midsize and large congregations have created part-time positions for a coordinator of volunteers, a coordinator of new members, and a director of stewardship development. A culture of "We are all expected to joyfully share our gifts, call, and spiritual vocation" is emerging.

Phase 4 turns attention to increasing financial commitment from specifically identified sets of donors, using several approaches.

- Arrange a list of donors in descending order of annual dollar amount of giving. Based on the results of a quartile analysis (see "Sharing the Responsibility" on page 7), annual budget drive leaders might ask a number of third-quartile donors to increase their financial commitment and move up to the second quartile of giving. The leaders might also, or instead, ask some of the second-quartile givers to move up to the first quartile of financial commitment.

- Categorize sets of donors by their type of involvement in the congregation. For example, Unitarian Universalist annual budget drive leaders might identify those parents who have children in the Coming of Age program or the Our Whole Lives program. Other identifiable donor sets might include congregants participating in small group ministry or as members of the choir. Before Commitment Sunday, ask to have a short stewardship conversation about joyful giving with each set of donors. Ask each member of each set to consider a significant increase in his or upcoming annual budget financial commitment. Bring financial commitment forms to each conversation and ask people to complete them. Indicate that their commitment will become part of the pre-launch, or silent, phase of the budget drive that precedes Commitment Sunday. The combined financial commitments of the donor sets can then be announced at the fellowship event.

- Identify congregants by geographic location. Schedule neighborhood gatherings at which annual budget drive leaders meet with groups to ask for increased giving. This approach may be the best way to identify donors. It is especially effective when combined with the activities described in the next component.

Ministry and Good Works

Program budgeting was introduced in Phase 3. In Phase 4, give careful attention to it so that more congregants understand and trust the process. Program budgeting almost guarantees conversation about the mission of the congregation and its relationship to programs and ministries.

Generate discussion by holding neighborhood gatherings that focus on sharing information.

Schedule the gatherings to take place after the preliminary program budget is created but before Commitment Sunday.

At the neighborhood gatherings, facilitators initiate conversations about the program budget and its relationship to current church programs and ministries. Participants look at the pie charts from the previous year and talk about the possibility of redistributing the size of each piece. For example, they may be surprised to see that only a small piece of the program budget was allocated to global ministries in recent years, which may initiate discussion about the importance of outreach in relation to other congregational initiatives. These conversations require a high level of mutual trust. The facilitators must trust that congregants will not use the gatherings for attacking programs, ministries, or people. The congregants must trust that their feedback will be used in a constructive way to help fulfill the mission of the congregation.

Plan the structure of neighborhood gatherings carefully. Announce in advance that each neighborhood gathering will start promptly at the appointed time and continue for two hours. Follow through on that commitment.

Schedule two facilitators for each neighborhood gathering: one to lead the conversations and the other to record ideas, suggestions, recommendations, and questions. Even if the facilitators attended an Appreciative Inquiry workshop during Phase 1, offer an opportunity for a short refresher session before they facilitate a neighborhood gathering. At the refresher session, remind facilitators that the Appreciative Inquiry philosophy requires looking first for what is already working well in the congregation.

Begin each gathering with a centering reading, meditation, or prayer. After the centering exercise, ask each person, as they are willing, to share a story that begins with "I remember the time when . . . ." Ask them to recall an especially spiritual event that has occurred during their relationship with the church. Expect that these stories will speak to the positive, warm, caring relationships that members have had with other congregants.

This Appreciative Inquiry approach to the neighborhood gathering sets the tone for the evening.

Here are some Appreciative Inquiry–oriented questions that could be asked during the first hour. Don't attempt to ask any more than a couple of them at any gathering.

- What do you value the most about our faith community?

- How do you stay spiritually vital?

- Think of a time when you were a part of, or observed, an extraordinary display of cooperation between two congregants or two church groups. What made that cooperation possible? How can we replicate that and utilize it in our programs and ministries?

- Describe a time when another congregant shared a gift (in the broadest sense of the word) with you. How did you receive the gift? How did you feel? How can we extend a feeling of gratitude to our programs and ministries?

- Describe a time when you shared a gift with another congregant. How did you feel? How can we extend that feeling?

- Recall a time when you were part of a church committee or group in which the members had a high level of trust in each other. What made it possible to establish that trust? How did the members maintain it? How can we create and maintain a high level of trust in our programs and ministries?

- What current church programs and ministries are particularly successful? Why are they successful? How can we extend that success to other programs and ministries?

- What gaps exist in our current programs and ministries? What new programs and ministries might be introduced to fill those gaps?

Focusing on current strengths will make it easier to expand upon those strengths. By guiding participants back to building upon current successes, the facilitator can manage the tendency of people to drift into conversations about congregational shortcomings.

During the second hour of the gathering, facilitators help participants connect the previous responses to the program budget by asking such questions as:

- Are your responses to the previous questions reflected in the program budget?

- Do your responses indicate a need to adjust the size of any pieces of the program budget pie? If so, which pieces might be increased? Which might be decreased?

- What new programs and ministries might be added to the various pieces of the program budget?

- Are there any programs or ministries that can be subtracted?

- If new programs and ministries are added and none can be subtracted, the whole budget increases in size. How will you financially support the larger program budget?

At each neighborhood gathering, the recorder writes responses on newsprint or a large easel pad for all to see. Promise that all responses will be collated, shared with congregational leaders, and available for review. Promise that lay leaders will review the responses to help determine how the size of the budget pie pieces, or the entire program budget, will be changed. Follow-through is vital if the neighborhood gatherings are to have any value.

End the gathering (promptly at the appointed time) by thanking the participants and offering a closing reading, meditation, or prayer.

Do not solicit financial commitments at these gatherings. The goal of each gathering is to share information and generate widespread understanding and ownership. The purpose of the meeting will be diluted, and some attendees will feel betrayed, if someone asks them for money during the event.

Annual Budget Drive

As in each of the previous fiscal years, have personal stewardship conversations with all of the leadership donors. However, instead of doing the same with the rest of the congregation, plan a Commitment Sunday (see page 27). This method, which devotes an entire worship service to stewardship, is a viable alternative best used as a one-year respite from congregation-wide personal stewardship conversations. Plan it as carefully as you have planned the past three fiscal years.

Since conversations are held with only the leadership donors in this fourth fiscal year, fewer visiting stewards are needed. However, the need for follow-up is greater. Make telephone calls to congregants who didn't attend Commitment Sunday (see page 46 for additional follow-up suggestions).

Planned Giving

Phase 4 of a planned giving program focuses on managing and marketing the endowment fund and the planned giving program. Chapter 8 provides details about how to implement the following activities. Begin to actively manage the endowment fund.

- Establish a minimum dollar amount that the fund must achieve before distributions can be considered (see page 74).

- Adopt the Harvard Model as a guide for how much of the endowment earnings may be spent each year.

- Create a marketing plan.

- Identify and cultivate planned giving prospects.

Annual Progress Summary

Distribute progress summary forms (page 139) to all congregational leaders and ask them to return the information to the chair. Collate the information and use it at the annual stewardship committee-meeting as the foundation for planning Phase 5.

Phase 5: Applying Recent Learnings

Vision is the imagination that gives inspiration and direction.

—Jacqui Lewis

Phase 5 provides guidance for assimilating all of the stewardship development information from Phases 1 through 4. Phase 5 offers a chance to step back, take a deep breath, determine what previous learnings the congregation has absorbed, and build on those learnings. Here's a chance to apply newfound knowledge of Appreciative Inquiry: Focus on the congregational strengths that have emerged through the first four phases of Forward Through the Ages.

Review the progress summaries that were completed at the end of each phase and the feedback forms that were collected after each workshop or course. What themes stand out as particularly successful? At which points was congregational passion most evident? It is fine to identify shortcomings or loose threads left over from the first four phases, but don't dwell upon them. Avoid the danger of being sucked back into a hole of scarcity by listing all the ways in which the congregation has failed to build a stewardship development plan. Identify what is already going well, and figure out ways to make the current strengths even stronger. Fine-tune stewardship development to create a truly outstanding and comprehensive program.

Reshape the following Phase 5 activities so that they are most meaningful for the congregation. Better yet, create your own activities to help move the congregation forward.

Stewardship Education

A careful review of the previously completed stewardship education activities will help determine the most helpful activities in this phase.

- Ask lay leaders to plan and conduct a worship service about generosity and abundance. Incorporate the themes of the first four phases: Accepting, Growing and Investing, Giving Back, and Giving Generously.

- Select one more topic for a money management workshop. By Phase 5, selecting a topic is relatively easy. The experiences of the past four phases help the stewardship committee to decide upon the next topic.

- For new members, conduct a stewardship education workshop as part of their new-member orientation that reviews and summarizes Phases 1 through 4. Ask past stewardship education graduates to facilitate it.

- Once again, distribute a feedback form to the participants of each workshop and course. Ask them to complete the form before they leave the event.

Joyful Giving

After working through the first four phases of Forward Through the Ages, congregational leaders sometimes find it hard to sustain volunteer energy. Phase 5 is a good time to focus on updating the volunteer skills databank. Congregants' interests change, and their amount of available time varies from year to year. Small congregations that rely on an unpaid coordinator of volunteers find Phase 5 particularly difficult. Midsize and large congregations that have a paid coordinator of volunteers find it easier to sustain and grow the volunteer program.

Create ways to breathe new energy into the stewardship development program. For example:

- Plan another service auction in which volunteers agree to provide a free service to the highest bidder. This time, instead of getting everyone together, consider making it a "virtual" silent auction run by e-mail. Continue the auction for a week, giving everyone plenty of time to view the offerings and place bids. If the volunteer program has been active, anticipate that the auction proceeds will be greater than in the past. As before, donate the proceeds to a local community or global ministry of the congregation's choosing rather than using them to help balance the operating budget.

- Organize a work party to clean up the building and grounds, or join a local Habitat for Hu-

manity project. Offer enough different tasks so that many people can apply their skills. Make the event prominent and well publicized—for example, contact a local newspaper. Take pictures, and create a scrapbook in which participants can sign their names and write notes about the event. Display the scrapbook prominently—perhaps on the visitors' table before the service and in the fellowship hall during coffee hour. Hold a similar event each year, and save the scrapbooks as historical documents.

- Match each new member with a mentor who is particularly knowledgeable and comfortable with stewardship development. Make a point of inviting new members to congregational activities and getting them involved in local community and global ministry opportunities. The goal is to include new members and provide a welcoming place where their special uniqueness is valued.

Ministry and Good Works

Devote Phase 5 to an intentional program of spreading the good news.

- Make the program budgeting process part of the institution of the faith community. Explain the process to congregants who are still unsure about it. Make a special effort to include an explanation of the process to new members as part of their orientation. Refer to Jerald King's workbook, *Mission-Based Budgeting: A Guide to Program Budgets* (see the list of resources for further reading starting on page 159), as needed.

- Focus on improving the website. Send the webmaster to a local, regional, or national workshop to refine skills. Regularly visit the websites of other faith communities of similar size.

- Find and share success stories from other congregations. Unitarian Universalist congregations can take advantage of a network of more than 225 public e-mail lists addressing subjects that range from large-congregation leadership tips to discussions for religious professionals. Success stories are frequently shared. Full information can be found on the UUA website.

- Begin to wean the congregation from hard-copy communication, and help them adapt to electronic communication. Unitarian Universalist congregations can submit their success stories to *InterConnections* for wide distribution to many congregations.

- Make extensive use of Appreciative Inquiry (see page 17). Don't be bashful: Go ahead and brag about your faith community.

Annual Budget Drive

As in the four previous fiscal years, schedule stewardship conversations with all of the leadership donors, following the guidelines given in Chapter 5. For the rest of the congregation, conduct small-group "cottage meetings" in congregants' homes. (See page 28 for more information about cottage meetings.) Organize the meetings by affinity groups, geography, or the availability of congregants' time.

At each meeting, two lay leaders from the annual budget drive committee present information about the upcoming fiscal year, entertain questions, and address concerns. They distribute financial commitment forms for each donor to complete, then collect the forms and deliver them to the annual budget drive treasurer. Follow up by telephone with congregants who did not attend a cottage meeting, as described on page 46.

Since stewardship conversations are scheduled for only leadership donors, fewer visiting stewards are needed, and it is easy to refine the stewardship conversation process. But beware of the complacency that can come after four successful years. Provide a mandatory orientation workshop (see page 41) for new visiting stewards and a condensed workshop for veterans. Review the previous orientation workshop agenda to determine whether it needs to be revised. Keep the workshop lively. Invite different lay leaders to conduct the workshops.

Planned Giving

Each of the following bulleted activities is discussed in more detail in Chapter 8.

- Ask the Bequest Society members to help refine the evaluation tool.

- Review the endowment fund managing guidelines and revise if necessary.

- Create a three-year plan that includes measurable goals.

- Expand upon the existing planned giving marketing plan.

- Continue to nurture existing relationships and identify new donors.

Annual Progress Summary

Distribute progress summary forms (page 139) to all stewardship committee members and ask them to return the information to the stewardship committee chair. Collate the information and use it to evaluate the five phases of Forward Through the Ages. Ask yourselves several questions:

- What did we like about Forward Through the Ages?

- What parts of the program were problematic?

- After the five phases, what has changed?

- How has the congregation grown in becoming a community of spiritual stewardship?

- What specific indicators of a spirit of abundance do we see?

- In what specific ways might the program be modified?

- How can we build on our successes to nurture a climate of stewardship development?

- What's next?

Answering these questions (and others that you will surely create) will help determine the future of a congregation-wide stewardship development program. Remember that Forward Through the Ages has been developed as an ongoing process that is never completely finished. Use the wealth of knowledge gathered during the five phases to create an intentional sequel to Forward Through the Ages.

CHAPTER EIGHT

Planned Giving

> One of the greatest missing teachings in the American church today is the reminder
> to men and women that nothing we have belongs to us.
>
> —Gordon MacDonald

An important element of a comprehensive financial management plan for faith communities is planned giving. A well-conceived planned giving program encourages congregants to give financial support for the long-term fiscal stability of a faith community. The gifts given to a planned giving program establish and maintain an endowment fund, the part of a faith community's income derived from donations. By providing investment income, the endowment fund becomes the vehicle through which long-term fiscal stability is assured.

There can be little doubt about the importance of a planned giving program. The Investment Company Institute, the national association of U.S. investment companies (**www.ici.org**), estimates that people currently 55 years or older will bequeath more than $8 trillion of accumulated wealth to noncharitable and charitable heirs by 2008. Barlow T. Mann, chief operations manager of the Sharpe Company (**www.rfsco.com**), writing in a 1997 article for *Give and Take*, estimates the intergenerational transfer of wealth at $10 trillion to $11 trillion between 1990 and 2040.

Conventional wisdom indicates that planned gifts are most often made by people between the ages of 55 and 75. By the year 2010, almost 14 percent of the U.S. population will be 65 years or older. In 2004 the median adult age of Unitar-

ian Universalist members was 54 years, and their average household net worth was estimated to exceed $232,000.

Planned giving can be accomplished by several means. For example, a person could name the church as a beneficiary of a life insurance policy or retirement plan. Charitable bequests, however, are the most commonly used form of planned giving. A *charitable bequest* is a gift given to charity through the provisions of a legal will or living trust. From the donor's standpoint, bequests have several advantages that make them popular. They are relatively inexpensive to arrange and save one dollar in estate tax liability for every dollar given. They are also easy for a congregation to promote. However, it is estimated that 70 percent of all Americans die without a will. It is also estimated that fewer than 10 percent of those capable of making a charitable estate gift have ever been asked.

Several books on planned giving are included in the list of resources for further reading that begins on page 159. The rest of this chapter summarizes tasks involved in creating or revitalizing a planned giving program. The tasks do not necessarily need to be completed in the order discussed. For example, some congregations create a bequest recognition society (page 77) as one of the first steps.

Approve the Enabling Resolution

An enabling resolution defines the purpose, governance, and operating procedures of an endowment fund and should be attached to the congregational bylaws. It must be approved by the congregation before an endowment fund is established and before a planned giving program is developed. The resolution should reflect timeless features, policies that the congregation wants to keep in place indefinitely. See page 141 for a sample enabling resolution.

Include a stipulation that endowment funds can be used only as designated by donors. Any exceptions are subject to a congregational vote, with a significant majority required to approve any exception.

Establish the Committee Structure

The size of a congregation determines how planned giving is approached. Ideally, two standing committees are formed. The planned giving committee establishes planned giving guidelines and seeks donations. The endowment fund committee develops and manages the endowment fund by:

- Encouraging, accepting, and acknowledging gifts (if there is no planned giving committee).

- Ensuring that restricted gifts are honored and properly recorded.

- Arranging for professional accounting of the funds.

- Reporting on fund activities to the governing body.

- Making prudent investment decisions.

- Administering the distribution of funds.

- Ensuring appropriate checks and balances regarding control of the funds.

Small congregations may not have enough human resources to create two committees. In that case, the planned giving committee is responsible for all the tasks identified above. In a congrega-

tion of seventy-five members, for example, a few committed and knowledgeable volunteers may be able to both create and implement a planned giving program and manage an endowment fund.

When forming a planned giving committee, five to seven volunteers are sufficient. Ideally, each volunteer serves a three-year term, using a staggered appointment schedule that guarantees continuity from one year to the next. Good candidates are those who have been active congregants long enough to know potential donors. They also need a working knowledge of planned giving.

Planned giving is a form of stewardship. The planned giving committee is the fiscal agent for assuring a healthy long-term financial future. These volunteers are obligated to develop a plan that will protect the financial security of the next generation of congregants. It is also imperative that all planned giving committee members lead by example and make their own planned giving commitment to the endowment fund.

A sample endowment document is located on page 145.

Clarify Checks and Balances

Whatever organizational structure is created, using one committee or two, develop specific lines of responsibility and accountability. Provide for a clear and simple separation of power. Create and implement controls that demand more than one set of eyes and hands for accepting gifts, managing investments, recording donations, and spending endowment funds.

Define the interaction of the planned giving committee (and endowment fund committee, if there is one) with the governing body, the treasurer, the finance committee, the annual budget drive committee, and any other relevant standing committees of the church. It would be wonderful if congenial relationships could be guaranteed among these groups. But at some point, conflicts are almost certain to arise. The most common situations are ones in which the governing body wants the endowment fund committee to release funds to balance the annual operating budget or to solve a pressing facility-related, deferred-maintenance need. Personal relationships can be strained when the endowment fund committee objects to or even refuses the request.

Ask the planned giving committee and endowment fund committee to report once each quarter to the finance committee, the governing body, or both. They should also report to the congregation at least once a year.

Develop a Mission Statement

Before any planned giving activity begins, develop a mission statement that makes a clear and compelling case for the importance of the planned giving program. Although the planned giving committee develops the mission statement, as in all mission statement processes, widespread acceptance must be gained. Depending on the size of the congregation and the specifics of the bylaws, the entire congregation may need to approve the mission statement, or it may be sufficient for the governing body to adopt it without congregational approval.

Create an Endowment Document

An endowment document provides specific written policies for a planned giving program. It assures that donated gifts will be responsibly managed. Create the document before any potential donors are approached. Here are some policy matters that the document should address:

Procedure for receiving unrestricted gifts. Will they be placed in the endowment fund? Will they be distributed among several different funds?

Types of acceptable gifts. Many congregations accept cash and stocks, and some congregations also accept gifts of personal property.

Reviewing and approving gifts. Write guidelines that clearly describe what types of gifts can be accepted without review and which gifts require approval of the governing body or the entire congregation. It is especially helpful to outline a procedure for reviewing gifts of real estate or other personal assets that may be difficult to sell. Does

the congregation really want to be in the business of managing a piece of real estate or assessing the value of Aunt Maude's priceless bric-a-brac? It is perfectly acceptable, and even advisable, to refuse a gift if it will distract the congregation from its primary vision and mission. It is also advisable to decline acceptance of a gift that might expose the congregation to expenses or liabilities that could pose a hardship on the financial resources of the congregation.

Procedure for liquidating stocks. Faith communities are not in the business of playing the stock market. There are horror stories of congregational volunteers who held onto a gift of stock while waiting for the market to improve, only to find that the market went down instead, forcing them to sell the stock for less than the initial value of the gift. In all cases, a gift of stock must be immediately liquidated when received.

A sample endowment document is found on page 145.

Define the Endowment Fund

Developing a planned giving program requires defining the destination of money donated to the faith community. Develop a clear, unique definition of the endowment fund that indicates how much of the fund may be spent, for what purposes, and with whose authorization.

The question of how much of an endowment fund may be spent is addressed under "Distributions" later in this chapter. The purposes for which it may be spent are defined by each congregation. Depending on the defined purpose of a particular endowment fund, it could provide funding for emergency assistance, building maintenance, social justice projects, a permanent arts program, student scholarships, or any number of other possibilities.

Once the endowment fund is defined and implemented, maintain it as separate and distinct from all other funds, such as the annual operating budget or a capital reserve fund. The endowment fund is a financial resource in perpetuity, extending and enhancing the congregation's capacity to fulfill its vision, mission, and goals.

Legal Definitions

The Uniform Management of Institutional Funds Act was written in 1972 and is now law in most states. It defines an endowment fund as "an institutional fund, or any part of such a fund, not wholly expendable by the institution on a current basis under the terms of the applicable gift instrument."

Most endowment funds are known as classic or true endowments. By definition, the principal (or corpus) is never spent. Income from investment earnings may be spent, subject to the policies adopted by the congregation.

Of course, this raises the question of how to define principal and income. At a minimum, principal is defined as the original value of any gift made to the endowment fund. Traditionally, income has been defined as including interest and dividends, but not capital appreciation. However, according to the Uniform Management of Institutional Funds Act, each institution is relatively free to define income and principal as it wishes, as long as three rules are followed: Faithfully observe restrictions made by the donor, follow sound accounting practices, and comply with state law regarding endowments and fiduciaries. So if, for example, a gift appreciates by 2 to 5 percent each year due to inflation, make sure the endowment document guidelines indicate whether that growth is considered principal or income.

Manage the Endowment Fund

The best investment strategy depends on a combination of the current value of the fund and the vision and mission of the congregation. In general, a prudent investment strategy for an endowment fund is a balanced portfolio with low to moderate risk.

Achieve a balance between the desire for growth and the need for income. *Growth* is defined as the increase (or appreciation) in the value of the fund. Historically, growth is greatest when funds are invested in corporate stock. *Income* is a combina-

tion of dividend payments from corporate earnings and the interest on bonds, money market funds, certificates of deposit, and interest-bearing savings accounts. *Total return* represents growth plus income. A minimum investment goal for an endowment fund is for total return to match the rate of inflation.

Asset allocation, the placement of endowment money, is a key factor in implementing a balanced portfolio. Often 40 to 60 percent of an endowment fund is invested in bonds. The other 40 to 60 percent is invested in stocks. The more money invested in stocks, the higher the risk. However, risk can be reduced through diversification—investing in many different stocks rather than those of just a few companies. A simple way to diversify is to invest in mutual funds.

Most congregations have members who are competent to review investment options. If there is no one who feels competent, seek an outside person to advise the congregation when needed. It is likely that an external advisor can be found in a local community foundation or charitable organization. A pro bono advisor can help point the congregation in a financially responsible direction.

If the congregation already has an endowment fund greater than $500,000, it is time to hire an investment agent and establish the congregation's own brokerage account. In this scenario, the endowment fund committee guides the direction of the agent, who suggests specific stocks in the various market sectors. Of course, the committee, not the investment agent, makes all of the final decisions.

Distributions

A common question asked by congregational leaders is, "How much of our endowment earnings should be spent each year?" Many congregations adopt what is sometimes referred to as the Harvard Model: Record the quarterly fair market value of the endowment fund. Once a year, calculate the average fair market value over the past thirteen quarters. Make between 4 and 6 percent of that amount available to spend each year. The Harvard Model is considered to be a sound and safe policy that:

- Ensures the continued growth of the fund.

- Provides a hedge against inflation.

- Yields a reasonable amount of money for specific purposes.

- Allows for a total return on investment strategy.

- Makes possible the distributions from capital gains, dividends, and interest.

Also consider establishing a minimum dollar amount that the fund must achieve before any distributions can occur. A sound and safe policy is that the endowment fund should reach the equivalent of at least twice the annual operating budget before distributions are considered. Even then, expend money in rare and extreme circumstances, always subject to approval by a majority of the congregants.

Endowment Fund Guidelines

In addition to the enabling resolutions that are added to congregational bylaws, create a separate set of guidelines for managing the fund. While the resolutions should reflect timeless features, the guidelines can indicate issues that the congregation might want to adjust at some time. The guidelines might include:

- Descriptions of socially responsible investments that the congregation wishes to maintain.

- Target ranges for growth, income, and total return.

- Degree of tolerable risk.

- Description of the asset allocation strategy.

- Benchmarks indicating when the strategy might change.

- Model for distribution of funds.

A sample Endowment Investment and Distribution Policy is provided on page 145. This sample policy is intended to reduce use of earnings from the endowment for the general operations of the church over a five-year time period. It also provides for continued growth of the endowment principal by limiting the amounts available for distribution to a small portion of the total assets over a three-year average.

A combination of enabling resolutions and endowment document guidelines will help to maintain a balanced portfolio and prevent any one person or committee from taking great risks. Let a general concept of prudence clarify the responsibilities of the people who manage the endowment fund. Check your own state laws for their definition of prudence. The following excerpt is taken from the laws of Massachusetts, Chapter 203C, Section 11. Endowment fund managers are expected to use

> . . . judgment and care under the circumstances prevailing that any persons of prudence, discretion, and intelligence exercise in the management of their own affairs, not in regard to the permanent disposition of the funds, considering the probable income as well as the probable safety of their capital.

The Massachusetts law continues: "Decisions respecting individual assets shall be considered in the context of the trust portfolio as part of an overall investment strategy reasonably suited to the trust" or endowment fund.

Market the Planned Giving Program

Once the planned giving and endowment fund policies and guidelines have been established, turn attention to marketing the program. There are a number of ways to create momentum through marketing. The following techniques are especially effective.

- Include a short (three-minute) testimonial in the worship service once a month. Invite a different person to give each testimonial. Congregants who can speak from their heart will be more effective than those who are accomplished public speakers but don't have a deep-seated passion for the faith community.

- Present one aspect of planned giving at an after-worship service forum every month. Offer the same information in the monthly newsletter.

- Create a literature rack and a bulletin board for planned giving publications and announcements. The Unitarian Universalist Association offers the planned giving marketing brochures listed on page 148. Additional materials are available from the sources listed on page 149.

- Develop opportunities to recognize and honor elders for their service to the church.

Provide Information About Financial Planning Options

As part of marketing the planned giving program, provide congregants with information about financial planning and charitable giving options that they may want to consider, such as:

- *Life insurance.* An especially flexible planning tool, life insurance can be used to meet a variety of personal financial needs. Many people have discovered that their life insurance can offer a convenient way to fund meaningful charitable gifts as well.

- *Charitable remainder trust.* A charitable remainder trust may allow a person to increase income from low-yielding assets; reduce or eliminate income, estate, and gift taxes; diversify investment assets; or create a source of income for children, parents, or other loved ones.

- *A valid will.* Without a valid will, a person's estate falls under the domain of the person's state of residence. In that situation the state must create a written, impersonal will that may not accurately reflect the unwritten wishes of the deceased.

- *Retirement plans.* There are a number of ways to enhance retirement plans. Through thoughtful planning it may be possible to assure a healthy financial future, benefit from significant tax savings, and increase income, asset management, and other economic advantages.

Also consider providing congregants with information about sources of reputable and reasonably priced legal and professional planning services. Ask professionals within the congregation to prepare a list of such resources, including attorneys, real estate brokers, bankers, accountants, stockbrokers, financial planners, and life insurance agents. They may include their own names on the list. Whatever fees they arrange with their clients can be determined by their own discretion and personal ethics. The faith community must not, however, offer free or reduced legal services to congregants. A contested estate could come back to haunt the congregation and could cost a great deal of time and money.

Offer a series of workshops on issues relevant for congregants who are planning their retirement years. Topics might include probate basics, federal and state estate taxes, revocable trusts, living wills, Medicaid, Medicare, Social Security benefits, extended health care, and powers of attorney. Consider co-sponsoring the workshops with other local religious organizations. For each workshop, ask three qualified professionals to speak briefly and answer questions from the guests. Make sure these professionals understand their role; they have been invited to share their expertise, not to solicit business. In addition to providing an important service, these workshops help identify people who are planning the ultimate use of their life estate.

Identify Planned Giving Prospects

While mass marketing of the planned giving program is important, identifying and cultivating specific planned giving prospects is even more crucial. Review the list of current congregants to identify people who might be interested in giving a gift through a charitable bequest or other form of planned giving.

Generally speaking, the profile of a planned giving prospect is someone over fifty years of age who has already met family obligations, is deeply committed to and already contributes to the church, and has both the means and the inclination to make additional financial contributions.

Don't, however, make the mistake of ignoring congregants who don't fit this generalization. It's impossible to know about their ability and willingness to make a planned gift without engaging them in meaningful conversation about their relationship to the faith community.

Get to know potential donors. Discover what they really like about the faith community. Visit them regularly. Find ways for them to get involved in the church community. Most important of all, ask potential donors to consider making a charitable gift to the church. Do not conduct this conversation by telephone. Asking a person to consider making a gift to the church must always be done in person.

Create a Bequest Recognition Society

Those who have made a charitable gift should be thanked and, with their permission, publicly recognized for their generosity. One way to do so is by creating a bequest recognition society. When starting a planned giving program, ask those who have previously made a charitable gift, and others who agree to do so, to become charter members of the society.

Create opportunities to acknowledge bequest recognition society members and keep them involved in the life of the church. For example:

- Publish a list of charter members.

- Create a banner with the names of the members, or start a permanent recognition wall.

- Offer special events and programs for society members.

- Invite a couple of them to be honorary members of the annual budget drive team.

- Ask the religious education youth group to interview society members and write a biography of each member.

- Create a buddy program by matching willing society members with young members of the religious education program.

- Invite society members to make guest presentations to religious education classes.

The possibilities for acknowledging the bequest recognition society members are almost limitless. A thorough recognition program dramatically increases the likelihood of convincing other people to make a charitable gift to the faith community.

Members of the bequest recognition society can also serve as ambassadors to the planned giving program. Ask society members if they know of other people who might be interested in joining the society. Encourage them to speak to others about their passion for the church and their stewardship. Some of the society members may be willing to help develop a brochure promoting planned giving. Distribute the brochure to potential society members and follow up with a phone call and a personal visit.

Evaluate the Program

Undertake a thorough review of the planned giving program and the endowment fund every three years. Use a variety of approaches to gather information that can help guide the planned giving program for the next few years.

- Study the gifts that have been received to determine patterns.

- Ask the bequest recognition society members for feedback.

- Compare the planned giving program with similar programs in other local faith communities. Check their websites for information, or call their church offices for guidance.

- Measure the success of the program in relation to others in your denomination. Unitarian Universalist congregations can ask their district executive for the names of congregations that have developed successful planned giving programs. They can also contact the Stewardship and Development staff group at 888-792-5885.

Put all of the gathered information together, and then use an Appreciative Inquiry approach (see page 17). Build on those components of the planned giving program that have already been successful. Determine whether there are components of planned giving that have yet to be emphasized. Create a plan, with measurable goals, for the next three years. This is the best way to ensure that the planned giving program remains alive, vital, and relevant.

CHAPTER NINE

Do You Really Need to Build?

What a tragedy that the quality of ministry is too often measured by numbers and building size, rather than by true spiritual results.

—Jim Cymbala

While it is important to have a spiritual home in which to worship, the congregants create true spiritual meaningfulness, not the building. Facilities are only a tool, a means to an end. There is nothing sacred about the materials used to construct facilities. In *First Impressions: How to Present an Inviting Church Facility*, Robert A. Lee notes that sometimes facilities can "take on the life of a ghost defending the territory for all eternity."

Lee is not suggesting that congregations be disrespectful of their facilities, ignore the legacy of previous members, or neglect their history. He does not advocate letting dirt accumulate in the corners or allowing buildings to fall into disrepair. Both Lee and Cymbala are reminding us that a church is a congregation, not a building. They are asking us to be mindful of the stewardship of efficiency by exploring ways to minimize structural needs. The less money a congregation spends on its spiritual home, the more money will be available to fulfill the mission of the faith community. Worshiping in a space that balances the mission and available financial resources is good stewardship.

When looking at strategic planning goals, congregations may recognize that not all their goals can be achieved in the current facilities. In fact, the building may be a formidable barrier to fulfilling the congregational mission. If congregations are unwilling to struggle with inadequate facilities, they may decide to seek a remedy to the space problems. Conducting a capital campaign in support of a major building project is certainly one way to seek a solution. However, it is not the only option. This chapter offers a process for analyzing the options and determining whether a building project is warranted.

Conduct this analysis under the umbrella of the Searching for the Future comprehensive strategic plan discussed in Chapter 3. Throughout the process, refer to the vision, mission, and goals for guidance. While the strategic plan will not provide specific answers to questions about limited facilities, it will certainly point the congregation in the right direction.

Create Growth Projections

The strategic planning team (see page 22) should create a task force to gather information about the current congregation and to determine future space needs based on congregational growth projections. The task force's job is to answer questions like:

- What kind of membership growth have we experienced during the past ten years?

- What has been the average Sunday attendance? How many have been in attendance on peak Sundays?

- What pattern is evident when religious education registrations are reviewed? How does registration compare to Sunday attendance?

- How many congregants have attended adult religious education offerings? What pattern is evident?

- What is the history of giving to the annual operating budget?

- How has the average financial commitment level changed? The median financial commitment?

It takes some time to gather this information, but it is important. Use this data to shape a conversation about future needs.

Analyze Existing Facilities

Meanwhile, the strategic planning team convenes another task force to look carefully at the current facilities. The goal of this task force is to determine whether facilities are being used efficiently, and if not, to suggest ways to make better use of them by adjusting programs and ministries. In this way it may be possible to overcome facility limitations at no cost or low cost.

It takes courage to pursue this particular issue. It is difficult to ask questions that might lead to better use of the current space rather than fulfilling the dream (sure to be dear to some) of building a sparkling addition or brand new facility. If the congregation has its heart set on a major building project, it is hard to hear that there may already be enough space and that the problem is just the use of the space. This "edifice complex" is fairly common among Unitarian Universalist congregations, but is certainly not exclusive to them. The complex can be hard to overcome, especially when the congregation is firmly convinced that a new building is the only solution to many of their problems.

The task force should include five to seven highly respected congregants who represent different congregational constituencies. Getting the right people to the table is especially important for this emotionally charged topic. Make inclusiveness a priority, and expect the task force members to treat each other with special care. A written covenant of spiritual relationship (see page 22) needs to be one of their very first tasks.

Give the task force the responsibility of creating an impartial, factual report. Ask them to include information about the entire property, not just the building. Remind them to address issues such as parking, signage, accessibility, storage, play areas, landscaping, and any deferred maintenance needs.

Taking an inventory of the facilities can help the task force determine the gap between the current facilities and ideal facilities. Page 151 provides facility guidelines adapted from recommendations by the American Institute of Architects and several other sources. These guidelines can be helpful in determining the adequacy of the current facilities.

In gathering and analyzing data, the task force uses the principles of Appreciative Inquiry (see page 17) to build upon the positive aspects of the existing facilities. Their goal is to find ways for the facilities to become more effective tools for fulfilling the mission of the congregation, allowing money to be invested in programs and ministries rather than in bricks and mortar.

If the current worship space is too crowded on Sundays, the easiest and least expensive solution may be to offer two or more weekly worship services. With multiple services, the use of facilities can be doubled or tripled.

Anticipate that some congregants will dismiss this option because they believe that it will be impossible to maintain the current level of intimacy. Experience has shown that this fear is often unfounded. The intimacy is not lost; it just takes a different shape. It's the difference between the congregation as a single unit and the congregation as a number of interrelated and overlapping groups.

Multiple weekly worship services offer several advantages: They can encourage growth, they can help the faith community better fulfill its mission, and they can be welcoming to a more diverse population. Even though the driving force behind offering multiple services may be to compensate for inefficient facilities, focusing on positive reasons for multiple worship services can be helpful. Margaret L. Beard, former Unitarian Universalist

Association director of New Congregation and Growth Resources, has said,

> A congregation that embraces a positive reason for the addition of a service is more likely to fulfill its mission. The members generate more excitement about the possibilities, and less resistance arises. The sense of mission helps carry the project through to its conclusion.

Let the congregational mission determine the nature of multiple worship services. Consider these possibilities:

- Two duplicate Sunday morning services.

- Two distinctly different Sunday morning services, such as an informal, contemporary lay-led service and a traditional service.

- Midweek vespers, perhaps on an evening when most committees meet.

- Sunday evening services for young adults (see **www.soulfulsundown.org**).

- Early Saturday evening services for youth, followed by programs specifically designed for them.

- Intergenerational services preceded by or followed by a shared meal.

- Services specifically designed for and led by seniors.

For more information about offering multiple worship services, refer to the booklet "Adding Worship Services," developed by the UUA Office of New Congregation and Growth Resources. This fifty-page resource can be found on the UUA website.

Beyond offering multiple worship services, think about other possible no-cost or low-cost ways to overcome facility shortcomings, such as:

- Moving groups to appropriate-sized rooms.

- Dividing large groups into two smaller groups to fit available rooms.

- Changing furniture or removing furniture.

- Building a storage facility to free up existing space (check local zoning codes first).

- Using off-site space for meetings.

- Implementing stacked parking (cars are parked bumper to bumper, with people waiting patiently at the end of a worship service for the car in front of them to move).

- Providing a "park and ride" center with shuttle vans.

- Using a municipal parking lot or the lot of a nearby business for early arrivals (choir, staff, religious education teachers), leaving the church lot for others.

- Changing committee or group meeting times (days or hours) so that fewer meetings occur at the same time.

- Offering a full religious education program during two Sunday morning worship services.

Review Options

Once the two task forces have completed their analyses, they share the information with the strategic planning team. After analyzing the information and considering options, the strategic planning team presents recommendations to the governing body. They might recommend making better use of the current facilities, beginning a relatively small renovation project, constructing a significant building addition, or relocating to a new spiritual home.

If there is a clear consensus that the current facilities, even with renovations, will not allow fulfillment of the mission, two options remain: Enlarge the current space by constructing an addition, or find another space (another building or piece of land) for the spiritual home. Constructing an addition may be the best option if:

The culture is not receptive to relocating. This may be the most important factor to consider. Some congregations would never consider leaving their beloved facilities.

The current facilities are highly visible. The more people who can see the facilities, the greater the number of visitors.

Access is convenient. A location close to major thoroughfares is important.

Adjacent land is available and affordable. Owning adjacent land or having the option of buying adjacent land may be a reason to build an addition.

The property is suitable for building additional facilities. Zoning laws, access to utilities, soil conditions, and disposition of the neighbors are all issues to consider.

There is a good match between the current location and the mission. The facilities need to be located where the community ministry occurs.

The facilities have architectural integrity. Look for clean circulation patterns with a logical layout of rooms and the ability to support an addition.

If the current facilities are lacking any of these attributes, relocation may be the best option. Of course, there is no clear right or wrong decision. There are always extenuating circumstances that make this a subjective, shades-of-gray decision.

"If You Build It, They Will Come"— But Will They Stay?

The well-known line from the movie *Field of Dreams* symbolizes the idea of building on faith. Some congregations believe that if they have the faith to build a new facility or renovate their existing one, people will flock to them and the congregation will experience rapid membership growth. And some congregations believe that the best way to reach out to the local community is to build a new, inviting fellowship hall, preferably with a stage, a commercial-grade kitchen, and maybe even a basketball court.

Unfortunately, experience doesn't support these ideas. If you build it, people may come to visit, but they won't stay long enough to become active congregants unless their spiritual expectations are met. It's what happens inside the building that converts

visitors into active congregants and enables the faith community to meet its growth goals.

Before making a final decision to proceed with a building project, the congregation must confront the question of why they want to build. If growth is the main motive, they cannot take that growth for granted. To increase the chances that a building project will lead to healthy congregational growth, they should consider the following.

Endorse a systemic definition of growth. For many congregations, growth equals increased numbers. Success is defined as increasing membership or increasing the size of the operating budget.

A wider, systemic definition of growth was first explored by Ted Buckle, a New Zealand minister, in his 1978 book *The House Alongside*. Loren Mead, founder of the Alban Institute, expanded on Buckle's work in his 1993 book *More Than Numbers: The Way Churches Grow*. Both Buckle and Mead suggest that churches grow in four ways. Their work is adapted below:

- *Numerical growth* is measured by worship service attendance, religious education attendance, budget size, number of programs and ministries, and number of active congregants.

- *Maturational growth* refers to the stature and maturity of each congregant. It includes growth in their faith and in their ability and willingness to nurture and be nurtured.

- *Organic growth* represents the systemic growth of the congregation as a healthy community that is capable of growing beyond its own confines to focus on the global community.

- *Incarnational growth* is growth in the congregational ability and willingness to create a positive impact, to make a significant difference in other societal communities to "walk the talk" with measurable deeds.

Healthy congregations are comfortable with a systemic definition of growth that includes all four of these areas. When faced with facility shortcomings, their goal is to find a solution that will better implement the congregation's mission. They are intentional about enhancing the growth of individual congregants as well as the entire faith community. Healthy congregations develop specific plans to increase their ability and willingness to spread the word to other faith communities.

Begin planning for additional programs and staff. Visitors will eagerly walk through the doors of a newly completed building. Unfortunately, many congregations experience a revolving-door phenomenon: Visitors do not return often enough to become included in the life of the congregation. Veteran fundraising consultants have learned that healthy, growing congregations are those that overcome the revolving-door phenomenon by developing a specific plan to include new people and welcome their unique gifts.

Visitors come to a faith community with spiritual expectations. Fulfilling those expectations requires additional programs and increased staffing. In anticipation of an increased number of visitors, growing congregations focus on several initiatives:

- Developing and maintaining an active welcoming program.

- Increasing religious education offerings.

- Creating a small-group ministry program.

- Developing ministries in the local community and the global community.

- Identifying tasks and matching a volunteer's interests and skills with the requirements of a task.

- Creating and filling as many new staff positions as needed, including a membership director, a director of volunteers, a coordinator of programs for young adults, a campus ministry coordinator, additional office support people, and sometimes an additional professional religious leader.

New programs and increased staffing demand more financial resources. An increasing number of congregations are including seed money for these initiatives within their capital campaign financial goal. Here's an example. A congregation

is conducting a capital campaign to build new program spaces. (We recommend using the term *program spaces* instead of *classrooms* because the term more accurately indicates that these rooms can be used more often than one hour a week.) The congregation also wants to increase the role of the religious education director by increasing the position from half time to three-quarter time. And in anticipation of more visitors, they want to create a new half-time membership director position. The congregation recognizes the importance of having these positions in place before the building project is completed.

To ease the burden on the operating budget, a three-year seed money program is developed. In the first year, 25 percent of the additional cost for the two staff positions is funded by the operating budget. The remaining 75 percent is funded by first-year capital campaign contributions. In the second year of the capital campaign, half of the additional cost is funded by the operating budget and half by capital campaign contributions. In the third year, 75 percent of the cost is funded by the operating budget. And in the fourth year, the salaries for the two positions are funded entirely by the operating budget.

Develop a growth plan. A solid growth plan includes the specific ways that the congregation will grow after completion of the building project. In addition to planning for an increased number of congregants, the plan addresses maturational growth, organic growth, and incarnational growth. A growth plan is always useful, and is required if the congregation chooses to apply for any of the loans or grants offered by the Unitarian Universalist Association (see Chapter 12). Many growth-related resources are included in the resources for further reading starting on page 159.

Remember: Keep the bricks-and-mortar issues within the context of the congregational mission. Unitarian Universalist minister Edwin C. Lynn, writing in *Tired Dragons*, says it well:

> Churches are a place for people. The architecture is the means, the setting; but the individual people bring a church to life. The

building can help or it can hinder each experience. The members of the church must care enough to create a meaningful religious environment that will truly meet the needs of the gathered community.

At first blush, a facility may seem to be woefully inadequate to meet the needs of the congregation. But before diving into a building project, take time to carefully examine this assumption. Remember that money spent on bricks and mortar is money that is not available to fund programs and staff.

CHAPTER TEN

Planning and Implementing a Building Project

A building project challenges every aspect of parochial life. In a real sense it is a test of a congregation's service, worship, education, evangelism, pastoral care, and stewardship. Rather than being something done in isolation from the daily life and work of a congregation, it is the material expression of that life and work.

—Charles N. Fulton III

Assume that a thorough analysis of existing facilities and future needs has been completed as described in the previous chapter. No-cost and low-cost options have been considered and rejected. A building project is imminent—but where to begin?

Clear vision is the core from which a building project evolves. Develop a building project that enables the congregation to focus on the ministry of fulfilling its mission. Remember that bricks and mortar can pave the way for growth, but programs and staffing will ensure lasting growth by meeting the spiritual expectations of congregants.

Although each building project is unique, here are some typical questions to answer:

- What type of building project matches the congregational mission?

- What role should a new building play in achieving overall goals?

- What programs and activities will be housed in the new facility?

- How can they be translated into specific space and square footage areas?

- How can the benefits of "green" construction be incorporated into the plan?

- How can the new facility provide universal accessibility?

As plans for the project unfold, the congregation will likely encounter some difficult decisions. A clear vision may not provide definitive answers, but it will help to narrow down the options, thereby reducing conflict. Still, some conflict is inevitable during a building project. The goal is not to avoid conflict, but to anticipate it and find ways to manage it without creating permanent divisiveness among the congregants.

Seek Guidance

Most congregations have not undertaken a building project often enough to understand the level of complexity involved in the process. Seek guidance from others to help make informed decisions at the beginning of the process. Gather firsthand information from others who have completed a similar project. For Unitarian Universalist congregations, the Office of Congregational Fundraising Services can compare the planned building project with other congregations that have completed similar projects. Unitarian Universalist congregations can contact the office at 617-948-4251 for an initial conversation with the program director. If it appears that the consulting program can be helpful, the director matches the congregation's needs with the skills of one of the fundraising consultants, and a consulting relationship begins. (See Chapter 2 for more on hiring a consultant.)

Organize the Leadership

Regardless of the size of the building project, congregational leaders must be well organized. Here are two key principles to follow in organizing the lay leadership for a building project.

Ensure widespread congregational participation. A building project can be exciting. It can bring the congregation together to focus on a common goal. When seen as a logical extension of the vision and mission process, the project entices many congregants to get involved and share responsibility. The more people who participate, the less likely that a few dedicated volunteers will experience burnout. In addition, widespread participation creates informed congregants who feel strong ownership of the building project, which in turn leads to significant financial support.

Many building project leaders would prefer to organize a small group of like-minded congregants to plan and conduct all aspects of a building project. The advantages of this model are evident: A small group is easier to manage, it is likely to move forward quickly and with little conflict, and it could complete a building project in a relatively short period of time. No need for all that messy and time-consuming discussion! But the messiness is important to ensure widespread ownership of the building project, and leaders avoid the messiness at their peril. When a small group completes most of the work, nonparticipants may feel isolated, uninformed, and devalued, even if they are comfortable with the small group's decisions. Participative involvement is more important than efficiency.

Maintain continuity with one steering committee. Over the years, faith communities have tried a variety of organizational models to support a building project. Some congregations have chosen to create several committees, with each working independently and reporting to the governing body. Others have started by hiring an architect who is responsible for gathering all the necessary building-related information and then moving the project forward. Still other congregations have begun a building project when a member's friend, let's call him Carpenter Carl, offers to direct a crew of volunteers in a series of weekend work parties. While some congregations have probably been successful with each of these models, there is one model that has consistently proven effective: Make one group of leaders—a steering committee—responsible for overseeing the entire building project.

The steering committee is a logical extension of the strategic planning team (see page 22). The steering committee oversees the entire building project process, from information collection to occupancy of the building. Eventually the steering committee develops a project package that makes the case for the building project and justifies the reason for raising money. It brings this package to the governing body for its review and adoption.

Steering Committee Structure

The size and structure of a building project steering committee depend on the size of the congregation and the scope of the project. Generally speaking, the bigger the project, the more committee members are needed. Although size categories are always somewhat arbitrary, for the purposes of this discussion they are defined as follows:

- Large building projects that cost more than $1,000,000

- Midsize building projects that cost between $500,000 and $1,000,000

- Small building projects that cost up to $500,000

Large building project ($1,000,000+). Recruit ten steering committee members: a chairperson, a secretary, and eight subcommittee leaders.

- *Chairperson.* The primary leader of the project and holder of the vision. Needs strong recruiting and delegating skills.

- *Secretary.* Maintains a complete historical record of the building project.

- *Publicity subcommittee.* Keeps the project on the minds of the congregation and the local community.

- *Strategic planning subcommittee.* Translates the comprehensive strategic plan into specific facility, staffing, and program needs.

- *Property subcommittee.* Gathers information and evaluates the existing property and the acquisition of new property, if applicable.

- *Capital campaign subcommittee.* Works with the fundraising consultant to plan all aspects of the capital campaign.

- *Finance subcommittee.* Proposes and arranges short-term and long-term financing and the financial package for the entire project.

- *Building plans subcommittee.* Works with the architect to develop complete construction plans for the building project.

- *Construction subcommittee.* Works with the architect and general contractor through the final inspection and acceptance of the building.

- *Furnishings subcommittee.* Inventories and evaluates existing furnishings, determines needs for new items, orders needed items (after approval by the finance subcommittee), and oversees placement before the occupancy date.

For a large building project, this model offers the best way to control the many pieces of the project. Remember, every project-related decision goes through the steering committee. Don't let any of the subcommittees bypass it and go directly to the governing body or the congregation.

Ask each subcommittee to create workgroups for special tasks. For example, if the project includes the need for new program spaces, ask the building plans subcommittee to form a workgroup to clarify the needs of specific groups like preschool, children, youth, young adults, adults, seniors, renters, music/choir, and office/administration. Workgroup members can be recruited from among congregants who are not otherwise involved in the project.

Midsize building project ($500,000 to $1,000,000). Even for a midsize building project, careful organizing is still needed. In fact, the smaller the proj-

ect, the more important the planning group because it is so easy to overlook important details.

The same areas of responsibility must be addressed in a midsize building project as in a large one. The primary difference is that some subcommittees can be combined to decrease the number of leaders needed. The steering committee for a midsize building project might look like this:

- Chairperson

- Secretary and publicity

- Strategic planning

- Property and furnishings

- Capital campaign

- Finance

- Building plans and construction

Small building project (up to $500,000). Organizing for a small building project can be further simplified by eliminating the subcommittees all together. All of the same tasks need to be completed, but the steering committee can be streamlined. Here is the steering committee for a small building project:

- Governing body chair

- Religious educator

- Capital campaign chair

- Finance committee chair

- Member-at-large

For small projects, it is especially important to recruit leaders carefully. Recruit five steering committee members who have the skills, time, energy, and commitment to focus on all of the details that would be delegated to several other people in a larger building project.

Statement of Responsibility and Authority

Before recruiting the building project steering committee members, the governing body must develop a statement of responsibility and authority that specifically defines the parameters of the steering committee's task. A clearly stated assignment, in writing, is essential to the work of the steering committee. Provide clearly defined and measurable outcomes, and include the start date and the completion date of their assignment. Share the components of the assignment with the congregation so that they are knowledgeable about the process.

Steering Committee Members

The governing body is responsible for recruiting the building project steering committee, as well as for clarifying the connection between the congregation's strategic plan and its building project. Because the building project must support the strategic plan, it's advisable to recruit some strategic planning leaders to join the steering committee. If there is some continuity of participation, the steering committee will not have to start from scratch.

The most effective building project steering committee members are those who feel passionate about the faith community and the building project. Look for people who have a strong and clear vision for the future that matches the vision of others in the congregation. Look for people able and willing to share their enthusiasm and who perceive each controversy as an opportunity to explore possibilities rather than as a problem to be avoided. They are often not the people who have specific technical and vocational skills. These specialists will be important as the project moves forward, but they are generally not best suited for this big-picture stage of the building project.

Sometimes governing bodies make the mistake of appointing new congregants or even fringe members to the steering committee. They presume that selecting these folks for leadership positions is a way of including them in congregational life. However, new people may not have broad enough experience in the total life of the congregation to make the best building decisions. The building project steering committee is not the place for new or inexperienced congregants.

First Meeting

After the statement of responsibility and authority has been created and all the steering committee members have been recruited, it's time for the steering committee chair to schedule the first meeting. Create a crisp, tight agenda. Begin by creating a covenant of spiritual relationship. Clarify the connections that link each steering committee member to the others. Discuss the timeline, the reporting procedures, and the specific outcomes expected of each person. Make sure that each committee member leaves the meeting with a clear understanding of the way his or her role fits into all the other building project pieces.

Hire an Architect

Building a new spiritual home or renovating an existing facility is a complex process. It requires not only the lay-led efforts of the congregation, but also professional knowledge and skills. Some congregations think that since their project is straightforward, the planning and construction can be accomplished with volunteers. Still others turn to a congregant architect over a more qualified architect in an attempt to save money. It cannot be stated too strongly: View the cost of an architect as an investment, not as an unnecessary expense.

Ask one steering committee member to convene a task force with the responsibility of choosing an architect for the early planning phase. Five to seven task force members are sufficient. Be particular about who is chosen for the task force. Recruit people who represent various ministry groups and who possess a variety of skills. A congregant architect can be a valuable member of the task force as long as he or she understands the parameters of the role (as task force member, not architect). Include some "left-brain" people (linear processors who are comfortable with logical sequencing) and some "right-brain" people (intuitive, big-picture people who process from the whole to each of the parts). Include people who are physically challenged, because they will bring a needed perspective to the project.

As with all other task forces, begin by creating a written covenant of spiritual relationship, a set of promises made in mutual responsibility and agreement (see page 22). Next, clarify the scope of the assignment by answering these questions:

- Is it our responsibility to *recommend* an architect, or do we also have the authority to *hire* an architect?

- How will we know when our task has been completed? Do we have a specific timeline? Who takes over when our task is completed?

- Do we report to the steering committee or to the governing body?

- How can the congregation be included in the process of selecting the architect?

- How can we keep the congregation informed as we move forward?

- What is to be designed and built?

- Where will it be built?

- What level of amenities, finishes, and architectural detail will be included?

- What aspects of an environmentally healthy "green" facility are important?

- What attention will be given to music, kitchen, and performance areas?

- What is the target date for completion of the building project?

- To whom will the architect report?

To avoid getting the "cart before the horse," *all* of these questions must be answered before hiring an architect.

Next, gather information about local architects. Seek referrals from the congregation, other local faith communities, and respected people in the greater community. Leaders of Unitarian Universalist congregations can join online discussion forums where you can ask questions and exchange information with other congregational leaders who have completed building projects. Participation is free. The uuleader and uumoney forums will be most helpful. For more information, go to the UUA website.

The most successful architects match a building project to a congregation rather than trying to squeeze a congregation into the mold of their favorite design. In *Building for Effective Mission*, Kennon Callahan suggests seeking an architect who shares the "best wisdom, experience, common sense, and judgment and who will coach the rest of the team as they seek to understand architecture." Look for an architect who is confidently competent, who shares ideas assertively and positively, and who is compatible with the congregation's mission.

Create a complete list of potential architects, and then narrow the list to five or six candidates. Send each candidate a description of the required architectural services as well as the anticipated scope of the project. Ask each architect to complete a Preliminary Selection Form (see page 155).

Ecological Stewardship

One piece of the information-gathering process is especially worthy of discussion: determining each architect's experience with ecologically friendly construction. Many congregations are now sensitive to "green" construction, an issue of ecological stewardship that must not be overlooked. An experienced architect can discover ways to build an ecologically responsible place of worship. As more breakthroughs in building science, technology, and operations occur, and with heightened awareness of ecological stewardship, there is no reason to hire an architect who is unwilling to actively pursue green construction options.

Here's a starter list of ways to be good stewards of the environment. Some pertain to the architect's responsibilities, while others are relevant for other phases of the building project. For additional information, refer to the list of resources for further reading starting on page 159.

- When possible, reconstruct existing buildings instead of constructing new buildings.

- Enhance a site by protecting trees and topsoil during construction.

- Minimize groundwater contamination by providing systems for treating on-site wastewater.

- Reintroduce native species in landscaping.

- Avoid toxic, hazardous, or polluting materials.

- Select materials that use less energy during extraction, manufacturing, and shipping.

- Select recycled materials.

- Select fast-replenishing materials, such as bamboo.

- Design buildings and landscapes that are water efficient.

- Install efficient plumbing fixtures and appliances.

- Collect and use rainwater.

- Reuse gray water (water that has been used, except water from toilets).

- Design easy-to-clean and low-maintenance air-distribution systems.

- Avoid air-polluting (combustion) equipment.

- Control moisture to prevent premature decay.

- Light with daylight, and continuously ventilate all rooms.

- Design for durability and adaptability by using durable building materials.

- Design for easy maintenance.

- Fully fund appropriate maintenance.

- Minimize waste from demolition and construction, and recycle when possible.

- Publicize your commitment.

Determine what experience the architect has had with this list of ecologically friendly construction possibilities. Ask for specific references. Ask if the architect is LEED (Leadership in Energy and Environmental Design) certified. The LEED program was created to define "green" buildings by establishing a common standard of measurement. Additional information is available through the United States Green Building Council (USGBC) at **www.usgbc.org**.

Selection Process

After reviewing the architects' credentials and résumés, narrow the field to three candidates. Send each architect a copy of the congregation's five-year strategic plan. Ask the three architects to prepare a schematic design to convey their best architectural and planning proposals. If appropriate, ask them to include five components: site plan, floor plans, elevations, narrative description, and budget. Most architects will agree to prepare a schematic design for a relatively large new-construction project. For smaller renovations, ask the architects to prepare a rudimentary planning proposal. Depending on the scope of the project, allow thirty to ninety days for them to prepare the proposals.

Meanwhile, ask the architects for a complete list of their projects. The task force can then decide which references to contact. In checking references, be brave enough to ask difficult, probing questions to develop an informed distinction among the architects. Develop the set of questions before talking with each reference.

Don't limit the decision-making process to an architect's list of contacts. Call the planning office of the city. What is the architect's reputation with the city planners and inspectors? You might find that a particular architect has been difficult to work with or that important deadlines have been missed. The local planning and building offices have the power to make life miserable if they don't like an architect, the building plans, or the contractor. On the other hand, if they like an architect, the project will be much easier to maneuver through the system. Select an architect who works well with local municipal officials.

Invite each architect on your short list to come in for an interview. At the start of each interview, welcome the architect and introduce the task force members. Allow thirty minutes for each architect's presentation. Do not interrupt the presentation; there will be time to ask questions after it is completed. Designate an official note taker for each interview.

Suggested interview questions are provided on page 156. Some were developed by the American Institute of Architects, and some were developed by Ryan Hazen, a consultant with the Board of Church Extension of the Disciples of Christ. Unless you are planning a three-hour interview (it is not recommended!), select only some of the questions that are listed. Ask each architect the same core questions. Remember that the questions are designed to gather information and to determine the fit between your congregation and the architect. Your goal is not to grill the architect or to raise the level of anxiety.

After the interviews have been completed, select an architect who instills confidence. Balance design ability, technical confidence, professional service, and cost. Architectural competence is not enough. Choose an architect who is truly excited about working with the congregation. On their website (**www.aia.org**), the American Institute of Architects suggests,

> Choose your architect at least as carefully as you would your dentist or your doctor. Factors such as experience, technical competence, and available staff resources will be important to your decision. . . . The most thoughtful architects are as careful in selecting their clients as owners are at selecting architects. They are as interested in a successful project as you are, and they know that good architecture results from fruitful collaboration between architects and clients.

The Architect's Contract

There are three acceptable ways to structure an architect's fees:

- The stipulated sum, or fixed fee, is generally preferred. This fee arrangement requires that the scope of the project be well defined so that design fees can be accurately predicted.

- A fee based on a percentage of construction cost allows flexibility in situations in which the project scope has not been fully defined.

- Compensation at an hourly rate can be an effective approach for a small project or a project with a number of unknown variables. This option can be a good way to explore design options before committing to an architect for the full scope of architectural services.

Consider using one of the AIA Owner-Architect agreements. These standard forms, developed by the American Institute of Architects in the 1880s, have been carefully reviewed and modified over the years. The most commonly used is AIA Document B141, Standard Form of Agreement Between Owner and Architect. It can be found on the AIA website.

Whether congregational leaders decide to use one of the AIA contracts or to develop their own contract, get approval from the congregation's legal and insurance counselors before any contract is signed. In *Planning and Building Facilities*, Steven Newton cautions,

> No matter which option is taken, the agreement should be formalized in a contract. Even though goodwill is intended by both parties, no handshake is firm enough to reach all the understandings about the roles and obligations of the [church] and the architect.

Develop Preliminary Building Plans

Once hired, ask the architect to develop three preliminary building plans. There is significance to preparing three options. If only one option is presented to the congregation, some will feel they are being forced to make a yes-or-no decision without knowledge of any other possible options. If given two options, winners and losers will be created among the congregants as they vote for one or the other plan. And if four options are presented, the congregational decision-making process may continue for an inordinate period of time.

The first of the three plans should incorporate most of the congregational needs and wishes for the new facility. It represents a best-case scenario. As a guideline for the total cost of the project, give the architect a figure that represents five times the annual financial commitments to the most recent operating budget. For example, if the most recent annual budget drive generated commitments of $200,000, give the architect a figure of $1 million. Of course, the congregation will be able to afford a more expensive building project if they are willing to finance part of the project. (For a discussion about the advantages of incurring a reasonable amount of debt, see Chapter 12.) But for now, keep it simple and just use multiples of annual giving as ballpark figures for the architect to use.

Let the second preliminary plan represent a less expensive version that includes most of the needed components and perhaps only some of the congregational wishes. Give the architect a figure of four times the most recent annual giving—$800,000 in this example.

The third plan should include just enough of the facility needs to create a bare-bones plan. Give the architect a figure that represents three times the annual commitment total. In this example, ask the architect to keep the total cost of this building project to $600,000.

Keep each plan within the realm of possibility. The most expensive plan cannot be so expensive that it is totally unreasonable. At the same time, the low-cost option cannot be so limited that it doesn't address any of the congregation's needs.

Develop Financial Projections

Create a five-year financial projection for each of the three architectural plans. Estimate capital income and expenses as well as annual operating budget income and expenses. Be conservative by projecting relatively low income and relatively high expenses. Use lots of zeroes as opposed to creating exact numbers in each category.

In this early planning phase, it is safe to estimate that about 50 percent of capital campaign contributions will be received by the end of the first year of the campaign. Another 25 percent is likely to be received by the end of the second year, with the final 25 percent being received by the end of the third year. Anticipate a slippage rate (the

variance between the financial commitments and the amount actually received) of about 10 percent of the total financial commitment.

To create the projections for annual operating budget income and expenses, use the annual budget information from the previous year, plus the current year's information. A cash flow projection spreadsheet is provided on page 158.

Take into consideration how the capital campaign will affect the annual budget drive. Unitarian Universalist Association data indicate little increase in annual giving during a capital campaign. Many congregants maintain their annual giving at the current level; only a few increase their annual giving, and only by a small amount. Anticipate about a 5-percent increase in giving to the annual operating budget during each of the three years of the capital campaign.

The good news is that in the fourth year (the first year after capital campaign money has been received), giving to the annual operating budget can sometimes increase by 15 to 30 percent. Here is an example.

During the most recent annual budget drive, Mr. and Mrs. Smith contributed $1,000. At the same time, they committed $6,000 to the building project. They plan to divide their capital campaign commitment into three installments, contributing $2,000 each year for the three years of the campaign. They will increase their annual giving by 5 percent during each of the following two years. Therefore, they will be contributing a total of $9,153 to the church during those three years, as shown here:

The Smith's Financial Contributions

	Annual Budget	Capital Campaign	Year Total
Year 1	$1,000	$2,000	$3,000
Year 2	$1,000 + 5% = $1,050	$2,000	$3,050
Year 3	$1,050 + 5% = $1,103	$2,000	$3,103

In the fourth year, their capital campaign commitment will have been completed. They might be inclined to increase their annual giving by another 5 percent (to $1,158), as they have been doing during each of the past three years. However, fundraising consultants' experience indicates that, *if asked*, the Smiths may be able and willing to significantly increase their giving to the annual operating budget in this fourth year. If they increase their most recent annual financial commitment by 30 percent, they will contribute $1,434 to the annual budget. That is still less than half of the total amount they had contributed to the church during each of the past three years.

Certainly some members of the congregation will not be able or willing to increase their fourth-year financial commitment by 30 percent. But experience tells us that some will substantially increase their giving. And you will never know unless you ask.

Present the Plans for a Vote

When the three building plans and their corresponding financial projections have been completed, the next step is to share them with the governing body and then the congregation. Prepare a summary sheet for each option as a kind of preliminary case statement to show the differences among the three. On the front side of each summary sheet, present a bulleted outline listing the highlights of that particular building plan and its estimated costs. On the back side, print the financial spreadsheet that corresponds to that plan. Choose a different color paper for each sheet. For example:

- The Gold Plan (goldenrod-colored paper): the most expensive project.

- The Silver Plan (gray-colored paper): the moderately expensive project.

- The Bronze Plan (tan-colored paper): the modest, inexpensive project.

In a formal vote, ask congregants to determine which of the three plans will most successfully fulfill the mission of the congregation. Congregants are specifically not asked to decide whether the project is financially feasible. They will need to trust that the building project steering commit-

tee has presented three plans that are each financially realistic.

This step is designed to indicate preliminary support prior to conducting a financial feasibility study. In other words, the choice among the three plans is made assuming that a capital campaign will raise enough money to make the building project a reality.

After the congregational vote, ask the architect to prepare a schematic design and a cost estimate for the one plan that received the most congregational support. Also, if applicable, ask the architect to create a crude scale model showing the exterior of the proposed building. Sometimes an architect will even create a scale model with a removable roof so that people can see the interior floor plan. A scale model is imperative when planning to build a completely new structure or significantly alter the interior space of an existing facility. The model is an important prop that the consultant uses during the financial feasibility study interviews, and it becomes a vital part of the overall communication plan.

Conduct a Financial Feasibility Study

To gauge the congregation's readiness to launch a capital campaign, ask the fundraising consultant and the building project steering committee to plan a financial feasibility study. Invite about 15 to 20 percent of the annual donors to participate in the study. The fundraising consultant helps determine the precise number of participants needed to get a representative cross section of congregants. Ask the consultant to conduct a confidential interview with each of the participants. With the consultant's help, develop a core group of questions to ask each participant. Although there are often fifteen to twenty-five questions asked, the consultant groups them under the umbrella of four broad questions:

- How knowledgeable is the congregation about the proposed project?

- What parts of the project are people especially excited about?

- Are there concerns about the project that might create a barrier to a successful capital campaign?

- How much money are the participants likely to contribute to the proposed project?

After completing the confidential interviews, the consultant analyzes all of the data and prepares a written final report that answers the four questions listed above. The results of the financial feasibility study determine the capital campaign financial goal and the ultimate scope of the building project. In the report, the consultant provides one of two broad recommendations. One recommendation would say something like:

> The steering committee has done a wonderful job of preparing the congregation for a capital campaign. You are ready to launch the campaign, and it is likely that between $_____ and $_____ in capital campaign contributions will be received. Please consider a stretch goal of $_____.

Or the recommendation might read like this:

> In spite of the wonderful work that has already been completed, you are not quite ready to launch a capital campaign. Here is a list of specific issues to be resolved as well as specific recommendations to resolve the issues. When these recommendations have been addressed, you are likely to raise between $_____ and $_____.

Invite the consultant to share the report with the entire congregation. Put the document on the church website, and make hard copies available as well.

If the consultant's report indicates that more work is needed, appoint task forces to resolve the issues described by the consultant. Create action plans for each task, including a due date for each. Do not move forward with the capital campaign until the tasks have been completed.

Launch a Capital Campaign

After any issues identified by the consultant have been addressed, or if the consultant's report was favorable, schedule a congregational meeting and take a formal vote to move forward with the capital campaign. Take a second vote to confirm the financial goal of the campaign.

In many respects, a capital campaign is similar to conducting an annual budget drive using personal stewardship conversations. Chapter 11 provides information about organizing a capital campaign.

Approve the Final Plans

Once the capital campaign is under way and visiting stewards have completed their stewardship conversations with donors, the congregation will have a solid estimate of the expected capital campaign financial commitments. That amount—plus any loans, grants, bequests, or money from the endowment fund (see Chapter 8)—determines the total amount of money available to complete the project.

Ask the architect to revise the preliminary design plans and to prepare more detailed cost estimates. In these detailed documents, ask the architect to include structural, mechanical, and electrical systems, as well as the building materials and finishes that will be used. Together, these documents create a more accurate construction cost statement.

The architect presents the completed plans, along with cost estimates, to the building project steering committee. Depending on congregational bylaws and congregational norms, the steering committee approves the revised plans or recommends approval to the congregation. Of course, this sequence assumes that the architect's plans match the desire of the congregation. In some cases, the architect's plans need to be revised once again.

Prepare for Construction

Before going on to the next phase, create a new contract with an architect. Congregations often retain the same architect for the remainder of the building project, but consider hiring a different architect if displeased with the work of the initial architect. Even though changing architects may slow down the progress of the project, it is better than continuing through the process with an architect who is not meeting the expectations of the congregation.

Construction Drawings and Specifications. Ask the architect to prepare construction drawings that are based on the previously accepted design development plans. Ask for detailed drawings and specifications of the construction requirements. The drawings describe the quantity of the construction materials and their location within the new facility. The specifications detail the quality of materials and the execution of the construction work. Ask the architect to prepare the list of necessary construction materials that will be presented to general contractors for the bidding process. The architect is also responsible for obtaining appropriate government approvals during this phase.

Bids. Ask the architect to assist in obtaining bids from general contractors and to help prepare construction contracts. Consider several alternates in the bidding process. An alternate identifies a specific part of the construction process that might be eliminated at the discretion of the steering committee. Clearly identify each alternate in the construction documents. For example, the bidding instructions might request a base bid on the total project plus these alternates:

- One alternate deducts the cost of movable partitions in the fellowship hall.

- Another alternate deducts the cost of paving a new parking area.

- A third deducts the cost of landscaping.

The purpose of creating alternates is to help control final costs. By making alternates a part of the bidding process, competitive estimates can be provided. If just a base bid is obtained and then negotiated with the low bidder for alternates, the congregation is losing its advantage of competitive bidding. Once a general contractor is known to be the low bidder, the bids for the alternates may not be as competitive as desired.

With the guidance of the architect, determine a few general contractors who will be asked to prepare bids. Give each contractor a copy of the project plans, including alternates, and specify a bid due date. After bids have been received, review them with the architect, and then award a construction contract to the best-qualified general contractor. It is not unusual to find that the best-qualified candidate is not the lowest bidder.

Begin Construction

There is good news for all those who have had a shovel in their trunk since the very first conversation about a building project. It is finally time to break ground.

During the construction phase, use the architect to represent the congregation to the contractor. The architect interprets the construction documents and guards against defects and deficiencies in the construction. This task is important but sometimes misunderstood. The architect is not a construction supervisor and does not have responsibility for construction sequencing, techniques, or procedures. These responsibilities belong to the general contractor. However, the architect can be expected to visit the construction site at appropriate times, evaluate the progress of work, and provide impartial interpretations of the contract documents. The architect has the authority (under AIA contracts) to reject work that does not conform to the contract. The architect determines whether the general contractor's requests for payment reflect the amount of work that has been performed and, if so, authorizes the payment. The congregation is thus protected from financial loss in case the general contractor defaults on the project.

The construction phase of a building project is difficult, with many opportunities for conflict. A strong commitment to teamwork helps congregational leaders navigate through the construction process. The steering committee is responsible for helping all interested parties work toward the common goal of completing the project. Teamwork among the members of the steering committee, the fundraising consultant, the architect, the general contractor, the governing body, and the congregation is essential. Let the steering committee take a leadership role in developing and maintaining open lines of communication.

A major part of the communication process is to be clear about the responsibility and authority for decision making. It is best to put that information in writing. Also put in writing all decisions made by any of the related parties. Keep written summaries of each meeting. Be sure that the steering committee secretary maintains electronic and hard-copy files of all the recorded information.

The best and most rewarding results occur when everyone works together for the common good of the faith community. The task is difficult, but the results can provide the foundation (both figuratively and literally) that enables the congregation to fulfill its mission.

Celebrate as Often as Possible

Rather than waiting until the dedication ceremony, take advantage of every opportunity to celebrate during a building project. Celebrations divide the process into manageable segments, help the congregation maintain its enthusiasm, and provide wonderful publicity opportunities. Get as many congregants as possible involved. Consider the following suggestions and use them as a launching pad for creating other celebrations.

Site dedication. Celebrate the commitment to purchase a piece of land or begin a building project.

Presentation of plans. The architect will likely make at least two presentations to the congregation—one when the schematic design is prepared and another when the project design has been completed. Publicize these occasions so that everyone is aware of the celebration.

Construction contract. The selection of the general contractor is an opportunity for a news release, with pictures, in the local newspaper. Include basic information about the building project, and

don't forget to post the same information on the church website. Celebrate this event as a significant step toward fulfilling the congregation's mission.

Groundbreaking ceremony. Groundbreaking offers an opportunity to celebrate the heritage of the church and to further unite the congregation behind the building project.

Time capsule. Celebrate the connection of the past to the future. Use a sealed receptacle to enclose historical artifacts and dreams for the future. Lay the cornerstone and bury the time capsule in a ceremony that marks a true transition from the past to the future.

Departure day. If relocating, celebrate the last service in the current facility. Make the service one of the most meaningful events that has ever occurred there. Focus the service on congregational challenges that will be met in the new setting.

Moving day. If the new facility is an addition to the current space, or if you are relocating in the immediate vicinity, arrange a procession from the old space to the new space. If the distance is greater, plan an auto caravan. In either case, ask everyone to carry some significant item that needs to be transferred to the new facility.

Commemorative tiles. Celebrate commitment to the new facility. Provide materials for each family to decorate a six-by-six-inch tile to be placed on a wall of the new building. Schedule the activity as part of the moving day celebration. Consider making this event an annual affair to celebrate each year of the new facility.

Dedication ceremony. Celebrate completion of the new facility by linking it to the congregational mission. Take this time to highlight the spiritual essence of the congregation that is being transferred from the old to the new.

Open house. Celebrate the congregation's commitment to the local community. Schedule an open house on a Sunday afternoon so that people from other local faith communities can attend. Send personal written invitations to local clergy and professional religious leaders of the denomination. Don't forget to invite the architect, the general contractor, and local municipal officials.

Sow seeds. Consecrate new property by having a "reverse offertory." Fill collection plates with bulbs or packets of flower seeds. Pass the collection plates and encourage each congregant to take something from the plate. At the end of the service, lead congregants to a section of the property that has been prepared to receive the offering. With careful supervision, invite congregants to plant the offering. Of course, the reverse offertory works best in the spring or fall.

Note burning. Assuming that a mortgage is being carried on the new facility, celebrate the final payment of the mortgage with a special service to symbolically burn the mortgage when it has been paid down. A note of caution: Some congregations have experienced a decrease in giving after their indebtedness has been paid. To guard against this possibility, make sure that the strategic plan clearly indicates the next goals to pursue.

These events provide opportunities to share the success of the building project. Be sure to include an offertory (not to be confused with a reverse offertory) at each event. The offertory provides a symbolic way for everyone to share in the celebration. Dedicate the money collected from the offertory to a specific aspect of the project that is connected to that celebratory event.

CHAPTER ELEVEN

Debt Is More Than a Four-Letter Word

We can pay our debts to the past by putting the future in debt to ourselves.
—John Buchan

Before you launch a capital campaign, there is another option to consider. Many of us were raised to believe that there is something shameful about debt, but debt responsibly handled can be a viable option for your faith community. Debt can send a positive message to the next generation of congregants. It can tell them that although the current congregation was not able to fully fund the project, its members chose to build (or to renovate) facilities to meet the projected needs of the future. Debt represents financial sacrifice in service of the next generation, and it is the shared responsibility of both the current congregation and those who follow.

Two financing options are available. The first is a bank loan and is available to any qualified faith community. The second is financing from the Unitarian Universalist Association, which is available only to Unitarian Universalist congregations.

First Steps

When financing is needed, some congregations begin by going to a bank or other lender, asking for money, and then developing whatever additional information is needed. This is not the best sequence of events. Long before contact with a lender, the congregation must clarify its mission and develop a five-year strategic plan. (An approach to strategic planning, Searching for the Future, is discussed in Chapter 3.) Once that is done, the congregation can consider its physical facilities needs, as described in Chapter 9. Note that the mission and goals are clarified *before* considering the brick-and-mortar concerns.

Once the physical facility needs have been determined, the congregation should create a five-year projection of operating income and expenses and of capital income and expenses, as described on page 92. This projection will help determine the amount that can be borrowed to ensure that the congregation does not burden itself with too much debt.

Financial Comfort Level

Each congregation has its own level of financial comfort. Some are comfortable with a relatively high amount of debt, while others are comfortable only if they are debt-free.

Most lenders, including the Unitarian Universalist Association, consider that some level of debt is healthy and can help a congregation to fulfill its mission. Here are three guidelines for determining an appropriate amount of debt:

- Be sure that annual debt service does not exceed 25 percent of the congregation's annual operating budget. The Unitarian Universalist Association does not even consider a request for a loan or loan guarantee if the annual debt service exceeds this level. The concern is not whether the congregation can service its debt; it is that the congregation may focus too much attention on making loan payments rather than on fulfilling its mission.

- Keep the total project cost within two to three times the annual budget total.

- Keep the total project cost to a maximum of 50 percent of the total property appraisal (when the project has been completed).

Historically, some congregational leaders have suggested funding a building project by making a deposit of 10 percent, with the remaining 90 percent to be carried with a mortgage. Here is the argument that they often use: The new building will attract visitors who will soon become members, and these new members will make substantial annual financial commitments to help make mortgage payments. As mentioned in Chapter 9, this "build it and they will come" model is not reliable. Until new members feel included in the life of the congregation, they seldom make significant financial commitments. Rather than helping to increase financial stability, their financial commitments do not even provide the money needed to support programs and ministries.

If a mortgage is proposed as a way to help pay for a building project, develop financial projections to show how the mortgage fits into the entire financial picture. Then the congregation can make an informed decision about whether or not to support a mortgage.

Local Bank Financing

It is always best to seek local financing first. In most cases, best terms can be obtained by shopping locally.

Typical Loan Terms

Most banks lend up to 75 percent of a project's cost. Congregations are eligible for a commercial loan rather than a residential loan, and the terms are very different. Most commercial loans are written with a five- to ten-year term, meaning that the loan must either be reset or paid off at the end of that time, and a fifteen- to twenty-five-year principal amortization schedule. There is always a refinancing risk. The bank is not committed to renewing the loan in five to ten years. Congregational leaders can, however, request an adjustable loan in which the rate is reset to the current market for another five- to ten-year period, thus avoiding having to pay the full balance.

Interest rates for a short-term construction loan may range from 0.5 to 1.5 percent above the prime rate or other index. During the term of a construction loan, only interest is paid. Once the construction is completed, the loan is converted to a permanent mortgage with a rate generally 2 to 3 percent over a Treasury note of the same five- to ten-year length.

Closing costs may include up-front fees, called points, that are sometimes paid in exchange for a lower interest rate. Each point is 1 percent of the loan amount, Other closing costs, such as legal fees, professional engineering reports (including environmental reviews), and a professional property appraisal, do not vary with the size of the loan and may total between $5,000 and $8,000. If negotiating with more than one bank, get agreements to put the appraisal out to bid and to share the appraisal cost. Congregational leaders can't arrange for the appraisal themselves because banks accept only the report of an independent appraiser from their approved list. The appraisal is addressed directly to the bank.

Loan Guarantees

When working with churches, banks sometime require a denomination's guarantee. In some cases, the guarantee is the final piece needed to get market-rate financing from the bank. But do not offer the guarantee unless requested by the bank, and then only if it makes the difference in getting the loan or reducing the interest rate.

Never agree to provide guarantees from individual congregants. They are congregants, not bankers. If a congregant becomes a guarantor of the project, the relationship between the congregant and the church becomes a financial one in addition to a pastoral or spiritual one. There is always a small possibility that the church could run into financial difficulty and default on the loan, in which case the guarantor would be held financially liable. But even if the congregation successfully services its debt and the guarantee never becomes an issue, there is still the question of clarity of purpose. Congregations are simply not in the business of guaranteeing loans.

Risk Analysis

When a bank loans money, it is taking a risk of not being repaid. The bank analyzes its risk based on three factors. The most important factor is cash flow. The bank wants to know whether the congregation consistently raises enough money from its annual budget drive to pay the debt service on the loan being requested. Although it has been stated earlier, it is important enough to repeat: *Do not agree to any loan that requires annual debt service of more than 25 percent of the annual operating budget.*

Bankers also need to be convinced that the financial projections are reasonable and not based on unrealistically high future increases in membership or financial commitments. Of course, "unrealistically high" is a relative term. Historically, some Unitarian Universalist congregations have experienced 5 to 10 percent membership growth during the years following a capital campaign. There is nothing mystical about this growth. When growth occurs, it is often because of a clear, specific membership growth plan and an intentional, direct, stewardship conversation approach to the annual budget drive. Annual financial commitments often remain stagnant during a capital campaign, but sometimes increase by 10 to 30 percent during the year after capital campaign commitments have been fully paid.

Banks also want to know about the versatility of the building design. Can the building be used for rental purposes? Is it adaptable to an alternative use? For obvious reasons, a lender does not want to foreclose on a church building. The bank will, however, need assurance that the building has resale value if foreclosure is necessary.

To summarize: The bank considers cash flow, growth potential, and versatility to determine the risk it is taking. If all are reasonable, a loan should be easy to obtain without a loan guarantee.

The Initial Presentation

When the building project information has been gathered and organized into an attractive packet, arrange a meeting with a decision-maker from a local bank or a local branch of a larger bank. Find a member of the congregation to make the initial contact, preferably a congregant who owns a business and is already in relationship with a senior bank employee. Many banks include community support in their mission, and they might be interested in talking about the proposed project. Speak with a bank employee who has the authority to make a decision about a building loan. A decision-maker is likely to view the loan as an opportunity to expand the bank's business or personal banking relationships, earn a profit, and get credit for being a good citizen. Of course, this process does not guarantee getting a loan, but it provides a receptive audience for an initial presentation.

The Final Presentation

After the total capital campaign financial commitments are determined, it's time to return to the bank for a final presentation. The final presentation emphasizes a proven ability to raise both capital and operating funds. The presentation also demonstrates that many congregants are sharing the financial burden. The bank needs to be assured that there is enough collateral to secure the loan. That is, if the congregation defaults on the loan, the bank can recover the debt by selling the congregation's assets. However, most sophisticated lenders understand the negative public relations impact of a foreclosure and prefer, if possible, to renegotiate the loan on mutually agreeable terms.

The lender also looks for a viable project that has been carefully planned. It wants to see a project that has utilized all of the appropriate, credentialed professionals. Depending upon the specifics of a particular project, these professionals could include an architect, a structural engineer, an environmental engineer, the faith community's legal counsel, and the fundraising consultant. It is helpful if these professionals have already developed credibility in the local area and even more helpful if they have previously developed a relationship with the bank.

Include the following exhibits in your final presentation:

Exhibit 1: The Congregation

- Description of the faith community, including its history and significant achievements

- Current membership total and the total number of donors

- Average annual financial commitment and median annual financial commitment

- Percentage of annual operating income from financial commitments, building rentals, and fundraising events (excluding money committed to the annual operating budget)

- Description of current meeting space

- Summary of recent financial history, including income and expenses for the previous two years

- Cash-flow projection spreadsheet estimating income and expenses for the next five years

- Current amount of debt, including annual debt service as a percentage of operating income

- Estimated property and land value, including a formal appraised value if available

- Amount of property and liability insurance

- Membership Growth Plan

Exhibit 2: The Denomination

- Description of the Unitarian Universalist Association or appropriate denomination, including the history, philosophy, number of members, and number of congregations

- Names of historically noteworthy members

- Audited financial report (Unitarian Universalist congregations can obtain a financial report from the Office of the Vice President for Finance)

- Description of the loan guarantee plan, if any, that the denomination offers

Exhibit 3: The Proposed Project

- Requested loan amount

- Explanation of whether the loan will be used to purchase land for new construction, to purchase an existing building, or to expand or renovate the current facility

- Description of the proposed new space, including the location, total square footage, number and types of rooms, and any available sketches or renderings

- Preliminary construction schedule

- List of all the paid professionals associated with the project (fundraising consultant, architect, engineer, contractor)

- Project finances, including the total cost (land, building, design, construction, contingency, landscaping, furnishings, and capital campaign expenses)

- Copies of any construction bids that have been received

- Anticipated sources of funding (building fund or reserve, sale of current building, and capital campaign financial commitment)

Exhibit 4: The Project's Benefit to the Congregation

- Explanation of how the project will help the congregation fulfill its vision

- Amount of money that the project is likely to add to the congregation's assets

- Indication that the project is the right size to meet the membership growth plan

Annual Review

Once the loan is secured, establish an annual routine of reviewing the loan rates. Compare them to the current interest rates being offered by other local banks to see if refinancing might save some money. Generally speaking, if the new rate is lower by 1 percent or more and at least five years remain on the loan, it makes sense to consider refinancing. To allow refinancing if rates decline, try to obtain a loan that has no prepayment penalties.

Unitarian Universalist Association Financing

Although local financing is usually advisable, there are other options to consider if the congregation is part of the Unitarian Universalist Association. The UUA offers qualified congregations a building loan program, a loan guarantee program, and a grant program, all of which are designed to facilitate the continued growth of the association. The programs acknowledge that beyond personal contributions and other available funds, financing is often necessary to completely fund a building project. In order to qualify for these programs, congregations need to have completed a capital campaign resulting in financial commitments totaling at least three times the amount of the most recent annual financial commitment. Information about all three programs can be found on the UUA website, and applications can be completed online.

Building Loan Program

Congregations seeking to purchase a building, to expand or renovate their current building, or to make their facility universally accessible can request affordable financing through the UUA Building Loan Program. The program is not designed to support deferred maintenance and repair efforts, nor does it provide short-term financing (construction/bridge loans) during the construction period.

The Congregational Properties and Loan Commission (CPLC) manages the assets of the building loan pool. The CPLC is a commission of congregational lay leaders appointed by the UUA Board of Trustees. The CPLC recommends and administers policy for loans, loan guarantees, and grants, including fees, terms, and interest rates.

Congregational applications are received and reviewed by the Director of Congregational Fundraising Services. Most often, more information is needed, and the director has questions to ask of the congregation. When all questions have been answered and all criteria have been met, the director recommends approval of the application to the vice president for finance, who approves the application.

Loan Guarantee Program

The UUA Loan Guarantee Program is designed to encourage local lenders to make larger mortgages available when the congregation's application is accompanied by a UUA loan guarantee. The standard guarantee liability is 50 percent of the original amount of the loan. The guarantee is available for loans between $50,000 and $750,000, so the minimum guarantee is $25,000 and the maximum is $375,000. (These dollar amounts, like others in this section, are correct as of late 2006. Check the website for the most up-to-date information.)

First Home Grant Program

While not considered a financing tool, the UUA First Home Grant Program is helpful for small congregations that want to own their first spiritual home. If all criteria are met, a congregation qualifies for a grant equal to 10 percent of the financial commitments made in its capital campaign, up to $25,000. The grant is paid in its entirety upon approval of the application and may be used at the discretion of the congregation. Often it is used to help with the closing costs of a land or building purchase.

It is possible to qualify for two grants under this program. For example, congregants might qualify for a grant after completing a successful capital campaign to purchase a piece of land. A few years later, if they conduct another successful capital campaign, they might qualify for a second grant and use it to help defray the cost of buying a building to serve as their first spiritual home.

Although some congregations are uncomfortable with any debt, most others are willing to incur a level of debt that can be reasonably managed. For those congregations willing to support their programs and ministries to fully implement their mission, it can be comforting to know that there are solid financing options available.

CHAPTER TWELVE

The Capital Campaign Team

People rarely give according to their blessings. They usually give according to the motivational and inspirational level of their faith and lives, regardless of income or assets.

—Anonymous

When the congregation has approved a project, the financial feasibility study has been completed with satisfactory results, and the congregation has agreed to a financial goal, it is time to launch the capital campaign. This chapter begins with an overview of the campaign's executive team, including its members, how they are recruited, and their first meeting. From there, the specific responsibilities of each member of the executive team are described. Many of the responsibilities in a capital campaign are similar to those in an annual budget drive, so cross-references to earlier chapters are given where appropriate. Adapt the information in earlier chapters as needed to fit the situation of a capital campaign.

It is hard to overemphasize the importance of recruiting the right people for capital campaign leadership positions. Matching a leader's strengths and interests with a specific capital campaign task will be an important factor in the success of the campaign.

Like other stewardship activities, capital campaigns benefit when information and resources are shared within the denomination. If your congregation is part of the Unitarian Universalist Association, contact your district executive to report capital campaign plans and activities and to seek support. Arrange to include campaign news in the district newsletter.

The capital campaign executive team is made up of the campaign chair (or co-chairs), responsible for directing all aspects of the campaign, plus seven to eighteen chairs responsible for specific aspects of the campaign. Regardless of the size of the project, the same campaign tasks need to be completed. Smaller projects can rely on a smaller executive team, but each chair will be responsible for a wider scope of tasks. A suggested roster for different-sized capital campaigns is on the following page. The dollar amounts are somewhat arbitrary, and the chart should be used only as a guide.

Recruiting Members

A capital campaign executive team is often recruited before the completion of the financial feasibility study (see page 94). Early recruitment allows the executive team to get started as soon as the financial feasibility study has been completed, assuming the results indicate that the congregation is ready to proceed.

Sometimes, however, the executive team is recruited after the financial feasibility study has been completed. The advantage is that the fundraising consultant might discover new, qualified leaders from among the feasibility study participants. Each capital campaign is different, and the

Small Campaign Raise up to $300,000	Midsize Campaign Raise up to $600,000	Large Campaign Raise more than $600,000
Campaign chair	Campaign co-chairs	Campaign co-chairs
Leadership gifts chair	Leadership gifts co-chairs	Leadership gifts co-chairs*
Fellowship event chair	Fellowship event co-chairs	Fellowship event co-chairs
General gifts chair	General gifts co-chairs	General gifts co-chairs**
Publicity/Publications chair	Publications chair	Publications co-chairs
	Group communications chair	Group communications co-chairs
	Publicity chair	Publicity co-chairs
Campaign treasurer	Campaign treasurer	Campaign treasurer
Follow-up chair	Follow-up chair	Follow-up co-chairs
Financial monitoring chair	Financial monitoring chair	Financial monitoring co-chairs
	Administrative support chair	Administrative support chair

*In a large capital campaign, the leadership gifts co-chairs should be supported by a few group leaders and several team leaders. None of these people are part of the executive team, but they are a vital part of a successful campaign.

**The general gifts co-chairs must be supported by several group leaders and many team leaders. These leaders are important, but they are not members of the executive team.

fundraising consultant can be helpful in determining whether it is best to recruit the executive committee before or after the study.

The governing body is responsible for recruiting the campaign chair, and the campaign chair is responsible for recruiting the rest of the executive team. The characteristics listed for the annual budget drive co-chairs on page 33 are as applicable for a capital campaign chair as they are for a budget drive chair. Here are additional guidelines for putting together the executive team.

Define each role. Define the purpose, goals, and expectations of each executive team role (as described later in this chapter). Before recruiting anyone, identify the benefits of accepting an executive team position so that the benefits can be shared with the potential team members. Benefits might include the exhilaration of being part of a "winning" team, or the satisfaction of supporting a worthy cause, or delight in making new friends.

Get the right people to the table. Once each role has been defined, begin to identify potential exec-

utive team members. Remember these two questions: Whose voices need to be heard? How can we include people of varying backgrounds, cultures, races, ages, abilities, genders, and sexual orientations, including people from historically marginalized groups? Seek people who are highly committed to the project and have the capability and willingness to make a significant contribution of their time, their expertise, and their financial resources.

Make the "ask" personal. Talk to each potential executive team member in person, making sure that the written role definitions are available to review. Tell the recruit exactly why he or she is the best person for the role, and anticipate with confidence a positive response.

Clarify support. Assure the recruit that there will be lots of support, including that of the fundraising consultant. Share the names of people already committed to the project (governing body, building project steering committee, fundraising consultant, professional religious leaders), and mention the thorough orientation that will be provided by the fundraising consultant.

Recruiting is often viewed as difficult because of the concern that someone will turn down the invitation. In most cases, however, people are flattered to be asked, even if they are unable to accept the position. If the recruit accepts the invitation, summarize the decisions that have been made, clarify the next steps, and thank the recruit. If some recruits need time to consider the invitation, establish a time to get back together for a decision.

Campaign Chair

The campaign chair is the overall leader of a capital campaign, responsible for directing all of its aspects. Specific responsibilities of the campaign chair are to:

- Recruit the rest of the executive team.

- Lead the executive team meetings and serve as an ex-officio member of every other campaign team.

- Help develop a capital campaign budget (with guidance from the fundraising consultant).

- With guidance from the fundraising consultant, complete a full-list evaluation—a best-guess assessment of the amount of money each donor is able and willing to contribute to the campaign (see page 127).

- Create an essential gifts chart (see pages 51 and 128).

- Write a letter to the congregation; assign responsibility for the other letters that are sent out during the campaign (see page 38).

- Help the leadership gifts chairs and the general gifts chairs match visiting stewards with specific donors (see page 41).

- Recruit a small group of people to manage the logistics for the orientation workshops for visiting stewards (see page 41).

- Immediately after the leadership reception (see page 38), ask for financial commitments from the leadership gifts chair(s) and the general gifts chair(s). The fundraising consultant helps the campaign chair to frame these stewardship conversations.

- Serve as the official spokesperson for the campaign and represent the executive team at all campaign-related events.

- Monitor all aspects of the campaign.

- Write a brief final report.

Leadership Gifts Chair

The leadership gifts chair is responsible for securing financial commitments from the leadership donors. These commitments most likely will represent between 50 and 80 percent of the total campaign financial goal, so it's important to select the leadership gifts chair carefully. He or she must lead by example and make one of the largest campaign gifts, preferably at least 10 percent of the campaign goal.

The leadership gifts chair recruits team leaders, each of whom will recruit and supervise four visiting stewards. (In very large campaigns, group leaders can be recruited to supervise team leaders.) These team leaders, as well as the visiting stewards, must also make a significant financial commitment to the campaign. There should be enough visiting stewards so that each one has stewardship conversations with a maximum of four donors.

After recruiting team leaders, the leadership gifts chair schedules a reception for all of the potential leadership donors. Suggestions for planning the leadership reception are found on page 38.

During the few weeks after the reception, the leadership gifts chair has a stewardship conversation with each leadership gifts team leader to ask for a financial commitment. Once the team leaders have made their commitment, they are ready to ask for financial commitments from the visiting stewards they have recruited. The leadership gifts chair must closely monitor this effort to ensure that all conversations have been completed and that each visiting steward has been asked to make a significant financial commitment to the campaign. Guidelines for conducting stewardship conversations are found in Chapter 5.

Be sure that all leadership gifts have been committed during this early phase of the capital campaign so that the leadership gifts total can be announced at the fellowship event. Confidence will be instilled in the congregation when they learn that 50 to 80 percent of the total financial commitments have already been promised by a small percentage of the congregants.

Fellowship Event Chair

After the leadership gifts donors have made their financial commitments and before the rest of the congregation is asked, the fellowship event is held. The fellowship event chair is responsible for coordinating the event to meet the following goals:

- Gather as many congregants as possible.

- Celebrate the start of the capital campaign.

- Showcase the visual image of a healthy, vital faith community.

- Share the campaign brochure and present information about the proposed project.

- Announce the financial commitments already made by the leadership donors.

Guidelines for planning a fellowship event are found on page 44).

General Gifts Chair

The general gifts chair is responsible for securing all campaign financial commitments after the leadership gifts portion of the campaign. Refer to the summary of general gifts co-chair responsibilities on page 34).

Group Communications Chair

Keep the group communications tasks separate from the publicity tasks, except in small campaigns with a limited number of volunteers. The group communications chair is responsible for creating dialogue opportunities for the congregation. As the project evolves, the group communications team creates opportunities for the congregation to offer input, ask questions, and provide feedback. Good communication about the project is an ongoing process, not a one-shot occasion. The opportunities need to be provided frequently, they need to start early in the process, and they must always promote two-way dialogue. Here are a couple of examples:

Small-group meetings. As people's lives become more complex and their time more precious, it can be difficult to get a large group of people together. So instead of holding one congregational meeting to explain the project, the group communications team can schedule a series of small-group meetings. These meetings provide an intimate setting where people can ask questions, state concerns, and offer suggestions. They help create a feeling of inclusion and an increased level of trust and enthusiasm.

These meetings are a way of taking the pulse of the congregation. If concerns about the project are expressed, there will be time to adapt the project if needed. It is much better to know of concerns early on than to find out when visiting stewards are asking for financial commitments.

Illustrative materials help convey information at small-group meetings. In addition to materials developed by the publications and publicity teams, prepare scale models, charts, pictures, architectural drawings, and videos. Effective communication programs employ a wide variety of approaches.

The small-group meetings can include presentations at meetings of selected congregational organizations. Examples might include affinity groups (such as groups for women, men, young adults, seniors, or high school students) and committees (such as religious education, finance, or building and grounds). Ask each group for a half-hour at the beginning of one of their meetings. Present the project information during the first fifteen minutes, leaving the remaining time for questions.

Also hold small-group meetings in congregants' homes. Invite eight to twelve people to each gathering. Schedule each meeting for one and a half hours, with a half-hour presentation, a half-hour of questions and answers, and a half-hour of socializing. Provide light refreshments. Set a goal to invite every congregant to one of these home meetings.

At each small-group meeting, ask someone to take notes. If there are unanswered questions, find the answers and get back to the persons who asked the questions.

Personal testimonials. The group communications team can also select three congregants to share a personal story as part of a worship service. The most polished public speakers are not necessarily the most effective. People who are able and willing to share their stories with passion, enthusiasm, sincerity, and conviction provide the most effective testimonials.

Ask speakers to write their testimonial ahead of time. It should last no longer than five minutes and focus on a specific theme. A senior congregant might tell a story about the long-term importance of the church to him. A congregant who is currently active in the church might talk about the importance of the church in her life. A third congregant might focus on the importance of the building project to the future of the church.

After the worship service (and after people have had a chance to grab a cup of coffee), invite congregants to gather and share stories about their experiences as part of the faith community. Ask them to make a connection between their experiences and the ways in which the project will generate even more stories. Ask people to dream about the future and share their thoughts about how completion of the project will enable the congregation to fulfill its mission. Take note of any questions or concerns and be sure to share the information with the campaign chair.

Publicity Chair

The publicity chair is responsible for marketing the building project to the congregation and to the greater community. While the group communications team promotes two-way dialogue, the publicity team uses advertising and other publicity techniques to heighten awareness of the upcoming capital campaign and to generate and maintain excitement about the building project.

Here's a list of creative publicity options that are especially effective for capital campaigns. Have some fun and let your imagination run wild.

- Ask the high school youth group to videotape interviews with senior congregants, focusing on their history with the faith community and the reasons why they are supportive of the building project. Show the videos before the Sunday service, during the social time after the service, or at other events. Share the tapes with the group communications team for use at home meetings.

- Ask the young adult group to create a fifteen-minute video featuring a cross-section of congregants speaking enthusiastically about the project. Use the videos as described above.

- Post a series of written testimonials, with pictures of the authors, on a portable display board that can be moved around the building and brought to small-group meetings.

- Create campaign announcements using fictitious characters such as Tony Toolbox, Rhonda Renovation, or Steven Spireburg.

- Present a humorous skit in the "Top Ten Reasons" style of a late-night talk show host.

- Ask the choir to compose a song or jingle to be sung during the offertory. There are several examples on the UUA website

As the campaign approaches, let the publicity become increasingly amplified, building to a crescendo at the fellowship event launch.

Publications Chair

The publications team is responsible for creating seven pieces of capital campaign information:

- Case statement

- Brochure

- Summary of current programs and ministries

- Financial commitment form

- Leadership reception invitation

- Fellowship event invitation

- Fact sheet

Except for the fact sheet, these are the same campaign materials needed for an annual budget drive. The first four listed above are described in detail in Chapter 6; adapt that information to fit the capital campaign situation. Sample invitations are provided on page 124 (leadership reception invitation) and page 125 (fellowship event invitation).

Fact Sheet

A capital campaign fact sheet is a quick reference piece that provides answers to frequently asked questions about the project, the capital campaign, and the financial plans. It supplements the case statement and the brochure and answers commonly asked questions. Limit the information to both sides of one sheet of paper. (See page 126 for an example.)

Following are some examples of frequently asked questions related to capital campaigns. The fact sheet must provide answers to any of these questions that are relevant to your campaign:

Capital campaign for a building project:

- What are the major components of the building project?

- How will the project help to fulfill the church mission?

- What is the projected total cost of the project?

- When will construction begin? What is the estimated completion date?

- Are we going to carry a mortgage? If so, what will be the level of debt service?

- What is the fundraising goal?

- Over what period of time can financial commitments be paid?

- How many members do we currently have? What is the average Sunday attendance? What is the median attendance?

- What is the capacity of the current building? What will be the capacity of the new (or renovated) building?

- How many children and youth are enrolled in the religious education program? What is the average Sunday attendance? The median?

- What is the capacity of the current program spaces? What will be the capacity of the new (or renovated) program spaces? (Use the term "program spaces" instead of "classrooms" to emphasize their versatility.)

- Which church and community groups currently use the facility? What is the approximate weekly usage? How many additional groups can be accommodated in the new (or renovated) facility?

Capital campaign to fund additional staffing, programs, and ministries:

- What new or expanded staff positions will be added?

- What new or expanded programs and ministries will be added?

- What is the demonstrated need for the additional staffing, programs, and ministries?

- How will the new or expanded staffing, programs, and ministries help the congregation to fulfill its mission?

- Will the staffing, programs, and ministries be "ramped up" over a period of time? What is the time frame to reach the goal?

- How much capital campaign income will be

used for staffing, programs, and ministries? How much operating income will be needed? How will the proportion of funding from each source change over time?

- When will staffing, programs, and ministries be fully supported by the operating budget?

Capital campaign to create or increase the endowment fund (see Chapter 8):

- What is the current level of the endowment fund?

- How was the money accumulated?

- Who manages the fund? How are investment decisions made?

- Are any endowment funds currently used to balance the operating budget?

- Are there plans to use the endowment fund to balance the operating budget in the future?

- Is the principal of the fund ever used? Are there any plans to use it in the future?

- What are the long-term goals of the endowment fund? How are those goals determined?

- What are the current endowment guidelines? Will they change with additional money?

- What is the fundraising goal of the capital campaign? How much of that money is designated for the endowment fund?

Capital campaign to liquidate debt:

- What is the current indebtedness?

- To whom do we owe money and on what terms?

- What is the current schedule for principal and interest payments?

- What percentage of income is our annual debt service?

- What is the amortization period on current loans?

- What is the capital campaign goal? Will all of that money be used to liquidate debt?

- Why does the debt need to be liquidated?

- How much interest will be saved?

Follow-Up Chair

Even in the most successful capital campaigns, some financial commitment forms are not returned by the end of the general gifts phase. The follow-up chair is responsible for getting the rest of the forms returned. For a complete discussion of the follow-up procedure, see page 46.

Campaign Treasurer

The campaign treasurer is responsible for creating and maintaining the data input and retrieval systems needed to provide all the necessary campaign financial information. The role is similar to that of the budget drive treasurer in an annual budget drive (see page 35).

Administrative Support Chair

Many administrative tasks need to be completed to ensure that a capital campaign runs smoothly. In almost all cases, it is unrealistic to think that the church administrator can absorb these additional responsibilities. Keep the church administrator informed of all campaign administrative support activities, but do not expect the administrator to be involved in completing them.

The administrative support chair is responsible for three main tasks: creating campaign contact lists, preparing mailings to potential donors, and preparing information packets for visiting stewards.

Campaign contact lists. Using the congregational databank and information from the campaign chair, the administrative support team compiles two campaign contact lists. On the first list, include all congregants being contacted by visiting stewards, as well as those being invited to campaign-related meetings. Create a second list that includes congregational alumni (those congregants who have moved away but want to stay in contact).

Mailings. At least four letters are written and mailed during the capital campaign. The administrative team is responsible for reproducing and mailing the letters, not for writing them.

- *First letter:* written by capital campaign chair or co-chairs; sent to all congregants; makes the case for financial support to the building project, including the estimated cost of the project and the amount of the fundraising goal.

- *Second letter:* written by the minister; sent to congregational alumni along with a financial commitment form; requests a financial commitment to the building project.

- *Third letter:* written by the governing-body president and sent to all congregants (except alumni); summarizes the building project and the plan for stewardship conversations.

- *Fourth letter:* written by the leadership gifts co-chairs; sent to all congregants (except alumni); gives a personal testimony and asks congregants to be receptive to the visiting stewards.

Information packets. Prepare information packets for each of the visiting stewards. The packets need to be ready in time for the stewardship orientation workshops conducted by the fundraising consultant (see page 41). Include the following items in each packet:

- The names and contact information for the four donors to which each steward has been assigned.

- The suggested range of each request.

- Four copies of the case statement (using information from the full-list evaluation)

- The essential gifts chart (if not included in the brochure)

- Four copies of the campaign brochure (see page 53).

- Four copies of the project summary (front side, bulleted talking points; back side, finan-cial spreadsheet) as developed by the campaign co-chair.

- Four copies of the fact sheet (see page 109).

- Four copies of the summary of current church programs and ministries (see page 49).

- Four financial commitment forms (see page 54).

- Four envelopes (for the commitment forms).

- Four lined 5-inch by 8-inch cards (for donors' comments during the conversation with the visiting steward).

- Four thank-you cards with envelopes (to be sent to donors after the conversation).

Financial Monitoring Chair

When the solicitation phase of a capital campaign has ended and financial commitments have been totaled, there is a natural tendency to feel that the campaign has been completed. But in some respects, it has just begun. During the three years in which capital campaign commitments are being fulfilled, a number of tasks remain: helping donors fulfill their financial commitments, soliciting campaign contributions from new congregants, and ongoing publicity, recognition, and celebration.

The financial monitoring chair and his or her team are responsible for these tasks. Team members should include:

- A professional religious leader.

- The church treasurer.

- The campaign chair.

- The coordinator of new members or a representative from the membership committee.

- A representative from the campaign publicity team.

Helping donors fulfill their financial commitments. Approach this task as a ministry. It is about being sensitive and helpful, not about judging the donors. Maintain a positive attitude.

During the three years of the campaign, the financial monitoring team meets monthly. Depending upon the volume of work, some of these meetings may be fairly brief telephone conference calls. Closely monitor the income, watching for any donors who fall behind or never begin to fulfill their commitment. When problems are noticed, determine the best response in each situation. In many cases, a phone conversation with the donor is helpful. Ask an especially tactful, loving, and understanding financial monitoring team member to initiate the phone conversation. People who have fallen behind on their financial commitment are often experiencing personal problems (job loss, for example) that might require some pastoral attention.

An intentional, consistent financial monitoring program helps to turn campaign commitments into financial contributions. If done well, congregations can expect to collect 90 to 95 percent of all the financial commitments made to the capital campaign.

Asking new members to contribute. Create a specific plan to give new members an opportunity to contribute to the capital campaign. Experienced fundraising consultants have learned that healthy congregations are those that discuss financial giving as part of their new member orientation. Congregations that delay asking new members for a financial commitment discourage the healthy development of giving. New members who are not asked for a financial commitment to the annual budget drive and the capital campaign might conclude that the congregation has enough money and that their financial support is not needed. Or they might feel that, as new members, they are not important enough to be asked to make a financial commitment.

Continuing to publicize the campaign. Keep the congregation informed about the campaign progress. Ask a publicity team member to be responsible for this ongoing task. Creative publicity sustains the spirit of the campaign, reinforces the pattern of honoring financial commitments, and encourages new gifts. Create opportunities for recognition and celebration to keep the campaign process alive. Some congregations have used such opportunities as an annual Celebration Sunday Anniversary Party, a groundbreaking celebration, a facility dedication ceremony, and an open house celebration.

Dedication Service

Plan and conduct a dedication service for the campaign executive team and the members of the other campaign teams. The dedication service is the first visible sign to the congregation that the campaign period has begun. Ask the professional religious leader(s) and the governing body chair to help plan the event. Invite the district executive to the dedication service. The large number of campaign participants signifies the importance of the campaign.

First Meeting

At least six months before the fellowship event that launches the capital campaign, the campaign chair schedules a meeting of the executive team. Because this first meeting is so important, and because it is likely to be longer than any subsequent meetings, consider scheduling it on a Saturday. Invite the fundraising consultant to attend the meeting. Prior to the meeting, ask each executive team member to bring a list of people who would be successful on their particular team, such as the fellowship event team or the publicity team.

Begin with a continental breakfast. After introductions and a quick review of each role, create a covenant of spiritual relationship (see page 22). The executive team members will need to rely on each other throughout the campaign, and clarifying expectations is the first priority.

Next, share the lists of possible team members that each chair developed before the meeting. Match attributes and skills to the needs of each team. Avoid competition for that "special person" that everyone wants on his or her team.

Create an inspiring theme to use throughout the three years of the campaign. To stimulate the imagination, here are a few theme titles that other congregations have used:

- Growing Our Vision

- Here We Grow (Again)

- Investing in Our Future

- From the Old, Unfold the New

- Let Our Tradition Grow

- Heart to Heart, Stone upon Stone

- Building Today for Tomorrow

- Sharing Our Ministry: Building Our Church

- The Warmth of Community, the Fire of Commitment

- Opening Hearts, Opening Minds, Opening New Doors

- Building Together What None of Us Could Achieve Alone

- Light the Way

- An Ever-Brightening Beacon

- Set the World Aflame

- A House for All People

- Moving In, Reaching Out

- Keeping the Faith: Yesterday, Today, and Tomorrow

- The Future Is Now

- We'll Build a Land . . .

- Imagine . . .

Then select a slogan (if different from the campaign title), logo, and color scheme to use on all print materials. The theme, slogan, logo, and color scheme together create a cohesive and consistent message that is readily recognized as related to the project.

With the help of the fundraising consultant, create a campaign calendar that displays the connections among the various teams and clearly shows how each team is dependent on the others to keep the entire campaign on schedule.

Make snacks available and provide a light lunch. Treat yourselves well. Have some fun. The executive team will be working hard for the next six months, so this is a great opportunity to start taking care of yourselves.

Subsequent Meetings

Throughout the campaign, hold regular executive team meetings (in person or through telephone conference calls) to hear progress reports from the various teams and resolve any problems. Schedule a meeting once every two weeks during the three months prior to the campaign launch. It is best to get all the meetings onto everyone's calendar and cancel some if they are unnecessary.

Final Words

Beyond Fundraising has told a story about transforming congregations from cultures of scarcity to cultures that welcome, and even expect, a focus on abundance. Congregations will know that their culture has changed when members believe in the reality that there can always be enough, a belief that diligent stewardship will provide everything needed.

We need a new vocabulary, one that emphasizes what we have instead of what we don't, that promotes gracious receiving as well as joyful giving, and that broadens the concept of stewardship beyond fundraising. But without significant changes in our congregational culture, the new vocabulary will produce nothing more than a futile semantic exercise. It will not grow our congregations, and without growth, our ability to make a difference in the world is greatly diminished.

I hope this book has been helpful. I encourage you to share your stewardship experiences with others so that we can build a set of best stewardship practices that can be shared with all of our congregations.

I leave you with my warm best wishes and my fervent hope for healthy, vibrant religious faith communities.

Glossary

alternate A specific part of a construction process that might be eliminated at the discretion of the building project steering committee.

Appreciative Inquiry An approach to strategic planning that focuses on identifying what already works well and building on those strengths rather than identifying problems.

assessment visit A weekend visit to a congregation by a UUA fundraising consultant, designed to assess a congregation's current situation and its desired future in order to provide recommendations about how to get "from here to there."

call Willingness to proclaim the good works of the faith community, such as by talking about one's passion for one of the congregation's internal programs or global ministries.

capital campaign An organized effort to raise money for a faith community for reasons other than to support the annual operating budget. Capital campaigns are often held to fund a building project, liquidate debt, enhance (or begin) an endowment fund, or increase programs and staffing.

case statement Information that justifies asking for money in support of a fundraising program.

community ministry Initiatives focused beyond the walls of the faith community, such as Habitat for Humanity, The International Heifer Project, and Guest at Your Table.

culture of abundance Belief in the reality that there can always be enough because diligent stewardship provides everything needed. The glass is at least half full; sometimes it even overflows.

culture of scarcity Belief in the myth that a congregation has never had, does not now have, and never will have enough of whatever it desires. At best, the glass is always half empty.

dedication service The formal installation of all annual budget drive or capital campaign leaders, or an official ceremony to bless a new building, renovation, or addition.

district executives Unitarian Universalist staff persons who offer guidance to congregations in each of twenty continental districts.

endowment fund The part of a faith community's income derived from donations.

equal sacrifice/proportional giving An acknowledgment that giving a percentage of net worth or salary is more equitable than asking all congregants to increase their annual giving by the same percentage. Replaces the term *equal giving*.

essential gifts chart A chart that lists the number of financial gifts needed in each range to meet a fundraising goal. Replaces the term *gift table* or *table of gifts*.

fair-share giving Financial commitment based on a percentage of a donor's income.

fellowship event The formal, public launching of an annual budget drive or capital campaign, usually at a special event to which all potential donors have been invited and at which leadership financial commitments are announced. Replaces the term *kick-off event*.

financial commitment A monetary obligation made by a congregant to an annual budget drive or a capital campaign. Replaces the term *pledge*.

financial commitment form The written record of a financial commitment. Replaces the term *pledge card*.

financial feasibility study An objective survey conducted by a fundraising consultant to determine a congregation's fundraising potential in support of a specific project. Includes a series of confidential interviews (often representing 20 percent of the donors) and a final written report that provides a summary of the findings, specific recommendations, and (when the goal is feasible) a campaign plan, timetable, and budget.

Forward Through the Ages (FORTH) A five-phase stewardship development program. The five phases are receiving and accepting, growing and investing, giving back, giving generously, and applying recent learnings. Each phase includes five components: stewardship education, joyful giving, ministry and good works, annual budget drive, and planned giving.

full-list evaluation A best-guess assessment of the amount of money that each congregant is able and willing to contribute to a capital campaign.

gifts What people can contribute to a faith community, including aptitude, ability, and money.

leadership donors Those who are expected or asked to make a significant financial contribution to an annual budget drive or capital campaign.

leadership gifts Financial commitments made at the start of an annual budget drive or capital campaign, which set the pace for the rest of the fundraising program. Leadership gifts often represent 50 to 80 percent of a total goal and are made by about 20 percent of the donors.

leadership reception A celebratory event for all donors being asked for a significant financial commitment to an annual budget drive or a capital campaign.

orientation workshops Sessions held to prepare visiting stewards to ask potential donors for contributions to an annual budget drive or capital campaign. Replaces the term *canvasser training*.

programs and ministries Programs are the internal activities of the congregation, while ministries are those activities focused on the external global community.

Searching for the Future A stewardship education workshop offered by Unitarian Universalist fundraising consultants to help congregations develop a strategic plan.

slippage rate The variance between the number of financial commitments made in an annual budget drive or a capital campaign and the amount of money actually received. Healthy congregations have a maximum of 5-percent slippage in an annual budget drive and a 5- to 10-percent slippage in a three-year capital campaign.

spiritual vocation Willingness to take up volunteer efforts to support the faith community.

stewardship The growing, nurturing, promoting, and building of congregants' gifts, call, and spiritual vocation. Stewardship is the spirit that influences the things that people do for their faith community. Replaces the terms *fundraising* and *canvass*.

stewardship committee A standing committee responsible for managing the five phases of the Forward Through the Ages program. An annual budget drive team could be a subset of the stewardship committee.

strategic planning Taking a clean-slate approach to the future—perhaps resulting in a new direction—after clarifying congregational vision and mission. Strategic planning differs from long-range planning, which is the process of simply adding incremental steps to the current direction without considering any significant changes in vision or mission.

vision A congregation's mental picture of the future, representing what the community is striving to become.

visiting stewards Lay leaders who have stewardship conversations with donors to talk about the faith community and to ask for a financial commitment. Replaces the term *canvassers*.

Mission Statement and Code of Ethics for Unitarian Universalist Fundraising Consultants

Mission Statement

We partner with congregations to help each community transform its unique vision into bold action.

Code of Ethics

We believe that it is in the best interest of our congregations that:

- We will at all times maintain the highest standards of professional conduct in working with the congregations we serve.

- No professional services will be provided until a contract specifying the services has been signed by a representative of the congregation and a representative of the Unitarian Universalist Association.

- A fixed per diem fee will be charged for the professional consulting services provided. Contracts based upon a percentage of funds committed are strictly prohibited.

- Initial telephone conversations, including conference calls with prospective congregations, should not be construed as services for which payment is expected. Payment is expected for subsequent and substantive consulting conversations.

- No congregational staff person or lay leader will be given money or provided with anything of value for influencing the selection of our consulting services.

- Fees will be mutually agreed upon in advance of consulting services.

- Fundraising expenditures are within the authority and control of the congregation. All consultant expenses, including airfare, ground transportation, lodging, and meals, will be paid by the Office of Congregational Fundraising Services.

- Carefully trained visiting stewards will be responsible for the solicitation of gifts.

- We will not use methods that are misleading to the public or harmful to our congregations, will not make exaggerated claims of past achievement, and will not guarantee the financial results of any fundraising effort.

- We will not acquire or maintain custody of funds and/or gifts directed to the church.

Sample Contract for Consulting Services

1. **Introduction.** Agreement dated [*date*], by and between [*name of consultant*], with offices at [*address of consultant*], and [*name of faith community*] in [*city and state of faith community*], with a principal office at [*mailing address of congregation*] (hereafter known as the Congregation).

2. **Retention and Description of Services.** During the term of this Agreement, [*name of consultant*] will furnish consulting services and advice as specifically requested by a designated representative of the Congregation. The services and advice will relate to work being done or planned by the Congregation in the area of [*area of consulting*], will be within the area of the consultant's technical competence, and will specifically include the following items [*select all that apply*]:

   Assessment Visit

   – Gather extensive information about the congregation.

   – Meet with relevant constituents (such as the minister, professional religious educator, other professional staff members, finance committee chair, annual budget drive chair, strategic planning team chair, building and grounds committee chair, and governing body).

   – Make specific recommendations to allow the congregation to reach its long-term goals.

   – Present verbal recommendations at the end of the assessment visit.

   – Provide a written summary of recommendations within two weeks after the assessment visit.

   Searching for the Future

   – Conduct a workshop for congregational facilitators.

   – Facilitate small-group workshops with congregational participants and provide counsel to facilitators.

   – Guide facilitators in assimilating all workshop information.

   – Assist facilitators in creating one representative mission statement.

   – Help facilitators develop a beginning list of goals and activities.

   – Meet with the governing body to review the weekend and discuss recommendations for next steps.

   Strategic Planning

   – Provide guidelines for creating a strategic planning team.

- Guide and coach the strategic planning team to develop a comprehensive five-year plan.

- Oversee the presentation of the plan to the congregation.

Annual Budget Drive

- Assist in developing an annual budget drive strategy.

- Assist in planning the drive, including developing a calendar of activities and events.

- Assist in the evaluation of giving potential.

- Guide development of a case statement.

- Guide recruitment of the leadership team.

- Guide preparation of various materials.

- Conduct visiting steward orientation workshops.

- Provide additional guidance and coaching as necessary.

Financial Feasibility Study

- Plan the study, including selection of congregants to be interviewed.

- Prepare questions.

- Conduct interviews.

- Analyze data and prepare a final report for the congregation.

- Present the financial feasibility study results to the congregation.

- Begin planning for a capital campaign.

Capital Campaign

- Help develop a capital campaign strategy.

- Help create campaign plans, including a calendar for operations and an organizational chart.

- Evaluate giving potential and assess specific suggested gift levels for prospects.

- Assist in recruiting the campaign leadership team.

- Guide preparation of educational, training, and campaign materials.

- Provide orientation for campaign volunteers.

- Assist in planning and coordinating the fellowship event.

- Guide development of a follow-up plan, and conduct a review of the final campaign results.

3. **Term of Agreement.** These services shall be available to the Congregation from [*beginning date*] through [*ending date*].

4. **Location of Consulting Services.** These services will be rendered in the Congregation's immediate area and such other places that are appropriate and mutually agreed to by the consultant and the Congregation.

5. **Compensation.** The Congregation will pay a consulting fee of [*$ amount*] per day (in which a day is eight hours and will be prorated for partial days under or over eight hours) for service rendered by the consultant under this agreement. The consulting fee will also apply toward the time in transit to the consulting site from the consultant's previous working day assignment, as verified by airplane tickets or mileage logs. The consulting fee will be payable at the end of each month in which the consultant furnishes services pursuant to this agreement.

6. **Reimbursement of Travel Expenses.** The consulting fee includes travel and lodging expenses for normal travel to and from the Congregation's area. Only in the event that the consultant is required to travel outside the Congregation's area will the Congregation be expected to reimburse the consultant for these extraordinary expenses. In addition, for such travel outside the Congregation's area, the consultant's time in transit both ways shall be considered working time. Reimbursement of travel expenses shall be made on the basis of itemized statements submitted by the consultant and including, wherever possible, actual bills, receipts, or other evidence of expenditure.

7. **Minimum and Maximum Consulting Time.** The consultant will furnish the Congregation with a maximum of [*number*] days during the term of the contract. Additional time may be mutually agreed upon. The Congregation pays for only those services actually provided by the consultant.

8. **Independent Contractor Status.** The consultant and any and all agents and employees of the consultant shall perform this agreement in their independent capacity and not as officers, employees, or agents of the Congregation. Both parties acknowledge that the consultant is not an employee for state or federal tax or any other purposes. The consultant shall retain the right to perform services for others during the term of this agreement. The consultant agrees to provide all necessary workers' compensation insurance for the consultant's employees, if any, at consultant's own cost and expense.

9. **Taxes.** The consultant agrees that he/she has no entitlement to employment or fringe benefits from the Congregation. Payments to the consultant pursuant to this agreement will be reported to federal and state taxing authorities as required. The Congregation will not withhold any money from compensation payable to the consultant. In particular, the Congregation will not withhold FICA (Social Security), state, or federal unemployment insurance contributions, or state or federal income tax or disability insurance. The consultant is independently responsible for the payment of all applicable taxes and shall indemnify and hold harmless the Congregation from liability for same.

10. Termination of Agreement by Notice. Either party may terminate this Agreement upon 30 days' notice by registered or certified mail, return receipt requested, addressed to the other party. If either party terminates the agreement, the Congregation shall be liable only for payment of consulting fees earned by the consultant as a result of work actually performed prior to the effective date of the termination. The 30 days' notice shall be measured from the day the notice is mailed.

_____

(consultant)   (date)

_____

(official congregational representative)   (date)

A Covenant Between the Congregation and Visiting Stewards

Stewards: We stand before you committed to doing our best to make our congregational dreams come true by asking each of you for your help in supporting the mission of our congregation.

Congregation: Committed to the dreams and hopes of this congregation and understanding that nothing buys nothing, we accept the responsibility for turning those hopes and dreams into reality.

Stewards: We commit ourselves to preparing for each stewardship conversation by having already made our own financial commitment and becoming knowledgeable about the goals of our annual budget drive or capital campaign. We further commit ourselves to contacting each of you to set up a convenient time for our stewardship conversation, and we commit to arriving on time.

Congregation: We commit ourselves to make time in our busy lives to have a stewardship conversation. We commit to prepare for the conversation by reflecting upon our relationship with the church and to engage the visiting steward in honest and direct conversation.

Stewards: We commit ourselves to listen respectfully to your dreams and concerns. We promise to keep private what should be private and pass along only that information that you have asked us to share.

Congregation: We commit ourselves to generosity of spirit and promise to make a financial commitment to the best of our ability.

Everyone: And together, we commit ourselves to enjoy each other's company, to respect each other's ideas, perceptions, and beliefs, and to have a good time while raising money to ensure the future health of our church.

Sample Leadership Reception Invitation

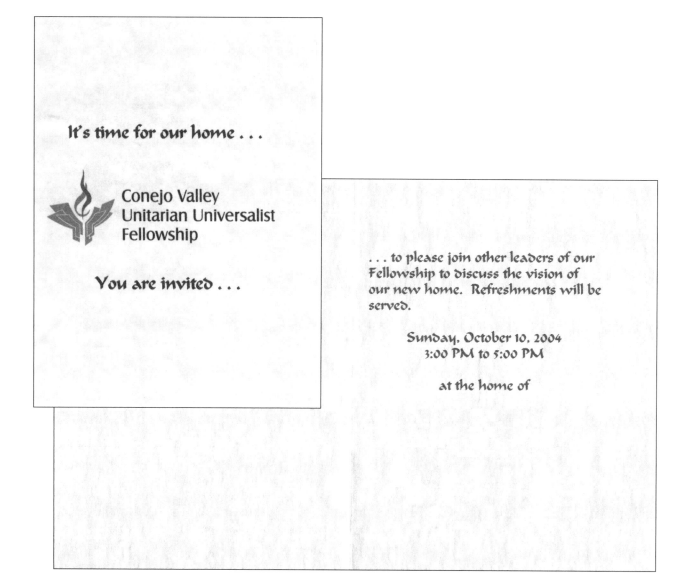

It's time for our home . . .

Conejo Valley
Unitarian Universalist
Fellowship

You are invited . . .

. . . to please join other leaders of our Fellowship to discuss the vision of our new home. Refreshments will be served.

Sunday, October 10, 2004
3:00 PM to 5:00 PM

at the home of

Sample Fellowship Event Invitation

On Sunday, October 24, 2004, our community will begin to change.

This change will bring us to the realization of our dreams.

Every person who loves and cares about our Fellowship

will want to join us in a grand celebration of

a quest for our very own home.

We will gather at the Los Robles Greens Golf Course Ballroom

at 5:00 p.m. for a dinner and entertainment

to celebrate the beginning of our Capital Campaign

and the birth of our new home.

Sample Capital Campaign Fact Sheet

The Capital Campaign
The First Church in Belmont
Unitarian Universalist
404 Concord Avenue, P.O. Box 113
Belmont, Massachusetts 02478
617-484-1054

A Church with a Proud Past
A Church with a Bright Future

View from the Town Common

Building Project Goals

To be good stewards of the existing structure, site, and environment

To provide the sizes and types of spaces that meet present and anticipated program needs

To organize the site and its buildings for improved safety and efficiency

To provide universal access and compliance with current building codes and regulations

To seek cost-efficiency in construction and long-term operation and maintenance

Proposed Scope of Work

Exterior repairs to stucco, wood trim and masonry of the existing 1890's building, replacement of the slate roof

New religious education classrooms for children, youth, and adults-10 total, a 41 % increase

New, enlarged Parish Hall for fellowship and musical events. Additional gathering space for community events, coffee hours, and meetings

Renovated office and meeting space for church staff, a 54 % increase

Energy efficient and environmentally responsible site and facility with universal accessibility

Lower Level Plan   ## Upper Level Plan

Building Project Costs

Site Costs	$ 860,000
New addition	2,310,000
Existing building renovation, repair	1,230,000
Subtotal	$ 4,400,000
Additional project-related costs *(survey, design, furnishings, etc)*	1,200,000
Total $ 5,600,000	

Building Project Financing Plan

The Capital Campaign	$ 4,250,000
Interest from gifts and surplus from operating budget	350,000
Endowment grant	250,000
Endowment loan	250,000
External loan	500,000
Total $ 5,600,000	

Building Project Schedule

The Capital Campaign	September through December, 2002
Construction Bidding	Spring, 2003
Construction Begins	June, 2003
Completion of Construction	September, 2004

Throughout the construction period we will remain together, on site, with use of the Sanctuary for our Sunday services; the Johnson House for church offices; and modular classrooms for Sunday School.

Gift Table for The Capital Campaign

GIFT LEVEL	# REQ'D
$ 1,000,000 +	1
$ 250,000 - $ 999,999	2
$ 100,000 - $ 249,999	6
$ 50,000 - $ 99,000	10
$ 25,000 - $ 49,999	15
$ 15,000 - $ 24,999	29
$ 10,000 - $ 14,999	11
$ 5,000 - $ 9,999	33
$ 3,000 - $ 4,999	58
Up to $3000	many

As of September, 2002 we have received $2.2 million in gifts and pledges for The Capital Campaign

Our Expectations

100% participation from our members and friends
Although we cannot all give equally, we can all make an equal commitment.

Pledge payments and gifts made over a period of 3 calendar years, 2002, 2003, 2004
Pledges for The Capital Campaign are in addition to those made to our annual operating fund

Pledges and gifts for an amount several times greater than your annual pledge
The last major addition to the church was in 1924. Now, it is our turn to step forward to make the necessary changes as previous generations have provided for us.

We Wish To Thank

those who have given or pledged to date,

those who have donated time, expertise, and faith to the building project to bring us to this point, and

all of us who together make The First Church a vital community of faith.

Please give generously to The Capital Campaign so we can continue to be . . .

A Church with a Proud Past
A Church with a Bright Future

Capital Campaign Full-List Evaluation

1. Begin this process by conferring with the capital campaign fundraising consultant. With the consultant's guidance, the capital campaign co-chairs appoint an evaluation task force. Often, one of the capital campaign co-chairs, one of the leadership gifts co-chairs, the minister, the governing body president, and the congregational treasurer are selected for this task force.

2. Using the current directory, review the names of all the congregants. Based on the task force members' *best guesses,* make an estimate of each donor's *ability* to make a financial commitment. This estimate is clearly subjective, as opposed to factual. Place each donor's name within one of the following categories. Spend no more than thirty seconds deciding upon the placement of each donor. List as many household names as appropriate in each category. Create an "unknown" category for any unfamiliar donors, but keep this category as short as possible.

A $1M+	B $501,000-$1M	C $251,000-$500,000	D $111,000-$250,000	E $51,000-$100,000	F $26,000-$50,000

G $16,000-$25,000	H $11,000-$15,000	I $7,600-$10,000	J $5,100-$7,500	K $3,100-5,000	L Up to $3,000

3. When all donors have been assigned to specific categories, review the list once more. This time, evaluate each donor by using a best guess as to their *willingness* to contribute. A donor's willingness to make a financial contribution is often related to his or her commitment to the congregation. In some cases, names will be moved from one category to another when a best guess is that a donor's willingness to contribute is lower than the donor's ability to contribute. As in the first round, this process is an art rather than a science.

4. Next, ask the fundraising consultant to help construct an essential gifts chart (See page 128). Use the "one-half rule" to create this chart. The one-half rule assumes that one half of the households in each category will actually contribute at the next lowest category. This final step creates a more realistic expectation of the congregation's level of financial commitment to the capital campaign.

Sample Essential Gifts Chart

Example 1: Annual budget drive, 200 donors, $300,000 goal

Fourth Parish Church Annual Budget Drive Essential Gifts Chart

Gifts Needed to Reach Goal of $300,000

To reach our financial goal, we need the following distribution of gifts. Ask yourself: How do I feel about my previous giving in relation to the gifts that I have been given? Have I been giving until it feels good? Can I increase my commitment to the next giving level?

1 gift of more than $15,000

2 gifts of $10,001 to $15,000

1 gift of $8,001 to $10,000

3 gifts of $5,001 to $8,000

7 gifts of $2,001 to $5,000

20 gifts of $1,501 to $2,000

32 gifts of $1,201 to $1,500

25 gifts of $901 to $1,200

27 gifts of $701 to $900

45 gifts of $501 to $700

Several gifts of up to $500

Example 2: Capital campaign, 200 donors, $1.2-million goal

Fourth Parish Church Capital Campaign
Essential Gifts Chart

Gifts Needed to Reach Goal of $1,200,000

To reach our capital campaign goal, the following distribution of gifts is needed. Ask yourself: How can I assure that this faith community will best serve the next generation? How much money can I commit to fulfill our ministry?

1 gift of more than $120,000

1 gift of $80,001 to $120,000

1 gift of $50,001 to $80,000

3 gifts of $20,001 to $50,000

7 gifts of $10,001 to $20,000

20 gifts of $6,001 to $10,000

32 gifts of $4,801 to $6,000

25 gifts of $3,601 to $4,800

27 gifts of $2,801 to $3,600

45 gifts of $2,001 to $2,800

Several gifts of up to $2,000

Suggested Fair-Share Giving Guide

Adjusted Annual Income	Supporter			Sustainer			Visionary			Full Tithe		
	Suggested % of Income	Monthly Payment	Annual Payment	Suggested % of Income	Monthly Payment	Annual Payment	Suggested % of Income	Monthly Payment	Annual Payment	Suggested % of Income	Monthly Payment	Annual Payment
$10,000	2%	$17	$200	3%	$25	$300	5%	$42	$500	10%	$83	$1,000
$25,000	2%	$42	$500	3%	$63	$750	5%	$104	$1,250	10%	$208	$2,500
$50,000	3%	$125	$1,500	4%	$167	$2,000	5%	$208	$2,500	10%	$417	$5,000
$75,000	3%	$188	$2,250	4.5%	$281	$3,375	6%	$375	$4,500	10%	$625	$7,500
$100,000	3.5%	$292	$3,500	5%	$417	$5,000	6.5%	$542	$6,500	10%	$833	$10,000
$150,000	3.5%	$438	$5,250	5%	$625	$7,500	6.5%	$813	$9,750	10%	$1,250	$15,000
$200,000	4%	$667	$8,000	5.5%	$917	$11,000	7%	$1,167	$14,000	10%	$1,667	$20,000
$300,000	5%	$1,250	$15,000	6%	$1,500	$18,000	8%	$2,000	$24,000	10%	$2,500	$30,000
$400,000	6%	$2,000	$24,000	7%	$2,333	$28,000	8.5%	$2,833	$34,000	10%	$3,333	$40,000
$500,000	7%	$2,917	$35,000	8%	$3,333	$40,000	9%	$3,750	$45,000	10%	$4,167	$50,000

(This guide was developed in 2006.)

Determining Your Income

Adjusted Gross Income

(Line 31 of IRS form 1040) _____

Add: Money set aside for future use

- Tax-exempt pensions and annuities _____

- Tax-free income _____

- Depreciation on rental property _____

- Other _____

  Total Income _____

Deduct:

- Nonreimbursed major medical expenses _____

- Care of parent(s) _____

- Costs of higher education _____

- Costs of child care _____

  Total Deductions _____

**Income to use in determining
your fair-share giving levels** _____

(Adjusted Gross Income + Total Income – Total Deductions)

Sample Financial Commitment Forms

Example 1: Form to be used in an annual budget drive
(based on a form developed by David Rickard,
a Unitarian Universalist fundraising consultant)

Full name of church   **Code number**
Church street address
Church city/state/zip code
Church telephone/e-mail address
Church website
Fiscal year
Name of the annual budget drive

Donor name _____ Second donor name _____

Mailing address _____

City/state/zip code _____

Telephone/e-mail _____

I/we commit $_____ to support the operating budget for the _____ fiscal year.

My/our financial commitment will be fulfilled using the following schedule:

$_____ Weekly $_____ Monthly $_____ Quarterly $_____ Annually   by (what date) _____

I am interested in automatic deductions from my checking account. ❑ Please contact me.

The amount is a suggested fair-share financial commitment.   ❑ Yes   ❑ No

You may list me as a suggested fair-share donor.   ❑ Yes   ❑ No

_____
   signature (or 2 signatures for couple)   date

It is understood that financial situations sometimes change. If you need to revise your financial commitment, please contact [*name of contact person*].

Example 2: Form to be used in a capital campaign

Full name of church **Code number**
Church street address
Church city/state/zip code
Church telephone/e-mail address
Church website
Title of the capital campaign
Fiscal years _____ to _____

Donor name _____ Second donor name _____

Mailing address _____

City/state/zip code _____

Telephone/e-mail _____

I/we commit $_____ to support the capital campaign.

My/our financial commitment will be fulfilled using the following schedule:

$_____ Lump sum on (date) _____ $_____ Monthly $_____ Quarterly

$_____ Annually by (what date) _____

I am interested in automatic deductions from my checking account. ☐ Please contact me.

_____
    signature (or 2 signatures for couple) date

It is understood that financial situations sometimes change. If you need to revise your financial commitment, please contact [*name of contact person*].

Five Phases of Forward Through the Ages

Phase 1: Accepting				
Stewardship Education	Joyful Giving	Ministry and Good Works	Annual Budget Drive	Planned Giving
Help congregants learn ways to accept gifts graciously. Offer at least one money-management workshop. Conduct a worship service around the theme of gracious receiving.	Create a plan to increase the giving of gifts, call, and spiritual vocation.	Learn the Appreciative Inquiry approach to spreading the good news. Create a worship order of service insert series. Highlight programs and ministries. Update website. Include information about successful programs and ministries. Acknowledge all budget drive volunteers. Celebrate completion of the budget drive.	Conduct orientation workshops for visiting stewards. Schedule as many stewardship conversations as possible. Supplement with telephone calls and e-mail messages. Use telephone calls and e-mails for follow-up. Conduct a closeout meeting for budget drive volunteers.	Create a bequest recognition society. Publish a list of charter members. Ask charter members to share their passion. Develop a planned giving mission statement. Create a brochure and distribute it. Prepare a list of local planning services. Create activities to recognize charter members.

Phase 2: Growing and Investing				
Stewardship Education	Joyful Giving	Ministry and Good Works	Annual Budget Drive	Planned Giving
Help congregants learn ways to increase and invest gifts, call, and spiritual vocation. Conduct a stewardship education workshop specifically designed for new members. Offer a money-management skills workshop. Conduct a worship service around the theme of increasing and investing gifts, call, and spiritual vocation.	Identify specific talents. Create a part-time coordinator of volunteers position. Identify volunteer skills and interests.	Organize a mission fair to spread the good news. Recognize budget drive volunteers. Celebrate completion of the budget drive.	Conduct orientation workshops for all new visiting stewards. Schedule condensed workshops for all returning visiting stewards. Conduct as many stewardship conversations as possible. Refine the process by applying experiences from the first year. Use telephone calls and e-mail messages for donors not having a conversation with a visiting steward. Use telephone and e-mail for follow-up. Hold closeout meeting with budget drive leaders.	Form a planned giving committee. Form a separate endowment fund committee (large congregations only). Clarify responsibility and accountability. Define policies. Create enabling resolutions. Nurture existing donors. Identify potential donors.

Phase 3: Giving Back				
Stewardship Education	Joyful Giving	Ministry and Good Works	Annual Budget Drive	Planned Giving
Offer at least one more money management workshop. Help congregants learn ways to give back gifts, call, and spiritual vocation. Offer a stewardship education workshop for new members. Conduct a worship service around the theme of giving back gifts, call, and spiritual vocation.	Update the volunteer skills information. Identify skills of new members. Use the volunteers! Expand coordinator of volunteers position to include coordination of new members. Begin to create an expectation that everyone shares gifts.	Introduce program budgeting. Use *Budgets With a Mission* as a guide. Invite an expert to help. Honor budget drive workers. Celebrate completion of the budget drive.	Conduct orientation workshops for all new visiting stewards. Conduct shortened workshops for all returning visiting stewards. Further refine approach to stewardship conversations. Use telephone calls and e-mails for those not having a stewardship conversation. Use telephone calls and e-mail for follow-up. Clean up donor and alumni data-banks. Schedule a closeout meeting for budget drive leaders.	Gather information about charitable giving options and publicize them. Define the purpose of the endowment fund. Create an evaluation tool. Continue to nurture existing relationships. Identify new donors.

Phase 4: Giving Generously				
Stewardship Education	Joyful Giving	Ministry and Good Works	Annual Budget Drive	Planned Giving
Offer at least one more money-management workshop. Help congregants learn ways to give generously. Conduct a stewardship education workshop for new members. Conduct a lay-led worship service around the theme of generosity.	Update volunteer skills information. Identify skills of new members. Continue to use volunteers. Refine the coordination of volunteers and new members. Reinforce the expectation that everyone shares gifts, call, and spiritual vocation. Increase giving from specific donors.	Refine the program-budgeting process. When needed, use *Budgets With a Mission* as a guide. Hold neighborhood gatherings for information sharing. Collate and respond to feedback from neighborhood gatherings. Acknowledge budget drive and neighborhood gathering hosts. Celebrate completion of the budget drive.	Conduct Commitment Sunday. Have stewardship conversations with all leadership donors. Conduct an orientation workshop for new visiting stewards and a shortened workshop for returning visiting stewards. Use telephone calls and e-mail messages for all other donors. Use telephone and e-mail for follow-up. Clean up donor and alumni data-bank. Schedule a closeout meeting for budget drive leaders.	Refine the program. Create specific management guidelines. Clarify endowment distribution policy. Apply the Harvard Model. Refine the evaluation tool. Create marketing plan. Continue to nurture existing relationships. Identify new donors.

Phase 5: Applying Recent Learnings				
Stewardship Education	Joyful Giving	Ministry and Good Works	Annual Budget Drive	Planned Giving
Offer at least one more money management workshop. Conduct a stewardship education workshop (that summarizes the previous four phases) for new members. Plan a lay-led worship service that ties together the previous four phases.	Update the volunteer skills databank. Identify skills of new members. Continue to use volunteers. Increase the resources (personal + financial) devoted to volunteer and new member coordination. Expect significantly increased giving.	Institutionalize the program-budgeting process. Continue to use *Budgets With a Mission* if needed. Focus on improving the website. Acknowledge all budget drive leaders and cottage meeting hosts. Celebrate completion of the budget drive.	Conduct cottage meetings. Have stewardship conversations with all leadership donors. Conduct an orientation workshop for new visiting stewards and a shortened workshop for returning visiting stewards. Use telephone calls and e-mail messages for those not attending a cottage meeting. Use telephone and e-mail for follow-up. Clean up donor and alumni data-banks. Hold a closeout meeting for all budget drive leaders.	Refine the evaluation tool. Revise the program based on the evaluation. Review management guidelines and revise as needed. Create a three-year plan with measurable goals. Continue to expand upon the marketing plan. Continue to nurture existing relationships. Identify new donors.

138 *Beyond Fundraising*   Unitarian Universalist Association

Annual Progress Summary

Fiscal Year ____

Directions to the Stewardship Committee Chair: Please use the numbers in the left-hand column to write the goals for each component. Then distribute the form to each Stewardship Committee member.

Directions to Stewardship Committee members: For each goal, circle the number. Answer the question at the bottom of each component. Return the progress summary to the stewardship committee chair by [*date*].

Stewardship Education Goals	Not Begun			Completed	
•	1	2	3	4	5
•	1	2	3	4	5
•	1	2	3	4	5
•	1	2	3	4	5

What have I learned about stewardship education?

Joyful Giving Goals	Not Begun			Completed	
•	1	2	3	4	5
•	1	2	3	4	5
•	1	2	3	4	5
•	1	2	3	4	5

What have I learned about joyful giving?

Ministry and Good Works Goals	Not Begun			Completed	
•	1	2	3	4	5
•	1	2	3	4	5
•	1	2	3	4	5
•	1	2	3	4	5

What have I learned about ministry and good works?

Annual Budget Drive Goals	Not Begun			Completed	
•	1	2	3	4	5
•	1	2	3	4	5
•	1	2	3	4	5
•	1	2	3	4	5

What have I learned about the annual budget drive?

Planned Giving Goals	Not Begun			Completed	
•	1	2	3	4	5
•	1	2	3	4	5
•	1	2	3	4	5
•	1	2	3	4	5

What have I learned about planned giving?

Name	Role	Date

Sample Enabling Resolutions for an Endowment Fund

Amendment to Congregational Bylaws

An endowment fund, whose purpose, governance, and operational procedures shall be defined by special resolution adopted by the congregation, shall be established.

A. Resolution to Implement the Endowment Fund

WHEREAS, stewardship involves the faithful management of the gifts of time, talent, and money, including accumulated, inherited, and appreciated resources; and

WHEREAS, we can support the religious mission and work of this congregation through transfers of property (cash, stocks, bonds, real estate), charitable bequests in wills, charitable remainder and other trusts, pooled income funds, charitable gift annuities, and assignment of life insurance and retirement plans; and

WHEREAS, it is the desire of the congregation to encourage, receive, and administer these gifts in a manner consistent with the loyalty and devotion expressed by the grantors and in accord with the policies of this congregation:

THEREFORE BE IT RESOLVED, that this congregation in an annual [or other] meeting assembled on [date], approve and establish on the records of the congregation a new and separate fund to be known as THE [name of your endowment fund in all caps] (hereafter called the "FUND");

BE IT FURTHER RESOLVED, that the purpose of this FUND is to enhance the mission of [name of congregation] apart from the general operation of the congregation; [choose one of the following options]

[Option A] that no portion of distributions from the FUND shall be used for the annual operating budget of the congregation;

[Option B] that only in particular, temporary, difficult circumstances, and where integrity of gift restrictions permit, may this congregation, by action in meeting assembled, use FUND distributions for its own operating or support services;

[Option C] that no more than 10 percent of the annual operating budget of the congregation may be funded by distributions from the FUND, except in particular, temporary, difficult circumstances, authorized by action of the congregation in meeting assembled, and where integrity of gift restrictions permit;

and that, except where specifically authorized otherwise in the terms of a gift, distributions from the FUND will be made annually, in amounts not to exceed 5 percent of the average fair market value of the FUND over the previous thirteen quarters;

BE IT FURTHER RESOLVED, that the endowment fund committee (hereinafter called the "COMMITTEE") shall be the custodian of the FUND;

BE IT FURTHER RESOLVED, that the following Plan of Operation sets forth the administration and management of the FUND.

B. Plan of Operation

1. The Endowment Fund Committee

The Endowment Fund Committee (hereafter, the "COMMITTEE") shall consist of five (5) members, all of whom shall be voting members of [name of congregation]. Except as herein limited, the term of each member shall be three (3) years. The minister and the president or vice president of the church governing body shall be advisory members of the COMMITTEE.

Upon adoption of this resolution by the congregation, it shall elect five (5) members of the COM-

MITTEE: two (2) for a term of three (3) years; two (2) for a term of two (2) years; and one (1) for a term of one (1) year. Thereafter, at each annual meeting, the congregation shall elect the necessary number for a term of three (3) years.

No member shall serve more than two consecutive three-year terms. After a lapse of one (1) year, former COMMITTEE members may be reelected.

The governing body of the church shall nominate new members for the COMMITTEE and report at the annual congregational meeting in the same manner as for other offices and committees. No member may serve on the COMMITTEE while also serving on the governing body of the church.

In the event of a vacancy on the COMMITTEE, the governing body shall appoint a member to fill the vacancy until the next annual meeting of the congregation, at which time the congregation shall elect a member to fulfill the term of the vacancy.

The COMMITTEE shall meet at least quarterly, or more frequently as deemed by it in the best interest of the FUND. A quorum shall consist of three (3) members. A majority present and voting shall carry any motion or resolution. The COMMITTEE shall elect from its membership a chairperson, financial secretary, and recording secretary. The chairperson, or member designated by the chairperson, shall preside at all meetings of the COMMITTEE.

The recording secretary shall maintain complete and accurate minutes of all meetings of the COMMITTEE and supply a copy thereof to each member of the COMMITTEE, as well as the chair of the governing body. Each COMMITTEE member shall keep a complete copy of minutes to be delivered to her or his successor. [*Choose one of the following two options*]

[*Option A*] The financial secretary shall assist the congregation's treasurer in maintaining complete and accurate books of accounts for the FUND and shall submit to the treasurer on behalf of the COMMITTEE written requests for checks payable from the FUND and shall sign all necessary documents on behalf of the congregation in furtherance of the purposes of the FUND.

[*Option B*] The financial secretary shall sign all checks payable from the FUND in amounts no greater than $250.00. Two authorized signatures are required for greater amount.

A certified public accountant or other appropriate person who is not a member of the COMMITTEE will annually audit the books. The COMMITTEE shall report on a quarterly basis to the governing body and, at each annual or special meeting of the congregation, shall render a complete audited account of the administration of the FUND during the preceding year.

The COMMITTEE may request that other members of the congregation serve as advisory members and, at the expense of the FUND (taken from the annual distribution amount OR undistributed capital appreciation), may provide for such professional counseling on investments or legal matters as it deems to be in the best interest of the FUND.

Members of the COMMITTEE shall not be liable for any losses that may be incurred upon the investments of the assets of the FUND except to the extent that such losses shall have been caused by bad faith or gross negligence. No member shall be personally liable as long as she or he acts in good faith and with ordinary prudence. Each member shall be liable for only her or his own willful misconduct or omissions and shall not be liable for the acts or omissions of any other member. No member shall engage in any self-dealing or transactions with the FUND in which the member has direct or indirect financial interest and shall at all times refrain from any conduct in which her or his personal interests would conflict with the interest of the FUND.

All assets are to be held in the name of the [*name of congregation*] [*name of the endowment fund*].

Recommendations to hold, sell, exchange, rent, lease, transfer, convert, invest, reinvest, and in all other respects to manage and control the assets of the FUND, including stocks, bonds, debentures, mortgages, notes, or other securities, as in their judgment and discretion they deem wise and prudent, are to be made by the COMMITTEE for approval by the governing body of the church, with subsequent execution by the delegated member of the COMMITTEE.

2. Distributions

The COMMITTEE shall abide by and keep a record of the terms and restrictions of all gifts to the FUND and shall determine what is principal and income according to accepted accounting procedures. [*Choose one of the following options.*]

> [*Option A*] Lifetime and testamentary unrestricted gifts to the FUND shall accumulate until a fair market value of $[*amount*] is achieved, after which annual distributions may commence. However, should the fair market value of the FUND subsequently decline to less than $[*amount*], distributions shall be made only upon a 2/3 majority vote of approval from the congregation.

> [*Option B*] Lifetime and testamentary gifts to the FUND shall accumulate for [*number*] years, after which annual distributions may commence.

> [*Option C*] Distributions from the FUND shall be made annually and at such other times as deemed necessary and/or feasible to accomplish the following purposes: [*Choose one of the following options, then see Continuation of Option C below.*]

> > [*Option C-1*] One-third (1/3) for the building reserve fund of [*name of congregation*], such as but not limited to major capital expenditures and significant improvement projects related to the buildings and real property of the church, including grounds and landscaping, over and above regular maintenance;

In addition to the permitted distribution, the COMMITTEE may, from time to time, recommend lending money from this building reserve fund to the church to help advance a particular improvement project on such terms and at such rates of interest and in such amounts as the congregation deems appropriate;

One-third (1/3) for outreach into the greater community at large, including, but not limited to, grants to [*name of denomination*] camps and conferences, theological schools, local service agencies, or institutions to which this congregation relates, and to special programs designed for those persons in our local community who are in spiritual and/or economic need; and

One-third (1/3) for the wider mission of [*name of denomination*], including, but not limited to, grants for new church development; leadership training; educational ministries; world mission; denominational capital financing; scholarships or grants to members of [*name of congregation*] for the purpose of attending college, theological, nursing, or medical school; for denomination-related camping or leadership conferences; or such other training which enables members of this congregation to grow in faith and service to [*name of denomination*].

[*Option C-2*] One-fourth (1/4) to provide seed money to develop new programming and/or to increase professional staffing in [*name of congregation*], distributed over a three (3)-year period of time in which a maximum of 60 percent of the total cost of new programming or professional staffing can be distributed in the first year, a maximum of 40 percent in the second year, and a maximum of 20 percent in the third year. In the fourth year the total cost of the new programming and/or staffing must come from the annual operating budget;

One-fourth (1/4) for scholarships and grants to members of [*name of congregation*] for the purpose of attending college, theological, nursing or medical school; for [*name of denomination*]-related camping or leadership conferences; or such training that enables members of this congregation to grow in faith and service to [*name of denomination*];

One-fourth (1/4) for outreach into the community, including, but not limited to, grants to [*name of denomination*] camps and conference centers, theological schools, social service agencies or institutions to which this congregation relates, and to special programs designed for those persons in the community who are in spiritual and/or economic need; and

One-fourth (1/4) for the wider mission of [*name of denomination*] at home and overseas, including, but not limited to, grants to [*name of denomination*] for new church development, professional leadership, educational ministries, world mission, and capital financing.

[*Continuation of Option C*] Programs for support shall be recommended by the COMMITTEE and approved by the governing body for funding. Suggestions or requests for funding must be submitted to the COMMITTEE by [*month and date*] of each year.

3. Amending the Resolution

BE IT FURTHER RESOLVED, that any amendment to this resolution which will change, alter, or amend the purpose for which the FUND is established shall be adopted by a two-thirds (2/3) vote of the members present at an annual meeting called specifically for the purpose of amending this resolution.

4. Disposition or Transfer of FUND

BE IT FURTHER RESOLVED, that in the event [*name of congregation*] ceases to exist through either merger or dissolution, disposition or transfer of the FUND shall be at the discretion of the governing body in conformity with the approved congregational bylaws and in consultation with [*name of denomination*]. Consultation with [*name of denomination*] may also be desirable for continuation of FUND obligations to grantors of gifts.

C. Adoption of Resolution

This resolution, recommended by the governing body and accepted by the congregation at a legally called congregational meeting, is hereby adopted.

_____
[*Name of Congregation*]

By_____
President

and _____
Secretary

Dated this_____day of _____, 20____.

Sample Endowment Document

I. The Church shall have a separate endowment fund to assure the long-range financial future of the Church, to help manage financial emergencies, and to fund capital needs and special projects that all support the vision and mission of the church.

II. An Endowment Fund Committee shall govern the endowment fund and shall serve as the custodian of the Endowment Investment and Distribution Policy passed by a vote of two-thirds of the members of the congregation. This policy shall provide for the protection of the income (corpus) of the endowment over the long term and shall require the Committee to exercise the utmost of care to respect the integrity of restrictions placed on any gift to the endowment.

III. The Endowment Fund Committee shall consist of three members of the congregation. Except in the initial election, when shortened terms will enable a staggered rotation of members, the term of each committee member shall be three years. No member may serve more than two consecutive three-year terms. After a lapse of one year, former committee members can be reelected. No member may serve on the Endowment Fund Committee while also serving on the Church governing body or as an elected officer of the congregation.

IV. A unanimous vote of the members of the Endowment Fund Committee is needed to carry any motion or resolution. The Committee shall elect its own chairperson. The Committee shall report to the governing body on a quarterly basis and provide a written report to the congregation at the annual meeting of the congregation.

V. The Endowment Fund Committee is empowered, acting through its elected chair, to hold, sell, exchange, rent, lease, transfer, convert, invest, and in all other respects manage and control the assets of the endowment pursuant to the Endowment Investment and Distribution Policy. The Committee shall act in its sole judgment and discretion, as it deems wise and prudent, without further approvals.

VI. Committee members shall not be liable for any losses incurred by the endowment fund except to the extent that such losses arise out of acts or omissions of willful misconduct or gross negligence. Each member shall be liable for his or her own acts and omissions of willful misconduct or gross negligence and not for the acts or omissions of other members. No member of the Committee shall engage in any self-dealing or transactions with the endowment fund in which the member has a direct or indirect financial interest. Members shall refrain at all times from conduct in which his or her personal interests would conflict with the interest of the endowment fund.

Sample Endowment Investment and Distribution Policy

General

1. The Endowment Fund Committee shall invest the assets of the endowment with the objective of earning an average annual total return of 8 to 12 percent consistent with moderate risk. The Committee shall endeavor to invest the assets of the endowment in a socially responsible manner. It is intended that reasonable restrictions placed on any gift by the donor will be faithfully followed, subject to the Committee's determination of the integrity and best interests of the endowment.

2. In order to protect and preserve the corpus of the endowment over the long term, the Committee shall distribute no more than 4 percent per year of the total market value of the assets, as determined by the average total market value on the last business day of each of the four immediately preceding calendar quarters. If less than 4 percent is distributed in one year, the Committee may distribute more than 4 percent in a subsequent year, as long as the distributions do not exceed 4 percent on a cumulative basis.

3. The Committee may provide for such professional counsel on investments or legal matters as it deems best and may incur reasonable expenses in the execution of its duties. The expenses shall be paid from the endowment.

4. All members of the congregation are encouraged to consider leaving a bequest of at least five times their annual financial commitment to the endowment in their wills.

5. This Endowment Investment and Distribution Policy may be amended only by a two-thirds majority vote of the congregation.

Three Funds

The endowment shall be composed of three funds, which may be commingled for ease of investment management. The Committee shall separately account for each of these funds, attributing to each its proportionate share of changes in investment values, as well as recording gifts to and distributions from each of the funds. The distribution limit outlined above shall be applied on a fund-by-fund basis. The use to be made of the allowed distribution from each of the three funds is determined by the congregation as part of its customary budgeting process. Gifts and bequests to the endowment may be designated for any of the three funds. Undesignated gifts shall be deposited to the Unrestricted Reserve Fund. The three funds are established as follows:

- 50 percent of the initial assets of the endowment shall be allocated to the Unrestricted Reserve Fund.

- 30 percent of the initial assets of the endowment shall be allocated to the Building Reserve Fund.

- 20 percent of the initial assets of the endowment shall be allocated to the Social Outreach and Service Fund.

Unrestricted Fund

1. Distributions from the Unrestricted Reserve Fund may be used for any purpose to further the work of the church, but shall not be used for the ordinary and customary operating expenses of the church, except as provided below.

2. Distributions from the Unrestricted Reserve Fund may be used for the ordinary and customary operating expenses of the church only as follows:

   - $10,000 maximum distribution in the first year of this policy

   - $8,000 maximum distribution in the second year of this policy

   - $6,000 maximum distribution in the third year of this policy

   - $4,000 maximum distribution in the fourth year of this policy

   - $2,000 maximum distribution on the fifth year of this policy

   In subsequent years, any distribution from the Unrestricted Reserve Fund for the ordinary and customary operating expenses of the Church will require a two-thirds majority vote of the congregation.

3. In addition to the distributions provided above, and upon the request of the Treasurer, the Committee may from time to time loan money from the Unrestricted Reserve Fund to the Church to help manage temporary cash-flow needs caused by month-to-month variations in the collection of pledges and other gifts. This should be done on such terms and at such rates of interest and in such amounts as the Committee deems appropriate.

Building Reserve Fund

1. Distributions from the Building Reserve Fund shall be used only to help pay for major capital expenditures and significant improvement projects related to the buildings and real property of the Church, including grounds and landscaping, over and above regular maintenance.

2. In addition to the permitted distribution, the Committee may from time to time loan money from the Building Reserve Fund to the Church to help advance a particular improvement project on such terms and at such rates of interest and in such amounts as the Committee deems appropriate.

The Social Outreach and Service Fund

1. Distribution from the Social Outreach and Service Fund shall be used only to further the Church's mission of supporting individual and collective service to the larger community. The fund is not intended to support activities for the Church community itself, but is intended for social-responsibility efforts in the broader community at large.

2. In addition to the permitted distribution and with the approval of the congregation, the Committee may make direct investment of not more than 20 percent of the assets in the Social Outreach and Service Fund in housing, social service, or community or economic development activities in furtherance of the mission of the Church and purpose of this fund.

UUA Planned Giving Marketing Brochures

These brochures are available for $1 each, except where otherwise noted. All fit in a #10 envelope or a display rack. Please allow 10 working days for delivery. Order from:

Office of Charitable Gifts and Estate Planning
Unitarian Universalist Association of Congregations
25 Beacon Street, Boston, MA 02108-2800
Phone: 617-742-2100, extension 509
Fax: 617-725-4979
E-mail: giftplans@uua.org

❏ **Funding Our Faith: The UUA Pooled Income Fund**
   Introduction to a popular life-income gift arrangement. Donors receive quarterly payments for life; ultimate gift goes to the local church and/or the UUA. (50 cents each)

❏ **Legacies of Hope: The UUA Charitable Gift Annuity**
   Introduction to a life-income gift arrangement that pays a guaranteed fixed dollar amount to one or two people. Ultimately, the annuity becomes a gift to the local church and/or the UUA. (50 cents each)

❏ **Giving Through Charitable Remainder Trusts**
   Basic introduction to trusts, a gifting opportunity for donor prospects who wish to give $100,000 or more to a local UU church and/or the UUA. Includes summary of benefits and tax considerations.

❏ **Giving Through Life-Income Plans**
   Summarizes life-income gift arrangements as part of an effective estate plan.

❏ **Better Estate Planning**
   General description of estate planning challenges and techniques, including federal gift and estate tax considerations.

❏ **Reflecting on Tomorrow**
   Presents nine specific charitable goals and the gift options to accomplish them.

❏ **How to Make a Will That Works**
   Answers very practical questions about structuring and revising a will. Touches on the probate process and how to plan for it most effectively.

❏ **Use Your Will to Give to Unitarian Universalism**
   Introduction to the basics about bequests. Includes a reply form and sample language for testamentary giving to UU organizations. (50 cents each)

❏ **Taking Stock . . . and Giving It**
   Describes benefits and tax considerations of making a charitable gift of stock. Includes Internal Revenue Code citations and narrative examples of gifting options.

❏ **Giving Through Life Insurance**
   Describes benefits and tax considerations of using life insurance to make a charitable gift. Includes Internal Revenue Code citations and narrative examples of gifting options.

❏ **Giving Through Retirement Plans**
   Describes benefits and tax considerations of using retirement plans to make a charitable gift. Includes Internal Revenue Code citations and narrative examples of gifting options.

❏ **Giving Real Estate**
   Describes benefits and tax considerations of using real estate to make a charitable gift. Includes Internal Revenue Code citations and narrative examples of gifting options.

Sources of Planned Giving Materials

The following companies or organizations publish and sell promotional and educational materials about how to make charitable gifts of stock, real estate, life insurance, and retirement or pension plans, as well as how gift arrangements such as wills, bequests, charitable trusts, charitable gift annuities, and pooled income funds work. Contact these providers directly to request a catalog and free samples of their materials.

UUA Office of Charitable Gift and Estate
Planning
25 Beacon Street
Boston, MA 02108-2800
Tel: 617-742-2100, ext. 509, 648, or 511
Toll-free: (888) 792-5885
Fax: (617) 725-4979
E-mail: giftplans@uua.org

Robert F. Sharpe and Co., Inc.
6410 Poplar Ave., Suite 700
Memphis, TN 38119
Toll-free: 800-238-3253
Fax: 901-761-4268
E-mail: info@rfsco.com
Web: www.rfsco.com

Taxwise Giving & Philanthropy Tax Institute
13 Arcadia Road
Old Greenwich, CT 06870
Toll-free: 800-243-9122
Fax: 203-637-4572
E-mail: info@taxwisegiving.com
Web: www.taxwisegiving.com

Planned Giving Today
100 Second Avenue South, Suite 180
Edmonds, WA 98020-3551
Toll-free: 800-525-5748
Fax: 425-744-3838
Web: www.pgtoday.com

R&R Newkirk
8695 South Archer, #10
Willow Springs, IL 60480
Toll-free: 800-342-2375
Fax: 708-839-9207
E-mail: inquiries@rrnewkirk.com
Web: www.rrnewkirk.com

Endowment Development Services
5546 Shorewood Dr.
Indianapolis, IN 46220
317-542-9829
Fax: 317-549-9470
E-mail: eds@pgiresources.com

Ecumenical Stewardship Center
1100 West 42nd Street, Suite 225
Indianapolis, IN 46208
317-926-3524
Toll-free: 800-835-5671
Fax: (317) 926-3521
E-mail: stewardshipcenter@ameritech.net
Web: www.stewardshipresources.org

Empty Tomb, Inc.
301 North Fourth Street
P.O. Box 2404
Champaign, IL 61825-2404
217-356-2262
Fax: 217-356-2344
E-mail: info@emptytomb.org
Web: www.emptytomb.org

National Committee on Planned Giving
233 McCrea Street, Suite 400
Indianapolis, IN 46225
317-269-6274
Fax: 317-269-6276
E-mail: ncpg@ncpg.org
Web: www.ncpg.org

The Steltor Company
10435 New York Avenue
Des Moines, IA 50322
Toll-free: 800-331-6881
Fax: 515-278-5851
Web: www.stelter.com

Pentera Inc.
8650 Commerce Park, Suite G
Indianapolis, IN 46268
317-875-0910
Fax: 317-875-0912
E-mail: info@pentera.com
Web: www.pentera.com

Renaissance Inc.
6100 W. 96th Street, Suite 100
Indianapolis, IN 46278
Toll-free: 800-843-0050
Fax: 317-843-5417
E-mail: info@reninc.com
Web: www.reninc.com

American Institute for Philanthropic Studies
Delona Davis, Director
California State University, Long Beach
Foundation
562-985-8446
E-mail: ddavis@csulb.edu
Web: www.plannedgivingedu.com

Indiana University Center on Philanthropy
550 West North Street, Suite 301
Indianapolis, IN 46202-3272
317-274-4200
Fax: 317-684-8900
E-mail: iucop@iupui.edu
Web: www.philanthropy.iupui.edu

Council for Advancement and Support of
Education
1307 New York Avenue NW, Suite 1000
Washington, DC 20005-4701
202-387-2273
Fax: 202-387-4973
E-mail: MemberServiceCenter@case.org
Web: www.case.org

American Council on Gift Annuities
233 McCrea Street, Suite 400
Indianapolis, IN 46225
317-269-6271
Fax: 317-269-6276
E-mail: acga@acga-web.org
Web: www.acga-web.org

Planned Giving Resources Inc.
P.O. Box 665
Baker, LA 70704-0665
225-774-6700
Fax: 225-775-6910
E-mail: jimbpotter@aol.com
Web: www.pgresources.com

Facility Guidelines

Site Recommendations

Worship center, fellowship hall, education space, parking:
>   1 acre per 100 to 125 in attendance

Recreation building and/or outdoor recreation: 2 to 4 additional acres

Parking

1 space for every 2.5 seats in sanctuary

110 to 125 spaces per acre

8.5 feet by 16 feet for each compact car

9 feet by 18 feet for each standard size car

14 feet by 18 feet for each wheelchair access

Specifically labeled signs for the physically challenged

Support for the Physically Challenged

A ramp if there are steps at building entry

Handrails at ramps

Slope of walks not more than 1 inch in 12 inches

36 inches minimum width doorways

5 feet minimum hallway width for two wheelchairs to pass

5 feet, 6 inches minimum hallway width for two people passing on crutches

Restroom dimensions to allow turning radius for wheelchair

Grab bars in restrooms

Specifically identified wheelchair spaces in sanctuary, fellowship hall, and education building

Elevators to all levels

Worship Center Ground Coverage

Attendance of up to 300:	15 to 17 square feet per person
Attendance of 300 to 500:	12 to 18 square feet per person
Attendance of more than 500:	10 to 18 square feet (including balconies)

Worship Center Seating

Row spacing:	48 inches minimum between the second-to-the-last row and last row if last row is against wall
	34 inches minimum space between other rows;
	36 inches or more recommended
Pew lengths and seating:	20 inches average width per person
	13 to 14 people maximum per row
	21 feet to 24 feet per row
Aisle widths (check local codes):	4 feet minimum for center or main aisle; 5 feet or more recommended
	2 feet 6 inches minimum for side aisles; 3 feet 8 inches recommended

Fellowship Hall Capacity

Dining capacity:	1/3 to 1/2 of education building capacity
Seated at rectangular tables:	10 square feet per person minimum
	12 square feet per person recommended
Seated at round tables:	12 square feet per person minimum
	15 square feet recommended

Administration Building

Primary building with multiple uses:	30 to 40 square feet per person
Small congregations	45 square feet per person
Larger congregations with extensive programs:	55 square feet per person
Office space for professional religious leaders:	140 square feet minimum; 250 to 325 square feet recommended
Office space for other staff people:	120 square feet minimum; 150 to 200 square feet recommended

Interior Program Space by Age

Age Group	Persons per Room	Square Feet per Person	Teacher-Pupil Ratio (2 teachers per room)
Infants	4–10	3 ft. space between cribs	1 for 4–6 pupils
Toddlers	6–10	30–35	1 for 4–6 pupils
Twos	6–10	30–35	1 for 4–6 pupils
Threes	8–12	30–35	1 for 4–6 pupils
Kindergarten (4–5 years old)	10–20	30–35	1 for 6–10 pupils
Elementary (Grade 1–6)	12–25	25–30	1 for 6–10 pupils
Youth (Grade 7–12)	12–25	20–25	1 for 6–12 pupils

Interior Program Space for Adults

In worship:	10 square feet per person plus aisles
Sitting down eating:	15 square feet per person plus aisles
Other activities:	12 square feet per person plus aisles

UUA Fundraising Consultant Request for Information

We partner with congregations to help each community transform its unique vision into bold action.

A fundraising consultant needs the following information to help plan an assessment visit. The information enables the consultant to review background information and formulate questions prior to arrival. The information allows the consultant to make efficient use of time spent with the congregation.

1. Current congregational directory, including names of officers and committee members.

2. Brief history of congregation.

3. Mission statement and strategic planning document.

4. Copy of bylaws.

5. Annual reports for previous year, including copy of operating budget.

6. Distribution of annual financial commitment (pledge) information, including total dollar amount, average commitment, median commitment, and a quartile analysis. Attach names to this financial information. Names will remain confidential.

7. Amount of endowment fund and reserve funds. Include designations and policies regarding expenditures of those funds.

8. Information about most recent annual budget drive, including brochure.

9. Amount of any outstanding loans including terms, balance outstanding, and name of lender.

10. Membership, worship service attendance, and religious education attendance figures for last three years.

11. List of UUA staff and consultants (including district consultants) who have worked with congregation in previous three years.

12. Copy of most recent newsletter. If newsletter is part of congregation's website, provide web address.

13. Information that supports congregational commitment to inclusion, diversity, and multiculturalism.

14. Information about previous capital campaigns, including dates, purpose of the campaign, and amount raised.

15. Any additional information that might be helpful to the consultant.

Architectural Firm Preliminary Selection Form

Name of Firm:_____

Address:_____

Telephone: _____   E-mail: _____

Website: _____

1. Is your firm locally owned? _____

   How many employees are in your office? _____

2. List the number of associates in your firm by technical specialties:

   _____

   _____

3. What is the range of project size for which your firm provides services?

   _____

   _____

4. Would you expect to use additional consulting services (outside your firm) for our project? What would those services include?

   _____

5. Are you, or is any member of your firm, LEED (Leadership in Energy and Environmental Design) certified? Please list all names.

   _____

   _____

6. How long would it take you to complete our project? Please explain.

   _____

   _____

   _____

Please respond to the following questions on a separate piece of paper.

1. How would you establish a working relationship with our building committee? With our governing body? With our congregation?
2. Please describe your methods for cost containment, quality, and value.
3. Please provide a sample contract for our review.
4. Please provide a complete list of church projects that your firm has completed during the past five years. Include references and contact information. Note and explain any that cannot be contacted for references.
5. Please describe your experience with "green" building construction.
6. Please provide a statement of your normal fee structure, organized by each phase of the project.

Interview Questions for Architects

Background

- Please describe your firm (personnel, size, and experience of the organization).

- What are the qualifications and experience of the firm? Do you have in-house engineering, or do you use consulting firms?

- What memberships do you hold in professional organizations? What awards has your firm received?

- What schools did the staff attend? What general training requirements are expected of the staff? What are their technical specialties?

- Which member of your firm would be primarily responsible for our project? What other personnel would be assigned to our project? Would it be beneficial to interview any of these people?

- What is the range of project sizes and costs with which your firm usually works?

- Has your firm provided architectural services to other church projects? Please describe the project(s). What were the actual costs in relation to your estimated costs?

Working Relationship

- What services would you provide at each phase of the architectural and construction process?

- What is your philosophy or understanding of church design? Are there particular styles or approaches to church architecture that you like or dislike?

- What are your thoughts regarding the relationship among the architect, the church, the building committee, and the general contractor? How can we create a process in which the congregation feels some ownership?

- Based on your understanding of our project, how would you work with us?

- What is your method of assigning design responsibilities?

- Would you help prepare a brochure with a sketch that can be used in presenting the project to the congregation?

Contracts and Fees

- How do you determine the fees for your services? When are payments due?

- What is specifically included in your basic fee?

- What is not included that we may need? How much will these services cost?

- What type of owner-architect agreement would you propose? May we have a copy for review?

- Does your firm carry Errors and Omissions Insurance? Please describe the benefits of this coverage.

- Would your fees include a model or rendering?

Cost Containment

(Note to task force: Many architects have a reliable rate of accuracy, and their cost estimates are close to actual costs. A variance up to 15 percent is acceptable.)

- What is your firm's record for designing within budget?

- What factors will affect the balance between economy and quality?

- Who would be responsible for value engineering to bring the project within budget?

- How would we work together to control the costs of the project?

Timing

- What is your estimate of the time required for each phase of the architectural and construction processes?

- What is your estimate of the total time needed for the project? What is your firm's record in meeting deadlines?

Construction Phase

- What would your role be during the construction phase?

- Do you have a preferred construction method?

- What might be some of the options for contractor selection?

- How would you handle change orders, and how are they billed?

Ending the Interview

- What other questions should we have asked?

- What questions do you have for us?

For Task Force Discussion after the Interviews

- Is the architect a good communicator?

- Does the architect listen well?

- Is the architect sensitive to the congregation's needs and desires?

- Does the architect show passion for the mission of the church?

- Do the architect's schematics reflect the mission?

- How does the architect manage unrealistic expectations from the task force?

- Does the architect offer suggestions and alternative approaches?

- Is the architect familiar with local codes and building issues?

- Is the architect excited about the opportunity to work with the congregation?

Cash-Flow Projection Spreadsheet

	[Fiscal Year] Previous	[Fiscal Year] Current	[Fiscal Year] Next 1	[Fiscal Year] Next 2	[Fiscal Year] Next 3	[Fiscal Year] Next 4	[Fiscal Year] Next 5
1. Income							
Pledges							
Gifts and Endowments							
Fundraising							
Rental Income							
Plate Collections							
District or UUA Grants							
Other Sources							
Total Income							
2. Expenses							
Personnel							
Administration							
Programming							
Contributions							
Building Maintenance							
Debt Service							
Other Sources							
Total Expenses							
3. Debt service as a percentage of operating budget							
	_____%	_____%	_____%	_____%	_____%	_____%	_____%

(Debt Service must not exceed 25% of operating budget. Do not include construction financing.)

For Further Reading

Appreciative Inquiry

Branson, Mark L. *Memories, Hopes, and Conversations: Appreciative Inquiry and Congregational Change*. Herndon, VA: The Alban Institute, 2004.

> Persuasively demonstrates how concentrating on needs and problems can mire a congregation in discouragement and distract it from noticing innate strengths. By focusing on memories of the congregation at its best, members are able to construct "provocative proposals" to help shape the church's future. Grounded in solid theory and real-life practice, *Memories, Hopes, and Conversations* is a groundbreaking work of narrative leadership and the first book to apply the principles of Appreciative Inquiry to the lives of congregations.

Cooperrider, David L., Diana Whitney, and Jacqueline M. Stavros. *Appreciative Inquiry Handbook*. Brunswick, OH: Crown Custom Publishing, 2005.

> Contains everything needed to launch any kind of Appreciative Inquiry initiative. The authors provide background information about Appreciative Inquiry, as well as sample project plans, designs, agendas, course outlines, interview guidelines, participant worksheets, and a list of resources.

Hammond, Sue Annis. *The Thin Book of Appreciative Inquiry*. Bend, OR: Thin Book Publishing Company, 2002.

> Introduction to Appreciative Inquiry. Written in simple language and includes references on where to go for more in-depth study.

Whitney, Diana, and Amanda Trosten-Bloom. *The Power of Appreciative Inquiry: A Practical Guide to Positive Change*. San Francisco: Barrett-Koehler Communications, 2003.

> Whitney and Trosten-Bloom ask, "Has your congregation spent energy and resources on 'problem solving' only to find that problems either persist or worsen?" They believe Appreciative Inquiry shows that if you want to transform a situation, a relationship, an organization, or a community, focusing on strengths is more effective than focusing on problems. The authors present both the principles of Appreciative Inquiry and case studies that demonstrate how it works. Congregational leaders who have grown tired of negative approaches to problem solving will be refreshed by the theory and examples presented in this book.

Whitney, Diana, David L. Cooperrider, Amanda Trosten-Bloom, and Brian S. Kaplin. *Encyclopedia of Positive Questions, Volume One: Using Apprecia-*

tive Inquiry to Bring Out the Best in Your Organization. Euclid, OH: Lakeshore Communications, 2002.

> This book offers a practical guide to implementing Appreciative Inquiry in congregations. The authors begin with an explanation of why positive questions are important. Then they offer an encyclopedia of sample positive questions, each group of which focuses on a specific topic. This book is full of concrete ways to begin an Appreciative Inquiry process.

http://appreciativeinquiry.case.edu

> Hosted by Case Western Reserve University's Weatherhead School of Management, Appreciative Inquiry Commons is an information highway connecting people with academic resources and practical tools for Appreciative Inquiry. Includes an explanation of Appreciative Inquiry, articles, news, book references, research, quotes, events, a practitioner database, links, and learning opportunities.

www.clergyleadership.com/appreciative/ai.html

> The Clergy Leadership website offers an introduction to Appreciative Inquiry and describes the 5D model. Also includes an explanation of the philosophy and theology behind Appreciative Inquiry, a listserv, additional book references, links to other sites, resources, and opportunities for training and consulting.

www.iisd.org/ai

> The International Institute for Sustainable Development offers an approach to Appreciative Inquiry for use in community development. This site addresses reasons why problem-solving approaches do not work for community development and how Appreciative Inquiry can work.

www.appreciative-inquiry.org
> Applies the Appreciative Inquiry model to philanthropy.

www.congregationalresources.org

> The Congregational Resource Guide provides web and book references to help you understand more about Appreciative Inquiry, its principles and practices, and how it might benefit your congregation.

Facilities Planning

Callahan, Kennon L. *Building for Effective Mission: A Complete Guide for Congregations on Bricks and Mortar Issues*. San Francisco: Jossey-Bass, 1997.

> Asserts that mission grows with compassion and community and that the mission field is the world. Describes concrete actions congregations may take to discover a mission and a focus for it and to plan for accomplishing it. Later chapters discuss the physical plant that furthers a chosen mission; evaluating possible sites for location, mission potential, property characteristics, and financial considerations; facilities that allow efficient staffing, scheduling, and leadership; and how to develop a schedule for completing building plans. Whether or not a congregation plans to move or renovate, this book's emphasis on mission is thought provoking.

Kibert, Charles J. *Sustainable Construction: Green Building Design and Delivery*. Hoboken, NJ: John Wiley and Sons, 2005.

> Focusing on green construction as it applies to large institutional buildings, this book provides an introduction to the design and construction of "healthy" buildings. Some translation is needed to adapt the concepts to church buildings.

Lee, Robert A. *First Impressions: How to Present an Inviting Church Facility*. Nashville, TN: Abingdon Press, 1993.

> Lee poses several questions: Does your church facility enhance or interfere with the ministries of your congregation? What is a visitor's first impression of your church as viewed from the street? from the parking lot? from the lobby?

from the chancel? from the nursery? Then he presents information to help church leaders evaluate the needs of existing and future members. He details how to determine whether the environment is inviting to members and effective for ministries. And finally, he discusses how to make creative, cost-effective changes to make church facilities more welcoming.

McCormick, Gwenn E. *Planning and Building Church Facilities*. Nashville, TN: Broadman Press, 1992.

Whether new facilities are an immediate need or a vision for the future, proper planning is crucial. This book gives your congregation guidelines, ideas, suggestions, and directions for the planning and building process and systematically explores the process of planning and building new facilities.

Moore, Lance, and Daniel Michal. *Firm Foundations: An Architect and a Pastor Guide Your Church Construction*. Lima, OH: CSS Publishing, 1999.

Offers a common language for ministers, church boards, contractors, and designers. Point by point, start to finish, Moore (a pastor) and Michal (an architect) warn of common follies and guide you in sorting out the best choices for your church.

Thompson, William J., Kim Sorvig, and Craig D. Farnsworth. *Sustainable Landscape Construction: A Guide to Green Building Outdoors*. Washington, DC: Island Press, 2000.

Reevaluates the assumption that all built landscapes are environmentally sound, and offers practical alternatives to more sustainable landscape construction. Offers specific methods organized around ten key principles of sustainability.

www.ag.org/top/Church_Administration

The General Council of the Assemblies of God provides information on master planning for new church facilities.

www.ifca.org/Handbook

The Church and Ministers Handbook from IFCA Press. See the Chapter "Facility Planning and Construction."

http://uuministryforearth.org/cgi/news.cgi

The Unitarian Universalist Ministry for Earth sponsors the congregation-based Green Sanctuary Program and provides information for Unitarian Universalists around critical environmental issues.

www.usgbc.org

The U.S. Green Building Council (USGBC) is a community of leaders who work to transform the way buildings and communities are designed, built, and operated. They envision an environmentally responsible, healthy, and prosperous environment that improves the quality of life. The USGBC administers the Leadership in Energy and Environmental Design (LEED) green building rating system, which is nationally recognized as the benchmark for design, construction, and operation of high-performance green building.

www.churchbusiness.com/articles/637/637_3b1Feat1.html

Paula Suhrbier and William Brocious write about responsible stewardship of the earth and explain how being a green church pays off.

www.gwipl.org/default.asp

The Greater Washington Interfaith Power and Light (GWIPL) is a nonprofit initiative that helps congregations, religious institutions, and others in the Washington, D.C., area work for a more just, sustainable, and healthier world by reducing the threat of global warming. Their website offers suggestions for education, how to save energy and buy clean energy, worship, and environmental stewardship.

www.webofcreation.org

Web of Creation, maintained by the Lutheran School of Theology in Chicago, provides ecology resources to transform faith and society. Web of Creation has materials and information on how to become a green congregation and a guide for congregational buildings and grounds.

Generosity and Stewardship

Barna, George. *How to Increase Giving in Your Church: A Practical Guide to the Sensitive Task of Raising Money for Your Church or Ministry*. Ventura, CA: Regal Books, 1997.

Geared toward helping church leaders acquire current and accurate knowledge about the who, how, and why of giving to churches. Barna addresses basic questions about donors and their giving to help defuse some of the most common sources of anxiety, fear, and misunderstanding related to fundraising. While Barna offers no magic formulas or foolproof gimmicks, he offers insight into some fundamental truths. It is Barna's belief that understanding people and their giving will help raise money for church activities.

Barrett, Wayne C. *The Church Finance Book: Hundreds of Proven Ideas for Funding Your Ministry*. Nashville: Discipleship Resources, 1995.

Presents ten strategies for commitment campaigns and hundreds of other techniques for church financial campaigns, administration, fundraising, promotion, and planned giving.

Berg, Linda Lee, Ruth Lewellen-Dix, and Fia B. Scheyer. *Stewardship: The Joy of Giving*. Boston: The Unitarian Universalist Association, 1999.

The authors share a stewardship program for four age levels: primary children, intermediate children, youth, and adults. The purpose of the curriculum is to empower all participants to be stewards of self, family, community, congregation, and the Unitarian Universalist faith.

Callahan, Kennon L. *Effective Church Finances: Fund-Raising and Budgeting for Church Leaders*. San Francisco: Jossey-Bass, 1992.

Offers a complete guide to budgeting and fundraising for local churches. Callahan shares practical methods to implement the principles presented in his companion book, *Effective Church Finances*. Written for committee members, key leaders, pastors, and staffs, the book includes detailed information about developing a church budget, fundraising for the budget, setting congregational giving goals, and increasing the giving from year to year.

Callahan, Kennon L. *Giving and Stewardship in an Effective Church: A Guide for Every Member*. San Francisco: Jossey-Bass, 1990.

Sheds light on solid financial resources, one of the twelve keys to building an effective church. Here is a practical plan for the growth and development of giving and stewardship in your congregation, complete with action worksheets that advance the progress of the plan over four years.

Dunham, Laura. *Graceful Living: Your Faith, Values, and Money in Changing Times*. New York: RCA Distribution, 2002.

Helps people clarify what's important in life and leads them through comprehensive financial planning that expresses their faith and values. Commissioned by the Ecumenical Stewardship Center, *Graceful Living* is widely applicable within faith traditions. The focus is faith-based financial decision making that challenges the consumer culture. Full of practical advice, the book opens up conversations about money issues and attitudes. One section focuses on lifestyle choices common to stages of life, from young adult through retirement.

Godfrey, Neale S., and Caroline Edwards. *Money Doesn't Grow on Trees: A Parent's Guide to Raising Financially Responsible Children*. New York: Simon & Schuster, 1993.

Godfrey is an expert in family finance and a parent who puts her advice to work in her own home. She has designed a unique program for kids, from those as young as three to those in their teens, that teaches them how to earn, save, and spend money wisely while it lets parents clearly communicate their family's values. Using age-appropriate exercises and concrete examples, Godfrey shows parents how to deal with a variety of tough situations.

Green, William. *Inspiring Generosity*. Cleveland, OH: Local Church Ministries, United Church of Christ, 2002.

A different kind of resource for the local church. It is based on the belief that church, before it is anything else, can and must be a place of inspiration. It starts with the conviction that generosity, long before it results in financial giving to the church, is a spirit and an approach to life that is waiting to happen in every church member and any congregation.

Grimm, Eugene. *Generous People: How to Encourage Vital Stewardship*. Edited by Herb Miller. Nashville: Abingdon Press, 1992.

Down-to-earth prescriptions for moving beyond the myths prevalent in stewardship; for helping to organize, energize, and equip local stewardship leaders; and for enabling effective implementation of stewardship programs in churches of every size.

Hoge, Dean R., Patrick McNamara, and Charles Zech. *Plain Talk about Churches and Money*. Bethesda, MD: The Alban Institute, 1997.

Tackles resistance, fears, and difficulties concerning money issues. Offers insight and help on the key fiscal topics confronting congregations today. Congregational leaders at all levels, seminarians, and adult educators will find this an important tool for understanding and engaging congregations in discussions about money.

Jeavons, Thomas H., and Rebekah Burch Basinger. *Growing Givers' Hearts: Treating Fundraising as Ministry*. San Francisco: Jossey-Bass, 2000.

Here is a spiritual way of looking at fundraising as an opportunity to nurture current and prospective donors and facilitate their growth in faith. Explores how development staff, executives, and board members from across the theological spectrum can make faith-building opportunities for donors their first priority, act on their confidence in God's abundance, draw from their theological tradition in their approach to fundraising, involve a vital cross-section of staff in planning, and cultivate spiritually mature leadership. Jeavons and Basinger empower readers to work in spiritually grounded, deeply creative, and professionally satisfying ways.

King, Jerald. *Asking Makes a Difference: A Guide for Stewardship Teams*. Self-published, 2000. (Available through the Unitarian Universalist Association bookstore at 800-215-9076.)

The result of King's twenty years of working with congregations around issues of annual canvass drives and annual stewardship campaigns. He believes that the two are different: The former is related to raising money, and the latter relates to why people give to their congregation. This spiral-bound workbook is designed for stewardship teams.

King, Jerald. *Mission-Based Budgeting: A Guide to Program Budgets*. Self-published, 1998. (Available through the Unitarian Universalist Association bookstore at 800-215-9076.)

King asks why a congregation can raise money for a special project but not for its annual operating budget. His book provides a tool to help congregations increase involvement and financial support of their operating budget. He presents a step-by-step process for moving from a line-item budget to a program budget and then to a mission-based budget.

O'Hurley-Pitts, Michael. *The Passionate Steward: Recovering Christian Stewardship from Secular Fundraising*. Toronto: St. Brigid Press, 2001.

Religious organizations have often been enthralled by the promise of more money (particularly if it is "easy" money) and thus have fallen into the arms of secular fundraisers without subjecting secular methods and operative principles to the scrutiny of their own theological and biblical agenda. *The Passionate Steward* parses the practice of fundraising as it is frequently experienced in churches and finds it wanting. Argues convincingly for a recovery of "passionate stewardship." The book is thoroughly researched and moves easily and cogently between statistical analysis, theological assessment, practice, and anecdotal integration.

Ronsvalle, John, and Sylvia Ronsvalle. *Behind the Stained Glass Windows: Money Dynamics in the Church*. Grand Rapids, MI: Baker Books, 1996.

What are the dynamics at the congregational level that contribute to declining giving? This book reports on a three-year study by Empty Tomb Inc. The project included encounters with hundreds of local congregations, a nationally distributed survey, and interviews with more than forty national congregational leaders.

Shore, William H. *The Cathedral Within: Transforming Your Life by Giving Something Back*. New York: Random House, 2001.

Shows how to make the most of life and to do something that counts. Like the cathedral builders of an earlier time, the visionaries described in this memoir share a single desire: to create something that endures. The extraordinary people Shore has met on his travels represent a new movement of citizens who are tapping into the vast resources of the private sector to improve public life. The leaders described in this book have built important new cathedrals within their communities, and by doing so they have transformed lives, including their own.

Sweetser, Terry, and Susan Milnor, eds. *The Abundance of Our Faith: Award-Winning Sermons on Giving, Plus Suggestions for Group Discussion*. Boston: Skinner House Books, 2006.

Talking about money is not particularly easy for Unitarian Universalists. When money is discussed, the conversation is often grounded in an anxiety about scarcity. The sermons in this book are effective in addressing money and giving as they relate to Unitarian Universalists.

Trumbauer, Jean M. *Created and Called: Discovering Our Gifts for Abundant Living*. Minneapolis: Augsburg Fortress Press, 1998.

Believing that one of the church's primary responsibilities is to help people discover and use the gifts given them, Trumbauer offers congregational leaders (lay and clergy) practical, concrete strategies and resources for doing this work in congregations.

Twist, Lynne. *The Soul of Money: Transforming Your Relationship with Money and Life*. New York: W. W. Norton, 2003.

Shows that examining our attitudes toward money—earning it, spending it, and giving it away—can offer surprising insight into our lives, our values, and the essence of prosperity. Twist is a global activist and fundraiser who has been responsible for raising more than $150 million in individual contributions for charitable causes. Through moving stories and practical principles, she demonstrates how we can replace feelings of scarcity, guilt, and burden with experiences of sufficiency, freedom, and purpose.

www.christianitytoday.com/yc/2003/002/3.36.html

This article in *Christianity Today* by Jim Sheppard suggests that for successful fundraising, professional help may be the best choice for reaching your financial goals. Offers reasons why doing it yourself can lead to failure and why you should hire a professional, information about selecting a consultant, how much you should expect to pay, discussion of the spiritual dimension, and two case studies.

www.generousgiving.org

Generous Giving provides articles and papers about generosity in the church.

www.christianitytoday.com/yc/9y5/9y5068.html

Christianity Today's article "Let's Talk Money: Advice from the Pros on Stewardship Training." Addresses some issues churches may face when the inevitable money crunch arrives, gives statistics, talks about turning it around, discusses better ways to give, and provides a case study.

www.stewardship.org/resources/steward_research/index.html

The Christian Stewardship Association provides information for church stewardship. Click on "One Hundred Stewardship Verses and Ideas" for scriptural quotations about stewardship and generosity. Also includes worksheets for church giving, calendars, and ways to increase congregational giving.

Leadership

Callahan, Kennon L. *Effective Church Leadership: Building on the Twelve Keys.* San Francisco: Jossey-Bass, 1990.

Shares an understanding of leadership and helps missionary pastors grow their leadership by cultivating new understandings and practices in twelve key areas. Callahan guides professional religious leaders and key lay leaders in building on their creativity and imagination in order to revitalize their local churches and advance their missions.

Leas, Speed, and George Parsons. *Understanding Your Congregation as a System: Congregational Systems Inventory.* Bethesda, MD: The Alban Institute, 1993.

Leas and Parsons have created an important tool for congregational leaders in this application of systems theory to evaluating a congregation's life and readiness for change. Church leaders can explore the forces at work and examine the systemic implications in seven key areas: strategy, process, pastoral leadership, lay leadership, authority, relatedness, and learning. The manual provides an overview of systems theory, complete instructions for administering and scoring the Congregational Systems Inventory, and guidance for interpreting and explaining the inventory results using sample scores.

Olsen, Charles M. *Transforming Church Boards into Communities of Spiritual Leaders.* Bethesda, MD: The Alban Institute, 1995.

If you want to understand what life on a "transformed" board is all about, you can experience it by reading this book. Presents the content and theory of the model of "worshipful work" in such a way as to allow an inquirer to experience it while reading. Named one of the top ten religious books in 1997 by the Academy of Parish Clergy.

Richardson, Ronald W. *Creating a Healthier Church: Family Systems Theory, Leadership, and Congregational Life.* Minneapolis: Fortress Press, 1996.

Two stories begin this book: One church reacts to a Sunday morning crisis in a calm and positive way, while the other meets an identical crisis in ways that shatter the emotions and the future relations of all concerned. Based on family systems analysis, and using charts as well as clear exposition, this book shows how relationships are never simply one-to-one, because each person brings along the ins and outs of all his or her other relationships. Furthermore, triangular relationships develop in which three people vary in their alliances, with one joining another against a third. Anxiety underlies most of these relations. Different congregational styles are described, and practical ways of changing destructive behaviors and achieving leadership are given.

Steinke, Peter L. *Healthy Congregations: A Systems Approach*. Bethesda, MD: The Alban Institute, 1996.

Takes readers into a deeper exploration of the congregation as an emotional system. Learn ten principles of health, how congregations can adopt new ways of dealing with stress and anxiety, how spiritually and emotionally healthy leaders influence the emotional system, factors that could put your congregation at risk, and more.

Philanthropy and Planned Giving

Arthur Andersen's Tax Economics of Charitable Giving. Chicago: Chicago Press, 1979.

Edited by partners in a well-known financial services company. Surveys the relevant federal tax laws regarding charitable gifts to qualified not-for-profit and tax-exempt organizations as well as private foundations. Excellent source for detailed answers to questions about deductions for gifts, substantiation and disclosure, appraisal requirements, and reporting gifts to the IRS. To order a copy, call 800-546-3209.

Gary, Tracey, and Melissa Kohner. *Inspired Philanthropy: Your Step-by-Step Guide to Creating a Giving Plan*. 2nd ed. San Francisco: Jossey-Bass, 2002.

Shows how social change happens. No matter how much or how little we have to give, we learn how to create a plan that will make our charitable giving catalytic. Then, through clear text and substantive exercises, Gary and Kohner teach how to align giving with our deepest values—to help bring about the very changes we want.

Quynn, Katelyn L., and Ronald R. Jordan. *Planned Giving: Management, Marketing, and Law*. New York: John Wiley & Sons, 1995.

Thorough and easy-to-read description of every aspect of planned giving. Includes a floppy disk with sample documents.

Schoen, Stella A., ed. *The Local Church Planned Giving Manual*. Cleveland, OH: United Church of Christ Planned Giving Ministry, 2003.

Intended as a guide for congregations that want to encourage bequests and other planned gifts. Loose-leaf format. Sells for $40. To order, contact United Church of Christ Planned Giving Ministry, 700 Prospect Avenue, Cleveland, OH 44115. 216-736-2290. Fax: 216-736-2297.

Spiritual Relationship

Hoertdoerfer, Patricia, and Fredric Muir, eds. *The Safe Congregation Handbook: Nurturing Healthy Boundaries in Our Faith Communities*. Boston: Unitarian Universalist Association, 2005.

Healthy, respectful adult relationships experience disagreements and conflicts. This is true of all relationships and especially true in Unitarian Universalist congregations, where diversity of opinion and perspective has been invited. Disagreements and conflicts are inevitable in open, growing relationships, yet instead of welcoming the breadth of perspective that is offered, congregations are often afraid of disagreements. While the editors understand that fear is a reasonable response, it is not a helpful one. They believe that congregational leaders must be responsible for setting the standards for how well disagreements are expressed.

Johnson, Allan G. *Privilege, Power, and Difference*. New York: McGraw-Hill Higher Education, 2001.

Provides an easily applied theoretical model for thinking about systems of privilege and difference. Writing in conversational prose, Johnson joins theory with examples to enable us to see the nature and consequences of privilege and their connection to it.

Kujawa-Holbrook, Sheryl A. *A House of Prayer for All Peoples: Congregations Building Multiracial Community*. Herndon, VA: The Alban Institute, 2003.

> Contrary to the oft-repeated saying, there are churches in America where Sunday is not the "most segregated day of the week," as Kujawa-Holbrook demonstrates in her exploration of congregations tackling racial justice issues. Yet the idea continues to haunt many congregations, and Kujawa-Holbrook reveals, through story and thoughtful analysis, what it means to create and live out multiracial community. These stories will inspire leaders to explore their congregation's history, study their community's demographics, and most of all, search their souls for ways they can develop and celebrate the diversity in their midst. Capped by an extensive annotated resource list for readers who want to explore the topic further.

Parker, Robin, and Pamela Smith Chambers. *The Anti-Racist Cookbook: A Recipe Guide for Congregations About Race That Goes Beyond Covered Dishes and "Kum-Bah-Ya."* Roselle, NJ: Crandall, Dostie, & Douglass, 2005.

> The authors' answer to the question, "Why can't we just all get along?" They believe that we can, and they present some basic recipes to help. In the style of all cookbooks, the book offers a list of ingredients and preparations that enables readers to feed themselves well, not with food, but with knowledge, ideas, and discussion strategies that can improve the places where we live, work, and study.

Rendle, Gil. *Behavioral Covenants in Congregations: A Handbook for Honoring Differences*. Herndon, VA: The Alban Institute, 1999.

> A down-to-earth workbook exploring how to live creatively together despite differences of age, race, culture, opinion, gender, and theological or political position. Rendle explains how to grow by valuing our differences rather than trying to ignore or blend them. He describes a

method of establishing behavioral covenants that includes leadership instruction, training tools, resources, small-group exercises, and plans for meetings and retreats.

Sellon, Mary K., and Daniel P. Smith. *Practicing Right Relationship: Skills for Deepening Purpose, Finding Fulfillment, and Increasing Effectiveness in Your Congregation*. Herndon, VA: The Alban Institute, 2005.

> Why is it that some pastors flourish wherever they go, while others with superior theological and practical training continually fail? Why do some insignificant events end up touching people in significant ways? Why do people leave churches with vibrant and exciting programs while others remain loyal to churches that seem to have very little to offer? What makes the difference? Sellon and Smith make the case that the health of churches and synagogues depends on congregations learning how to live out love in "right relationships." The quality of relationships seemed to be the key. Leadership is not a matter of using certain skills and implementing particular practices, nor is it about being right. Leadership is a relationship.

Transformation

Ammerman, Nancy T. *Congregation and Community*. New Brunswick, NJ: Rutgers University Press, 1997.

> Addresses the multiple ways twenty-three Protestant congregations and Roman Catholic parishes in nine communities across the United States respond to significant cultural, economic, and social/structural change within their surrounding community contexts. Chapter 1 surveys the communities where the focus congregations are located, describes the local religious ecologies of the communities, and outlines the three broad dimensions used to analyze the congregations in the study: resources, structures of authority, and culture.

Gladwell, Malcolm. *The Tipping Point: How Little Things Can Make a Big Difference.* New York: Little, Brown & Co., 2000.

> Gladwell looks at why major changes in our society often happen suddenly and unexpectedly. Ideas, behavior, messages, and products, he argues, often spread like outbreaks of infectious disease. Gladwell introduces readers to the particular personality types who are natural pollinators of new ideas and trends, the people who create the phenomenon of word of mouth.

Heller, Anne Odin. *Churchworks: A Well-Body Book for Congregations.* Boston: Skinner House Books, 1999.

> This accessible, intelligent, and enjoyable handbook uses the human body as a model for a church community. Provides creative and practical prescriptions for health in all aspects of a congregation—spiritual development, covenants and mission statements, growth and new membership, conflict resolution, ministry, building and grounds, and more.

Herrington, Jim, Mike Bonem, and James H. Furr. *Leading Congregational Change: A Practical Guide for the Transformational Journey.* San Francisco: Jossey-Bass, 2000.

> The authors share their experience guiding dozens of churches through the change process. The central component of their change model is for congregations to first nurture spiritual and relational vitality. Drawing examples from thriving churches, they offer long-term support through eight well-considered stages: personally preparing for change, creating a sense of energy and urgency, establishing the vision community, discerning the vision and determining the vision path, communicating the vision, empowering change leaders, implementing the vision, and reinforcing momentum through alignment.

Mann, Alice. *Raising the Roof: The Pastoral-to-Program Size Transition.* Bethesda, MD: Alban Institute, 2001.

> Designed for a congregational learning team to effect transition. Features a five-step process to help the team engage a wider circle of congregational leaders and church members in study, discernment, and planning activities. Mann provides all the resources needed to address significant size transitions.

Mead, Loren B. *More Than Numbers: The Ways Churches Grow.* Bethesda, MD: The Alban Institute, 1993.

> Explores what church growth and evangelism really mean in a time when it is mathematically impossible for every congregation to achieve significant numerical growth. He argues provocatively that spiritual, organizational, and "missional" growth are just as important as numerical growth, and that all four are needed for a truly healthy and growing church. Case studies and discussion questions are included.

Oswald, Roy M., and Robert E. Friedrich Jr. *Discerning Your Congregation's Future: A Strategic and Statistical Approach.* Bethesda, MD: The Alban Institute, 1996.

> Written for congregations that want to stop drifting and establish a corporate direction. Rather than focusing on the need for leaders to have and impart a vision to the congregation, they are committed to a theology and methodology that places the entire congregation in the center of the visioning process.

Oswald, Roy M. *Making Your Church More Inviting: A Step-by-Step Guide for In-Church Training.* Bethesda, MD: The Alban Institute, 1992.

> Fifteen sessions designed to help clergy or lay leaders guide committees or study groups through a dynamic exploration of their congregation's IQ (invitation quotient). Discover how well you invite, welcome, and incorporate new members. As participants uncover the inviting elements of your church, they develop a

personal witness style that emerges comfortably from their individual gifts.

Rendle, Gil, and Alice Mann. *Holy Conversations: Strategic Planning as a Spiritual Practice for Congregations.* Herndon, VA: The Alban Institute, 2003.

In this handbook for congregational lay leaders, Rendle and Mann show that they do not believe that planning centers on problem solving. The leader is not responsible for discovering the perfect solution or for creating a perfect planning process to arrive at a perfect plan. Instead, they believe that the task of the leader is to help group members have a purposeful and meaningful conversation about who they are and what they believe is important to do.

Rendle, Gilbert R. *Leading Change in the Congregation: Spiritual and Organizational Tools for Leaders.* Bethesda, MD: The Alban Institute, 1998.

Focuses on the kind of change that tears at a community's very fabric. Provides a respectful context for understanding change, especially the experiences and resistance that people feel. Rendle pulls together theory, research, and his work with churches facing change to provide leaders with practical diagnostic models and tools. In a time when change is the norm, this book helps to "lead change" in a spiritual and healthy way.

Warren, Rick. *The Purpose-Driven Church.* Grand Rapids, MI: Zondervan Press, 1995.

Every church is driven by something. Tradition, finances, programs, personalities, events, seekers, and even buildings can each be the controlling force in a church. But Rick Warren believes that in order for a church to be healthy, it must become a purpose-driven church. Warren offers ways for your congregation to become warmer through fellowship, deeper through discipleship, stronger through worship, broader through ministry, and larger through evangelism. He shifts the focus away from church-building programs to emphasizing a people-building process.

Wheatley, Margaret. *Turning to One Another: Simple Conversations to Restore Hope to the Future.* San Francisco: Berrett-Koehler, 2002.

"I believe we can change the world if we start talking to one another again." With this simple declaration, Wheatley proposes that we use the increasingly popular process of conversation and dialogue as the means to develop solutions for the societal changes that need to occur both locally and globally. Wheatley asserts that the changes required in all aspects of modern life will not come from governments or large organizations, national programs, new policies, or laws. The changes will be led by everyday people. Wheatley begins by describing several conditions that support good conversation, including simplicity, personal courage, real listening, diversity, and several others. Ten short essays act as "conversation starters," leading people into conversations about their deepest beliefs, fears, and hopes.

www.netresults.org/sample/JanFeb/transformationprocesses.htm

George W. Bullard Jr. writes about work that he has done with various denominations trying to transform themselves. He identifies factors that empower and hinder transformation as well as the role of the denomination in congregational transformation.

www.pbs.org/thecongregation/indepth/beyondoutreach.html

The Congregation, a PBS documentary by Alan and Susan Raymond, profiles a progressive United Methodist church in the midst of profound change. This website contains articles and information about the church and offers a look at a church in transition.

www.uscongregations.org/growth.htm

"Myths and Facts about Evangelism and Church Growth," based on the 2001 U.S. Congregational Life Survey, in which more than two thousand congregations of many different denominations and faith groups participated.

www.centerce.org/LEADERSHIP/StrategicPlanning.htm

> The Center for Church Enrichment offers a PowerPoint presentation on strategic planning.

www.christianitytoday.com/bcl/areas/vision-strategy/articles/070204.html

> Stephen A. Macchia's *Christianity Today* article "Developing a Strategic Plan for Your Church." Offers suggestions on what to do and what not to do when embarking on a strategic plan.

Acknowledgments

I extend my sincere thanks to the following colleagues:

Marcy Bailey Adams, Susan Erickson, Jerry Gabert, Jerry King, Carla Kindt, Ralph Mero, Dave Rickard, and Don Ross for their contributions to the chapter on planned giving.

Mary Benard, for her tireless editing and her many helpful suggestions.

Kathy Carter, for her meticulous copy editing.

Amy Clark, for her insightful editing recommendations.

Fundraising consultants Martha Easter-Wells, Dave Rickard, and Larry Wheeler, for their suggestions to enhance Searching for the Future.

Carla Kindt and Kenneth Collier, for sharing their document "Covenant Between the Congregation and Their Visiting Stewards."

Fundraising consultant Frankie Price-Stern, for her helpful suggestions in creating the Annual Progress Summary Form.

Dave Rickard, for editing the Congregational Services Code of Ethics and for creating the term FORTH to represent Forward Through the Ages.

Amanda Schuber and Robin Nelson for compiling the annotated list of further reading.

Stuart Sendell, for his earlier version of the chapter on debt.

Praise for *Beyond Fundraising*

"Wayne Clark has translated twenty years of experience as the UUA's congregational finances guru into a clear, concise and invaluable guide to best practices in congregational stewardship. He embeds conversation about money in a culture of appreciation rather than a culture of criticism and does so in a conversational manner that is accessible, practical and step-by-step."

—William Saunders, Minister Emeritus, South Church,
Unitarian Universalist, Portsmouth, New Hampshire

"Wayne Clark has succeeded with this wonderful and practical book, which offers equal measures of inspiration and information to congregations seeking to become all they can be. For far too many generations, Unitarian Universalist congregations of all sizes have been held back from their missions by bad ideas and practices surrounding money and financial giving. Step by step, Clark shows the way to a new paradigm of giving and sharing that will enable both congregations and their members to thrive in every aspect of their ministry. This book is a must-read for both laity and clergy who are committed to the health of our congregations and our movement."

—Scott W. Alexander, Senior Minister,
River Road Unitarian Church, Bethesda, Maryland

"Wayne Clark begins with getting rid of old money-related 'scarcity' language and replacing it with a new and more visionary vocabulary of stewardship. *Beyond Fundraising* is a blueprint to connect the practice of giving with the congregation's vision, mission and ministries. This book is now at the top of my reference list under the heading 'if you have to recommend just one book to the volunteer fundraisers in your congregation. . . .'"

—Lynda Shannon Bluestein, Former President,
UU District of Metropolitan New York

"Wayne Clark's new book debunks our many myths about money in congregational life and offers a clear blueprint for successful fundraising. The book sees giving and receiving as profound acts of faith that deepen our lives in fellowship with one another."

—Larry Ladd, Former UUA Financial Advisor

"How I wish this book had existed four years ago. By changing the vocabulary of fundraising, Clark has given us a new way of thinking about our faith, our money, and our commitment to leading religious communities."

—Harlan Limpert, UUA Director of District Services

"Wayne Clark has written the most comprehensive and compelling book on Unitarian Universalist Stewardship in this era. His ideas, principles and practices will transform your congregation's giving. This is a much needed new resource as we seek to bring the fullness of our mission and message to the world."

—Thomas Chulak, UUA District Executive, St. Lawrence District